Decision Making Within International Organizations

International organizations are increasingly important in the era of globalization but little is known about decision making within these institutions. This edited volume investigates how much influence governments as well as non-state actors, such as non-governmental organizations and international bureaucracies, have upon decision making and the specific ways in which they try to affect international outcomes.

Decision Making Within International Organizations utilizes various theoretical approaches – such as two-level games, groupthink, neo-institutionalism and 'garbage can' theory – to offer new insight into questions such as

- What drives international agencies?
- How do they attempt to affect decision making between states?
- What explains their success or failure?

The book includes an introduction by Robert W. Cox and presents case studies of many different international organizations, including the European Union, the Council of Europe, the World Trade Organization, the World Meteorological Organization, the International Maritime Organization, the World Bank, the International Monetary Fund, the United Nations, the G7/G8, the Organization for Economic Cooperation and Development and the UNHCR.

The authors explore the delicate balance between the objectives of international organizations and their member states by drawing from both rationalist and constructivist scholarship in International Relations, thus contributing to a synthesis between both perspectives.

Bob Reinalda is Senior Lecturer in International Relations at the University of Nijmegen. **Bertjan Verbeek** is Associate Professor of International Relations at the University of Nijmegen, The Netherlands.

Routledge/ECPR studies in European political science

Edited by Thomas Poguntke

Keele University, UK

Jan W. van Deth

University of Mannheim, Germany on behalf of the European Consortium for Political Research

The Routledge/ECPR Studies in European Political Science series is published in association with the European Consortium for Political Research – the leading organization concerned with the growth and development of political science in Europe. The series presents high-quality edited volumes on topics at the leading edge of current interest in political science and related fields, with contributions from European scholars and others who have presented work at ECPR workshops or research groups.

1 **Regionalist Parties in Western Europe**
Edited by Lieven de Winter and Huri Türsan

2 **Comparing Party System Change**
Edited by Jan-Erik Lane and Paul Pennings

3 **Political Theory and European Union**
Edited by Albert Weale and Michael Nentwich

4 **Politics of Sexuality**
Edited by Terrell Carver and Véronique Mottier

5 **Autonomous Policy Making by International Organizations**
Edited by Bob Reinalda and Bertjan Verbeek

6 **Social Capital and European Democracy**
Edited by Jan van Deth, Marco Maraffi, Ken Newton and Paul Whiteley

7 **Party Elites in Divided Societies**
Edited by Kurt Richard Luther and Kris Deschouwer

8 **Citizenship and Welfare State Reform in Europe**
Edited by Jet Bussemaker

9 **Democratic Governance and New Technology**
Technologically mediated innovations in political practice in Western Europe
Edited by Ivan Horrocks, Jens Hoff and Pieter Tops

10 **Democracy without Borders**
Transnationalisation and conditionality in new democracies
Edited by Jean Grugel

11 **Cultural Theory as Political Science**
Edited by Michael Thompson, Gunnar Grendstad and Per Selle

12 **The Transformation of Governance in the European Union**
Edited by Beate Kohler-Koch and Rainer Eising

13 **Parliamentary Party Groups in European Democracies**
Political parties behind closed doors
Edited by Knut Heidar and Ruud Koole

14 **Survival of the European Welfare State**
Edited by Stein Kuhnle

15 **Private Organisations in Global Politics**
Edited by Karsten Ronit and Volker Schneider

16 **Federalism and Political Performance**
Edited by Ute Wachendorfer-Schmidt

17 **Democratic Innovation**
Deliberation, representation and association
Edited by Michael Saward

18 **Public Opinion and the International Use of Force**
Edited by Philip Everts and Pierangelo Isernia

19 **Religion and Mass Electoral Behaviour in Europe**
Edited by David Broughton and Hans-Martien ten Napel

20 **Estimating the Policy Position of Political Actors**
Edited by Michael Laver

21 **Democracy and Political Change in the 'Third World'**
Edited by Jeff Haynes

22 **Politicians, Bureaucrats and Administrative Reform**
Edited by B. Guy Peters and Jon Pierre

23 **Social Capital and Participation in Everyday Life**
Edited by Paul Dekker and Eric M. Uslaner

24 **Development and Democracy**
What do we know and how?
Edited by Ole Elgström and Goran Hyden

25 **Do Political Campaigns Matter?**
Campaign effects in elections and referendums
Edited by David M. Farrell and Rüdiger Schmitt-Beck

26 **Political Journalism**
New challenges, new practices
Edited by Raymond Kuhn and Erik Neveu

27 **Economic Voting**
Edited by Han Dorussen and Michaell Taylor

28 **Organized Crime and the Challenge to Democracy**
Edited by Felia Allum and Renate Siebert

29 **Understanding the European Union's External Relations**
Edited by Michèle Knodt and Sebastiaan Princen

30 Social Democratic Party Policies in Contemporary Europe
Edited by Giuliano Bonoli and Martin Powell

31 Decision Making Within International Organizations
Edited by Bob Reinalda and Bertjan Verbeek

32 Comparative Biomedical Policy
Governing assisted reproductive technologies
Edited by Ivar Bleiklie, Malcolm L. Goggin and Christine Rothmayr

33 Electronic Democracy
Mobilisation, organisation and participation via new ICTs
Edited by Rachel K. Gibson, Andrea Römmele and Stephen J. Ward

34 Liberal Democracy and Environmentalism
The end of environmentalism?
Edited by Marcel Wissenburg and Yoram Levy

Also available from Routledge in association with the ECPR:

Sex Equality Policy in Western Europe, *Edited by Frances Gardiner*; **Democracy and Green Political Thought**, *Edited by Brian Doherty and Marius de Geus*; **The New Politics of Unemployment**, *Edited by Hugh Compston*; **Citizenship, Democracy and Justice in the New Europe**, *Edited by Percy B. Lehning and Albert Weale*; **Private Groups and Public Life**, *Edited by Jan W. van Deth*; **The Political Context of Collective Action**, *Edited by Ricca Edmondson*; **Theories of Secession**, *Edited by Percy Lehning*; **Regionalism Across the North/South Divide**, *Edited by Jean Grugel and Wil Hout*

Decision Making Within International Organizations

Edited by Bob Reinalda and Bertjan Verbeek

With a foreword by Robert W. Cox

Routledge
Taylor & Francis Group
LONDON AND NEW YORK

ecpr

First published 2004
by Routledge
2 Park Square, Milton Park, Abingdon, Oxon, OX14 4RN

Simultaneously published in the USA and Canada
by Routledge
270 Madison Ave, New York NY 10016

Routledge is an imprint of the Taylor & Francis Group

Transferred to Digital Printing 2006

Typeset in Times by Wearset Ltd, Boldon, Tyne and Wear

British Library Cataloguing in Publication Data
A catalogue record for this book is available from the British Library

Library of Congress Cataloging in Publication Data
Decision making within international organizations / edited by Bob Reinalda and Bertjan Verbeek.
p. cm.
Includes bibliographical references and index.
1. International agencies—Decision making. 2. International organization. I. Reinalda, Bob. II. Verbeek, Bertjan, 1960–
JZ4839.D43 2004
352.3'3211—dc22 2003022241

ISBN10: 0-415-30426-1 (hbk)
ISBN10: 0-415-40678-1 (pbk)

ISBN13: 978-0-415-30426-9 (hbk)
ISBN13: 978-0-415-40678-9 (pbk)

Contents

Contributors

Nicholas Bayne, Fellow at the International Trade Policy Unit at the London School of Economics and Political Science, United Kingdom

Robert W. Cox, Professor Emeritus of Political Science at York University, Toronto, Canada

Jan Dirks, Senior Research Fellow at the Research Centre Work–Environment–Technology, University of Bremen, Germany

Jim Dratwa, Research Fellow at the Belfer Center for Science and International Affairs, Kennedy School of Government, Harvard University, United States of America, and Research Fellow at the Fonds National de la Recherche Scientifique, Belgium

Raquel Freitas, Researcher at the European University Institute, Florence, Italy

Hadewych Hazelzet, Former Researcher at the European University Institute, Florence, now an official at the General Secretariat of the Council of the European Union, but writing on a strictly personal basis

Jutta Joachim, Assistant Professor at the Institute of Political Science, University of Hannover, Germany

Bart Kerremans, Associate Professor of International Relations at the Department of Political Sciences, University of Leuven, Belgium

Jill Lovecy, Lecturer at the Department of Government, University of Manchester, United Kingdom

Martin Marcussen, Associate Professor at the Department of Political Science, University of Copenhagen, Denmark

Bob Reinalda, Senior Lecturer at the Institute of Political Science, University of Nijmegen, the Netherlands

Yves Schemeil, Professor of Political Science, Institut d'Études Politiques, Grenoble, and Institut Universitaire de France, France

Jarle Trondal, Director of the Centre for European Studies CES, Agder University College, Kristiansand, Norway

Bertjan Verbeek, Associate Professor of International Relations at the Institute of Political Science, University of Nijmegen, the Netherlands

Ngaire Woods, Fellow in Politics and International Relations, University College, Oxford University, United Kingdom

Series editor's preface

Ever since the Treaty of Westphalia, a system of states and of diplomatic relations between them has dominated the world. Although the rise of international organizations in the late nineteenth and early twentieth century was widely recognized as an important development, wars and growing interdependencies emphasize the relevance of states for studying international relations and security. Yet states are increasingly confronted with a wide variety of non-governmental organizations (NGOs), which represent an astonishing range of different interests, and rapidly develop their own networks, resources and arenas. But NGOs are not the only organizations whose relevance and visibility has increased. International (or intergovernmental) organizations like the OECD or the IMF challenge and enhance the traditional position of the state by representing member states on the one hand, and facilitating their own interests on the other.

In the chapters in this volume, the authors deal with the question of how international organizations make use of the policy autonomy they have. This question is not easy to answer, since an enormous number of different organizations exists, which all differ in the degree of policy autonomy in specific areas of their activities. Moreover, academic debates on the study of decision-making processes in international organizations are characterized by an astonishing variety of rival approaches, concepts and methods. It is for these reasons – the apparently incredible diversity of organizations, policies and explanations – that the editors attempt to identify the main problems and prospects of studying international organizations in their introductory chapter. Their plea for a revitalization of the study of policy making within international organizations is based on the unambiguous recognition of the need to combine rationalist and constructivist approaches. They also recommend the use of middle-range theories to account for the outcomes of decision-making processes in international organizations. Only if these two recommendations are followed will our understanding of the ways international organizations use their policy autonomy vis-à-vis their member-states be advanced.

After the editors present a very ambitious research agenda in their extensive introduction, twelve thoroughly accomplished studies of decision-making processes are presented under six headings. The first two chapters are addressed to *leadership*: Bart Kerremans analyses the negotiating processes of the European Commission within the framework of the WTO, and Jill Lovecy studies the relative autonomy of the Council of Europe. The next two chapters illustrate the problems and prospects of *consensus building* within the WTO and the World Meteorological Organization (discussed by Yves Schemeil), and within the OECD to produce 'soft' regulations (discussed by Martin Marcussen). *Organizational dynamics* are discussed in the next part of the volume. This part consists of a detailed analysis by Ngaire Woods of decision-making processes by the IMF and the World Bank with respect to the Mexican economic crisis of 1994, and an examination of the determinants of decisions taken by the UN High Commissioner for Refugees by Raquel Freitas. Various *conflicts of loyalty* are illustrated in Nicholas Bayne's highly original study of the role and position of so-called sherpas (personal representatives of leading politicians) in meetings of G7 and G8 countries. Jarle Trondal identifies similar encounters in an analysis of decision-making processes in EU committees as a key element of Brussels bureaucracy. The content of decisions is emphasized in two chapters on *policy windows*: Hadewych Hazelzet demonstrates the impact of various non-state actors on EU sanctions in reaction to human-rights violations, whereas Jutta Joachim focuses on the issue of reproductive rights and health, which women's organizations placed on the UN agenda. Finally, organizations gradually adapt their strategies and show *learning processes*, as is clearly illustrated by Jan Dirks in an analysis of the adoption of a highly disputed convention by the International Maritime Organization in 1995, and by Jim Dratwa in an examination of the role of norms in complicated policy-making processes at the European Commission.

The main findings of the various case studies are used by the editors in their concluding chapter for a systematic discussion of the ways international organizations use their freedom to manoeuvre and to develop specific policies. Although different in scope, design and objective, the set of case studies and analyses of distinct organizations, issue areas and policy fields presented here all underline the need to combine various theoretical and methodological approaches and to rely on middle-range theories. It is this combination of approaches and theories to study specific decision-making processes in detail that defines the unique character of the chapters presented in this volume. And it is the praiseworthy attempt to integrate these various approaches and theories by the editors, in both their introductory and their concluding chapters, which enormously increases the relevance of the specific findings on decision-making processes in organizations, varying from the OECD and the IMF, to the International Shipping Federation and the Feminist International Network of Resistance to Reproductive and Genetic Engineering.

Jan W. van Deth, *Series Editor*
Mannheim, October 2003

Abbreviations

AI	Amnesty International
CAC	Codex Alimentarius Commission
CC	Comitology Committee
CCGP	Codex Committee on General Principles
CE	Council of Europe
COG	Chief of Government
COREPER	Committee of Permanent Representatives
CWP	Council Working Party
CWPE	Committee on Women, Population and the Environment
DG	Directorate-General
DIP	Division on International Protection
DSB	Dispute Settlement Body
EC	European Community
EC	Expert Committee
ECHR	European Convention on Human Rights and Fundamental Freedoms
EDRC	Economic and Development Review Committee
EFSA	European Food Safety Authority
EIDHR	European Initiative for Democracy and Human Rights
EP	European Parliament
EU	European Union
FAO	Food and Agricultural Organization
FOC	Flags of Convenience
GA	General Assembly
GATS	General Agreement on Trade in Services
GATT	General Agreement on Tariffs and Trade
GSP	General System of Trade Preferences
GW	Global Witness
HOD	Head of Delegation
HRW	Human Rights Watch
IBRD	International Bank for Reconstruction and Development

ICASC	International Contraception, Abortion, and Sterilization Campaign
ICFTU	International Confederation of Free Trade Unions
ICG-FINRAGE	Feminist International Network of Resistance to Reproductive and Genetic Engineering
ICPD	International Conference on Population and Development
IDP	Internally Displaced Person
IGC	Intergovernmental Conference
IGO	Intergovernmental Organization
ILO	International Labour Organization
IMF	International Monetary Fund
IMO	International Maritime Organization
IPPF	International Planned Parenthood Federation
ISF	International Shipping Federation
ITF	International Transportworkers Federation
IWHC	International Women's Health Coalition
LDC	Least Developed Country
MOU	Memorandum of Understanding
MSC	Maritime Safety Committee
NAFTA	North American Free Trade Agreement
NEPAD	New Partnership for Africa's Development
NGO	Non-Governmental Organization
NSA	Non-State Actor
OECD	Organization for Economic Cooperation and Development
PAC	Partnership Africa Canada
QMV	Qualified Majority Voting
SPS	Sanitary and Phytosanitary Measures
STCW	Standards of Training, Certification and Watchkeeping for Seafarers Convention
TEC	Treaty of the European Community
TNC	Trade Negotiating Committee
UK	United Kingdom
UN	United Nations
UNCTAD	United Nations Conference on Trade and Development
UNDP	United Nations Development Program
UNEP	United Nations Environmental Program
UNESCO	United Nations Educational, Scientific and Cultural Organization
UNFPA	United Nations Fund for Population Activities
UNHCR	United Nations High Commissioner for Refugees
UNMOVIC	United Nations Monitoring, Verification and Inspection Commission

USA	United States of America
WDC	World Diamond Council
WFP	World Food Program
WGNRR	Women's Global Network for Reproductive Rights
WMO	World Meteorological Organization
WTO	World Trade Organization

Part I

Introduction and overview

Foreword

International organization in an era of changing historical structures

Robert W. Cox

Some thirty years ago Harold K. Jacobson ('Jake') and I published *The Anatomy of Influence. Decision Making in International Organization*. The editors of the present volume recall it as a starting point in a program of studies they are now continuing. Their work and that of the contributors to the present volume prompts me to reflect upon the direction that has been taken in the interval by the study of international organization in world politics.

Like many things in intellectual life, my encounter with 'Jake' was a matter of chance. We first met in the autumn of 1966. I had been long established in Geneva with the International Labour Organization and Jake was coming to Geneva with his family on sabbatical leave from the University of Michigan to continue his study of international organization. It was Inis Claude who brought us together, the author of *Swords into Ploughshares. The Problems and Progress of International Organization* (1956), one of the first major studies in the field. I had known Inis as a participant in various Carnegie Endowment sponsored meetings. In those days the Carnegie Endowment was located in Geneva and was oriented towards studies of international organization rather more than, as it subsequently became, a think-tank for US foreign policy. A few years previously I had discussions with Ernst Haas when he came to Geneva to research for his book *Beyond the Nation-State. Functionalism and International Organization* (1964). This says something about the intellectual context of the meeting between 'Jake' and me.

During that year, 1966, 'Jake' joined me in a seminar I was directing at the Graduate Institute in Geneva; and we took up as a research project an idea put forward by Pierre Gerbet of the *Institut d'études politiques* in Paris for a comparative study of decision making in international organizations. Jake brought to that theme the thinking he had absorbed at Yale from Robert Dahl's *Who Governs?* (1961). We began a collaboration, which extended to include others, that culminated in the publication of *The Anatomy of Influence* (1973).

That book had a certain immediate impact in the scholarly literature but, I think, was soon displaced by other directions in research. Emphasis in the scholarly world shifted from how institutions work to how and why certain issues become salient objects of international concern. For a time 'regimes' became preferred objects of theorizing. My own interest moved from international organization to international political economy. Jake, after producing his definitive work *Networks of Interdependence. International Organizations and the Global Political System* (1978), which he described as 'an optimistic book, though I hope not an unrealistic one', moved more in the direction of international law. That optimism, rooted in his conviction that the multilateral approach was the indispensable condition for a durable world peace, was expressed again by him in a short piece he wrote, not long before his untimely death, for a symposium to explore the relationship of international law and political science. 'International law', he wrote, 'will be enormously relevant in the agenda of international relations in the twenty-first century.'

These hopeful words were followed only weeks later by the attack of 9/11, which occurred after Jake's death. In the aftermath of 9/11 multilateralism and international law – along with civil liberties – have suffered a severe setback.

Jake represented, for me as a non-American, the ideal of integrity in American intellectual life. Non-Americans often perceive two qualities in Americans: patriotism or a sense of identity with the constituted authorities of the nation, and belief in a God firmly embedded in American culture. Jake's patriotism was clear, though he never made a show of it. His religion was an important part of his life, though you had to know him well to sense what it meant to him. Both qualities have been open to distortion in politics. Patriotism can be distorted into the unilateralism of universalistic nationalism. Belief in God can be distorted into exclusionary fundamentalism. Jake maintained a commitment to openness and understanding – hence his intellectual focus on international organization and international law.

There are few constraining influences upon a unilateralist America which has the predominance of military world power. It is becoming more and more obvious that the most likely effective moderating force is that which is latent within America itself. I, as a non-American, look with cautious hope to that continuing strand of the American human and moral reality that Jake so fully represented.

Working with Jake on *The Anatomy of Influence* introduced me to the American political science of the 1960s in the behavioural mode – in the attempt to find quantitative measures to justify statements. I was quite fascinated by it then, though subsequently I came to wonder whether there was not something important missing in a methodology that contrived to achieve 'objectivity' by failing to take account of the inter-subjective element in reality. In the course of time my background training in history reasserted itself. *The Anatomy of Influence* was for me an epistemological moment that passed.[1]

If Jake, looking hopefully from the outside at the development of international organization, was optimistic, I, with a quarter century experience within international organization behind me when we came to prepare our book, was perhaps more pessimistic. We shared the normative vision that world peace and orderly societies can only be secure when the powerful entities in the world negotiate consensus to avoid violent conflict and that multilateralism, in practice expressed through international organizations, is the way this can be pursued. Hence the importance of understanding how the process of international organization works. There is a realist basis for this – a recognition that you have to start with an assessment of the real forces. There is also a recognition that the process itself adds something over and above an inventory of the material capabilities of those forces and that an inquiry into that something else makes a useful contribution to the outcome.

A quarter century after Jake and I completed our inquiry, Bob Reinalda and Bertjan Verbeek, with their collaborators, have taken up the task again, employing more refined analytical categories of decision making and a different mix of cases, first in *Autonomous Policy Making by International Organizations* (1998) and now in the present volume. What difference, if any, does the interval in time make?

My question involves how the synchronic and the diachronic may be reconciled in social science research. The methods that Jake and I used like those used by the editors and collaborators in this volume work well in the synchronic dimension. They elucidate how decisions are made in a given contemporary world context. As such they are useful tools for understanding how things work under these conditions. The diachronic – the longer term dimension of change in those conditions – is more elusive. Jake and I had tried to find a place for that in the device of categorizing the *environment* of an international organization, both a general environment of world power relations that was common to all international organizations and a specific environment that included factors relevant to the specific functions of each organization. But this device followed the same synchronic approach, an attempt to break down these environments into factors that could be itemized or quantified in a positivist manner.

In retrospect, I think the methodological artifact of the 'environment' failed to take account of the way the world has changed. Positivism knows only the synchronic – perhaps it can depict sequential synchronic slices in time but it cannot explain how a complex process of change restructures the goals and opportunities open to international organization. For that, the historical method remains indispensable, the method that combines the view from without (which is that of positivism) and the view from within (which is proper to historicism).

In this approach the 'environment' is replaced by the historical structure. The historical structure is how the world appears to the entities – persons, states, corporations, or whatever – that are interacting in it, how they perceive the concatenation of the forces at work and the conflicting directions these forces take. This is what informs the making of decisions or non-decisions. The historicist approach is always latent even in positivist analyses like those we attempted thirty years ago when motivations and reactions to the Cold War, or to the gap between poor and rich, inevitably creep into a purportedly 'objective' account.

An historical structure has an objective dimension which depicts a prevailing arrangement of forces and an inter-subjective dimension in which the actors share a vision of reality. By introducing the inter-subjective dimension, however, we allow for the coexistence of different and often conflicting perceptions of reality, each of which can become transformed over time.

Thirty years ago, the uncertain balance between the United States and the Soviet Union called the Cold War was a central feature of an inter-subjective understanding of reality, with a 'Third World' frustrated in hopes for development as a potentially disruptive force. Functionalism was a theory derived from the wartime experience of allied countries cooperating for common purposes that seemed as though it might be a means for further knitting together the performance of common tasks, at least among developed capitalist countries, so as to minimize conflicting national interests. There was an apparent stability in the historical structure which would seem to allow for the possibility that international organizations performing technical and non-political tasks, insofar as they could avoid paralysis on Cold War issues, might quietly advance the interdependence of states. They might even, to cite the title of Ernst Haas' book, take us 'beyond the nation-state' towards a more integrated transnational structure.

In the interval the world has changed and different rival historical structures have appeared on the scene. One of these collective visions of reality, based on the military predominance and economic influence of the United States, envisages a central power that penetrates throughout the world as a new emerging 'empire' – one core civilization that will absorb bit by bit the rest of the world into a homogeneous entity with common values. This 'empire' is being built through a process of economic and social globalization and cultural diffusion backed by military power.[2] Parallel with that is a second configuration of power, the residue of the Westphalian order of independent states that originated in seventeenth-century Europe and spread over the world in the era of European dominance. This historical structure has generated as its *modus operandi* diplomacy, international law, and, most recently, the United Nations and other international organizations. Evolving within the Westphalian structure is the movement towards unification in Europe, which evokes, in opposition to the vision of 'empire', the perspective of a future world with a balance of regional powers. Then, appearing even more recently, is yet a third configuration of world power in the shape of civil society or the social movement which is autonomous in relation both to 'empire' and to the Westphalian state system. This movement expresses a diversity of social forces in opposition to 'empire' and attempts to orient states towards peace, defence of the biosphere, respect for cultural difference, and social equity. These are three coexisting historical structures and three different visions of reality. The three tendencies are each of them global in extent. They are not territorially distinct but overlapping in space.

Thirty years ago one might speculate about the opportunity international organizations had to gain greater autonomy and, through a functionalist process, gradually to encompass all mankind in a web of technical and economic cooperation that would eliminate causes of violent conflict. Today, the US–Soviet superpower balance of Cold War has been replaced by what I have elsewhere called a decadent phase of Cold War[3] in which structures created during the superpower rivalry – intelligence services practising covert violence and assassination, proliferation of weapons, control of information, and economic aggression – maintain themselves and engage in a global conflict which has now been baptised as 'the war on terror'. The decadent phase is in direct continuity from the superpower phase. Symbolic of this affiliation are Osama bin Laden and al-Qa'eda, whose activities were initiated with US support to attack the Soviet Union in Afghanistan, and then came to use Afghanistan as a base for attack on the United States. 'Empire' and 'terrorism' are engaged in a dialectic that knows no end.

The future of international organizations will very largely depend upon how far they can strengthen the historical structure out of which they have come – the inter-state system – while avoiding being taken over by the expansion of 'empire' and at the same time serving as a vehicle for the expression of the demands of civil society. The decision-making process of international organization now takes place within the framework of these competing historical structures. Bob Reinalda, Bertjan Verbeek and their co-authors have given us an insight into the process whereby this balancing act among coexisting and rival historical structures may be acted out.

Notes

1 There is a perceptive comment by Hadewych Hazelzet in her critical review of *The Anatomy of Influence* which appeared in the editors' earlier volume *Autonomous Policy Making by International Organizations* in which she points to an ambiguity in the work. She writes: 'They [Cox and Jacobson] wrote in reaction to functionalism without posing a clear alternative and arrived at a realist conclusion. Arguing against a positivist approach (which they regarded as closely connected to realism) they used instead a historicist approach which made their work more descriptive than explanatory' (39). We were indeed working in a time when there was a tension between two conflicting theories (functionalism and realism) and between two conflicting epistemological standpoints (positivism and historicism). Perhaps as editors each of us leaned in a different direction, one towards functionalism and positivism, the other

towards realism and historicism. But each of us was committed to the idea that a full understanding did not exclude the one or the other.

2 Michael Hardt and Antonio Negri, *Empire* (Harvard University Press, 2000) give a 'post-marxist' critical view; Martin Shaw, *Theory of the Global State* (Cambridge University Press, 2000) offers a more benign version; and Michael Ignatieff, *Empire Lite: Nation-Building in Bosnia, Kosovo and Afghanistan* (Penguin Canada, 2003) presents a liberal imperialist viewpoint.

3 Robert W. Cox, ed. *The New Realism. Perspectives on Multilateralism and World Order* (Tokyo: Macmillan for the United Nations University Press, 1997) 256–9.

1 The issue of decision making within international organizations

Bob Reinalda and Bertjan Verbeek

Introduction

The war against Iraq in 2003 may prove to be a watershed in post-Cold War international relations. The disposal of the Iraqi regime by a coalition of mainly Western states symbolizes the zenith of American hegemony. There can be no doubt that unipolarity characterizes world politics and that the remaining superpower, or *hyper puissance*, as French foreign minister Hubert Védrine coined it, will not hesitate to defend its vital interests, if necessary without the permission of the international community. From this perspective the United States (US) seems to be moving from a multilateral to a unilateral foreign policy. This was also illustrated by its resistance to the International Criminal Court, its struggle against the Kyoto Protocol, its driving of hard bargains over the New Economy within the context of the World Trade Organization (WTO), and its pressure on members of the North Atlantic Treaty Organization in 1999 to strike against Yugoslavia over Kosovo without a resolution from the United Nations (UN) Security Council.

In a unipolar world, why bother about the role of international organizations? What use is it to investigate their decision-making processes, when it is likely that their policies will either reflect the vital interests of the most powerful state or be ignored by that state if the outcomes are inconvenient for its hegemony? The escalation process leading up to the war against Iraq, however, suggests that analysing decision-making processes within international organizations may be relevant even in such extreme cases of unipolarity and 'high politics'. For one thing, it is important to realize that the US and the United Kingdom (UK) sought the adoption of a Security Council resolution that would legitimize their Middle East policies. States, especially democracies, cannot easily go to war without seeking international legitimacy, because this helps them to mobilize domestic and international support. In the end the US and the UK chose not to introduce a resolution giving explicit approval for military intervention, knowing that it would be defeated. They thus judged that such an international defeat would damage their domestic and international stance. Instead, they insisted that previous resolutions, especially number 1441, had already implied the authorization to engage in military conflict. The US-led effort in 2002 to obtain Security Council permission to intervene in Iraq was severely affected by the behaviour of the UN Monitoring, Verification and Inspection Commission (UNMOVIC) headed by Hans Blix. His interpretation of the mixed outcome of Iraqi compliance with UN resolutions regarding weapons of mass destruction proved authoritative for a long time, despite American attempts to impose their own interpretation. Blix's assessments thus slowed down the escalation process and contributed to the split among Security Council members.

These aspects of the Iraqi crisis underline two important matters. First, even in a security crisis the leading state prefers international legitimacy over acting as a lone cowboy. Second, an organizational unit of an international organization, such as UNMOVIC, because of its independent authority, can significantly affect the decision-making process even in areas of 'high politics'. It thus remains highly relevant, also after the war against Iraq, to acknowledge that (units of) international organizations may have some policy discretion and that therefore decision making within them is not simply explained by pointing to the power distribution among states.

The increased relevance of international organizations

The editors of this volume argue that the increased role of international organizations[1] over the last 15 years warrants a re-launch of the study of decision-making processes within them. At least four developments contributed to the greater relevance of international organizations to international and domestic politics (see Reinalda and Verbeek 1998). First, the end of the Cold War melted the icecap of superpower competition, which had held many international organizations frozen since the late 1940s. Second, globalization, defined as the deterritorialization of human interrelationships (see Baylis and Smith 2001: 14), acted as an incentive for states, and other actors, to deal with changing, intensifying interdependencies by widening the scope and density of international institutions. Third, globalization further reinforced the interrelatedness of transnational and domestic politics and offered means and opportunities for a whole variety of non-state actors to become active between the domestic and international spheres, also by approaching international organizations. Fourth, the growth of what has been called the legalization of international relations (see Goldstein *et al.* 2000) has made it more difficult for states, and other international actors, to ignore the policies of such international organizations as the European Union (EU), the European Court of Human Rights, and the WTO. In particular, the legal system of the so-called First Pillar of the EU, which has established a system of compliance through the national judiciaries, has created a maze that states cannot easily escape from.

These developments have augmented the number of tools of influence that international organizations can employ and they have increased their effectiveness (see Reinalda and Verbeek 2001). Problems of global governance require the mobilization of specific technical expertise that international organizations often possess. They make use of globalized mass media in order to apply shaming tactics. And the increased participation of a growing number of international and national non-governmental organizations (NGOs) provides opportunities for alliances against pressures from member states on international organizations, as well as possibilities to affect member states' domestic policies. The involvement of intergovernmental organizations in implementation and monitoring mechanisms offers further occasions to apply pressure. All in all, it can be argued that over the last 15 years these developments have contributed in principle to an increase of policy autonomy for international organizations, albeit in different degrees for different organizations. Recent events may cast doubt on this conclusion. But if recent events are a sign of growing American unilateralism, international organizations will become an even more interesting subject. In vital issue areas, the US is likely to challenge the acquired room of manoeuvre of international organizations. It will be interesting to see how they will react to that challenge.

This volume thus starts from the premise that international organizations have gained varying degrees of policy autonomy. Acknowledging such freedom of manoeuvre is not enough, however. It is only one piece of the puzzle. It is yet another matter to stipulate the conditions under which an international organization will make use of such room for policy manoeuvre and, equally importantly, what policies it will try to promote. These are the main questions this volume seeks to answer. The primary purpose of this book is to demonstrate that the examination of these questions requires a more in-depth analysis of decision-making processes within international organizations.

All contributors to this volume, in their own way, seek to analyse decision-making processes within international organizations. Often this is done against three considerations that place this volume in the context of current international relations theory. First, analysing decision making within international organizations takes place against the background of a sometimes latent, sometimes manifest, tension between the member states and the international organization, which is best encapsulated as a so-called principal–agent relationship. While a principal–agent relationship is usually couched in rational-choice language, the editors prefer not to immediately adopt the rationalist perspective, but rather to consider the tension between the member states and the international organization as a structural constraint within which decision making is taking place. Our second consideration is that the study of decision making within international organizations needs a more relaxed, pragmatic attitude toward the rationalist/constructivist divide that currently characterizes the international relations discipline. This requires us to focus on those elements that suggest the compatibility of rationalist and constructivist arguments, rather than on their incompatibility. Third, we believe that scholarship on decision making within international organizations will benefit from the use of so-called middle-range theories, just as their employment has been beneficial in comparative foreign policy analysis. Middle-range theories focus on accounting for a relatively small number of classes of events, and seek to concentrate on the contingent factors under which these events occur rather than on grand theories or single events. Below we will further develop these three considerations. In the concluding chapter we will assess the extent to which the contributions to this volume warrant their adoption.

This chapter is structured as follows. First, we will define more narrowly what constitutes an international organization and what are its decision-making processes. Next, we give an overview of past studies of international organizations from a decision-making perspective. Then we will elaborate on the three considerations presented above, which are important building blocks for a renewed attention to decision making within international organizations. This will be followed by the formulation of the research questions guiding this book. Finally, we will present an overview of six themes of decision making that characterize the individual contributions to this volume, as well as a short survey of each of the chapters.

The essence of international organization

Before we can embark on an analysis of decision-making processes within international organizations we need to define what constitutes an international organization, as well as what is meant by decision making in its context. From an organizational perspective three basic characteristics identify an international organization: a formal instrument of agreement between three or more nation states which serves as the *constitution* of the organization; an *international conference* where representatives of nation states convene and take decisions and where representatives of various non-state actors may exert influence; and a permanent *secretariat* for the performance of ongoing tasks (a bureaucracy led by a secretary-general) (see Judge 1985: 1591).

The first characteristic, the constitution of an international organization, explains its purposes, means and functions and regulates the existence and creation of specific organs, judicial procedures, membership, decision rules and the like. Furthermore, it is the basis of an organization's rule-creating capacity and the international conventions emanating from it, which in turn are part of the gradual codification of international law. In most cases, an international organization is conceived as a dynamic institution 'evolving to meet changing needs and circumstances and, as time goes by, becoming further and further removed from its treaty base'. This widening effect is the result of the expression of the will of the majority, with a dissenting minority appealing 'to the original meaning of their treaty commitments in vain' (Bowett 1982: 338).

The international conference is the forum or arena in which representatives of nation states convene to take decisions and where representatives of various non-state actors may exert influence directly through special arrangements, such as consultative or observer status, or indirectly, through the dissemination of ideas and expertise. These non-state actors include private organizations (NGOs and transnational companies), other intergovernmental organizations and experts, either as part of national delegations or in a more independent position. The conference structure has no direct parallel in national political systems. Although an international conference resembles them in form and procedures, there are considerable differences to national or local legislative bodies, because the main participants in the conference structures of international organizations are representatives of sovereign states 'who have more or less rigid instructions' (Cox and Jacobson 1973: 16). Murphy regards the conferences called by the nineteenth-century public international unions – the prototypes of the present organizations – as perhaps the most important institutional innovation engineered by them: 'ironically most state members did not expect it to have the effect it did'. While states saw the periodic conferences as a way to oversee the unions' work, the preparations for the conferences gave the unions' functionaries power over the international agenda as well as over the negotiation and implementation processes. Around 1910 the nineteenth-century practice of *ad hoc* conferences was replaced by regular, often annual, conferences organized by international organizations (Murphy 1994: 111–12).

The role and size of the international secretariats increased in parallel with the institutionalization of international conferences. When, during the Versailles Peace Conference in 1919, the League of Nations' secretariat was designed, the model of a 'principal secretary' plus assistants, who would serve as liaison agents between their respective governments and the secretary-general and enjoy the full confidence of both, was rejected in favour of a 'truly international secretariat, whose members ... must divest themselves of national preconceptions and devote themselves wholeheartedly to the service of the League', as Eric Drummond phrased it (cited in Dubin 1983: 472). The establishment of international civil servants, who were expected to be loyal to the international organization rather than their country of origin, was underpinned by individual incentives such as diplomatic status and competitive salaries. Nevertheless, member states remained keen on retaining close ties with 'their' civil servants. Drummond's success in the League, as well as Albert Thomas's striving for relative independence for the International Labour Organization secretariat (see Reinalda 1998), served as the model for international civil servants in the UN system and other international organizations. Because of their successes in creating an independent international civil service, Drummond and Thomas became role models for later secretaries-general, such as UN secretary-general Dag Hammarskjøld, who wanted to make their mark on their international organizations' policies.

It is thus important to realize that international organizations comprise at least two sets of actors: its member states and its organizational units, in particular the international secretariat. This distinction has terminological implications. When in this volume we discuss an international organization's policy discretion, we imply the acts of the international secretariat, including its substructures of committees, commissions and departments (unless stated otherwise). When we employ the term decision making within international organizations, we usually refer to the entire policy process as defined by the international legal framework of an intergovernmental organization, in which member states, the international secretariat and various other actors participate. Occasionally, however, decision making within international organizations explicitly refers to the policy process within the international secretariat (e.g. Chapter 7 by Freitas).

The essence of decision making within international organizations

For most international organizations the conference is the apex of their decision-making processes. The regularity of the meetings has turned these conferences into the *timetable* for the actors engaged in it. Most actors want to obtain, or obstruct, results before the conference closes. Following the timetable of the international conference implies that agenda setting takes place mostly before and during the meetings of preparatory committees and while national delegations are discussing their mandates. Scheduling the annual conferences to end at a previously established moment imposes clear deadlines on decision making. Furthermore, because next year another conference will be held, issues that did not make it onto the agenda this year may have another chance then.[2] In that sense, the so-called conference method of diplomacy (Kaufmann 1996) ensures that decision making within international organizations effectively never stops.

Leaving aside the variation in styles of interstate cooperation and in non-state actors' official possibilities to influence the internal process, the most general understanding of what happens *within* international organizations is *conversion* in a process of inputs, outputs and feedback (see Easton 1965). Inputs are converted into outputs within a 'black box', either as primary wishes and demands, or as assessments of implementation results. Decision making within international organizations thus can be described as a *process of phases*: a 'barrier model', where an issue goes from preparation to decision and to implementation, or from agenda setting through deliberation on causes and alternative solutions to voting on a preferred solution. It can also be considered as a combination of *temporal streams*: 'garbage cans' in which problems, solutions, decision makers and choice opportunities come together as a result of being simultaneously available. Finally, it can be presented as *rounds of decisions*, in which problems and solutions are relevant by the time a participant in the process, such as an initiator, broker or facilitator, is available to play such a role. In all cases we deal with ongoing processes of public decision making and the creation of international principles, norms, rules and decision-making procedures, referred to as international standard setting and law making.

While agenda setting is primarily determined by the timetable of conferences, actual decision making is seriously influenced by the *decision rules* that are applied. International organizations vary significantly in the decision rules they have adopted. One issue is the number of votes allotted to member states. Most organizations operate on the basis of 'one state, one vote', but others have a different distribution of votes. The IMF, the World Bank and the International Fund for Agricultural Development have allotted votes on the basis of financial contributions by individual member states. The International Coffee Organization distributes votes between producers and consumers of coffee on the basis of market shares. The International Labour Organization distributes votes to different sectors of society (representatives of the government, employers and workers). A further issue is the exact decision rule that is agreed upon. Formally, often, qualified majority rules apply, such as in the UN General Assembly (two-thirds). Frequently, different rules apply for different types of decisions. In practice, however, participants at international conferences strive for consensus, even when there is a formal vote at the end of the process. The main reason behind this is the idea that a possibly weak, but widely accepted, decision is to be preferred over a stronger, yet barely accepted decision. Actors may be part of the consensus while not going along with the majority position. They may, for instance, negotiate a formal individual exception to, or add their individual interpretation of, a certain article. Importantly, consensus seeking during conferences provides participants to whom the issue at stake is salient and whose agreement is badly needed with a negotiating advantage.

The decision-making process within the European Union differs in various ways from this general description. The regular three summit meetings of the European Council per year, as well as the more irregular official intergovernmental conferences (IGCs), are similar to annual conferences of international organizations to the extent that they create permanent opportunities for agenda setting. The day-to-day policy process within the EU, however, is different in two respects. First, the exclusive right of the European Commission to initiate legislation, within the so-called First Pillar, makes it a quite unique international bureaucracy. Actors who want to affect European legislation can lobby the Commission during the very first stages of legislation drafting. It provides the Commission with a tool of influence *vis-à-vis* the member states. Furthermore, in certain policy areas the European bureaucracy (the Commission, but also the European Central Bank or the Veterinary Committee) has an exclusive competency to decide. Examples include preventing business cartels, fighting inflation and combating foot and mouth disease.

Second, the EU (again, within the First Pillar) is highly legalized. The direct effect of European law, in combination with the role of national courts in upholding it, makes decision making within the EU more consequential than in other international organizations. The possibility for the Commission and other non-state actors, such as individual citizens and groups acting through them, to seek recourse to the European Court of Justice in Luxembourg provides them with an important tool of leverage over the member states. Day-to-day policy making is also affected by the decision rules that apply. EU member states have votes relative to the size of their respective populations. Furthermore, different rules (unanimity, qualified majority) apply to different issues. Interestingly, policy areas covered by the so-called Second and Third Pillars (foreign and security policy, and justice and home affairs, respectively) are not as much legalized. Decision making in these areas should thus resemble more closely the patterns of international conferences described above.

What kind of decisions do international organizations produce? Cox and Jacobson present a helpful taxonomy, which divides decisions of international organizations into seven categories: representational, boundary, symbolic, programmatic, rule-creating, rule-supervisory and operational. The first two categories refer to the functioning of the organization (internal procedures and external relations with other organizations), the second two to the elaboration of its purposes (with symbolic and programmatic texts), the third two to international law making and standard setting, and the final category relates to the provision of services by organizations (see Cox and Jacobson 1973: 9–11). The normal procedure for arriving at decisions at international conferences is based on a *draft resolution* which is voted upon or, in case a decision is reached without voting, is formed by consensus. The draft resolution contains a preamble with considerations and beliefs, and an operative part with endorsements, appeals and requests. Depending on the objective of a conference, its rules of procedure and traditional practices which may have been formed over the years, the draft resolution is turned into a final one, which marks the end of the conference's decision making (see Kaufmann 1996: 17).

Resolutions may take specific forms, such as declarations or international conventions. The latter, international treaties, signify the intention to establish a new legal relationship between nation states, and due to their legal capacity involve the creation of binding obligations. The legal way to implement these obligations is the ratification procedure, which brings the international agreement before the national parliaments. Ratification is a formal act, whereby a state consents to be bound by a treaty that its representatives have already signed at the international conference. Accepting the international treaty is to be followed by the necessary changes in national and subnational laws and practices. That the impact of power and politics is much more immediately recognizable and directly relevant in international law than in national law does not make it 'primitive', as Morgenthau argued (Morgenthau 1978), but means that it is heavily dependent on national legal systems for its implementation (see Malanczuk 1997: 5).

Previous studies of decision making within international organizations

The study of decision making within international organizations witnessed a short heyday in the early 1970s. Building on the pioneering efforts of scholars in comparative foreign policy since the 1950s (e.g. Snyder *et al.* 1962) and in European integration (Haas 1958), decision making became a possible focus when studying international organizations. This culminated in a small wave of studies of international organizations' decision-making, of which Ernst Haas's *Beyond the Nation-State* (1964 [1968]), Robert Cox and Harold Jacobson's *The Anatomy of Influence* (1973) and Jacobson's *Networks of Interdependence* (1979) became the best known contributions. The early 1970s also witnessed the rise of new approaches to the study of international relations, such as transnationalism (Keohane and Nye 1972; 1977). Critical of the realist approach, transnationalism challenged the dominant view that states are the primary actors in world politics, and to be studied as unitary actors. Although this new approach increasingly made international organizations an object of investigation in their own right, international relations theory began to widen its horizons. It did so through a gradual abandonment of the assumption that formal arrangements of international organizations explain what they do, and a shift to the actual and potential roles of international organizations in 'a more broadly conceived process of international governance' (Kratochwil and Ruggie 1986: 756). Unfortunately, this move to international regime theory, ironically in the journal *International Organization*, was coupled with a move away both from the consideration of international organizations themselves (Abbott and Snidal 1998: 6) and from international law. The Cox and Jacobson research programme was not implemented (for an exemption: Codding Jr. 1981), nor was it replaced by another one that took decision making within international organizations seriously. Furthermore, after the publication of Waltz's *Theory of International Politics* in 1979, mainstream regime theory returned to the original realist proposition that states dominate world politics (Verbeek 1998). Regime theory underpinned the neo-institutionalist wave particular to international relations, which tended to ignore international organizations as a subject in their own right. Curiously, at the same time, neo-institutionalism in mainstream political science and public administration called for renewed attention to formal organizations (see Peters 1999). Many of these studies portrayed organizational behaviour as driven by formal and informal norms, rules and understandings (March and Olsen 1989). This sparked a new interest in decision making within organizations. Their application to international organizations, however, remained negligible (see for an exception March and Olsen 1998) and would not occur properly until the growth in studies of the EU and the advent of constructivism in the 1990s.

What has been the contribution of the decision-making studies of the 1970s? Basically, they reveal a contradiction between *realist*-inspired studies of decision making and *pluralist*-oriented studies. While the former focus on the relative capabilities of an international organization's member states, the latter underline the impact other international actors and the international bureaucracy may have on policies to be adopted. More importantly, it is recognized by students of international relations that international organizations may simultaneously accommodate both phenomena. Cox and Jacobson showed that international organizations can be described at the same time as a *representative* subsystem, dominated by the major member states, and as a *participant* subsystem, which comprises all those who actually participate in the decision-making process (Cox and Jacobson 1973: 17). From this perspective the different weights of the realist and transnational approaches are an empirical matter.

Studies of the representative subsystem

In studies of the representative subsystem the international organization is considered as an instrument in the hands of its member states, at best as an arena for discussion between them (Krause and Nye 1975). The distribution of capabilities between member states and their coalitions is the major independent variable in explaining decision making within an organization. Many of these studies investigated voting patterns within the United Nations family of international organizations (e.g. Newcombe *et al.* 1970; Rai 1972; Vincent 1972; Newcombe *et al.* 1977). Their findings suggest that patterns of UN voting reflect shifts in the global distribution of power. Whereas until the mid-1950s Western member states outvoted Communist states in the General Assembly and the Security Council, they gradually lost ground to a combination of Communist and non-aligned countries. The latter managed to form a quite effective and durable coalition, called the Group of 77. While, until the 1970s, it was principally the Soviet Union which had to seek recourse to issuing vetoes in the Security Council, this role is later taken over by the US, which finds itself increasingly isolated especially over its support for Israel. Today, UN voting patterns remain a popular subject of study (e.g. Kim and Russett 1996; Voeten 2000).

Studies of European integration add the impact of decision rules to this perspective. Within the UN, apart from in the Security Council, the principles of 'one state, one vote' and qualified majority have produced the voting patterns described above. Within the EU, until the Single European Act of 1985, the decision rule was unanimity. From a realist perspective this is likely to produce policies based on the lowest common denominator, basically giving the most stubborn member state the best position at the negotiating table (Haas 1968). Indeed, the period of so-called Eurosclerosis between 1966 and 1985 is usually attributed to the relatively poor results the unanimity rule is likely to produce in an international organization consisting of competing, interest-driven states (for a different interpretation see Golub 1999). Eurosclerosis was paralleled in the 1970s and early 1980s by paralysis of many UN organizations because of what was called 'politicization'. This refers to the perceived abuse of technical issues of international cooperation to the benefit of political issues, such as the nuclear arms race and Israel's security policy. Politicization eventually led several Western states, among them the US, to leave international organizations such as the International Labour Organization and UNESCO. Clearly then, the representative subsystem of international organizations reflects world politics, in which member states dominate decision making and in which states that grow dissatisfied may decide to leave.

Studies of the participant subsystem

Most studies of the participant subsystem suggest that the bureaucracy of an international organization, together with other actors, may be relevant in the decision-making process. In general the international bureaucracy is considered a unitary actor, represented by the organization's administrative leader, the secretary-general. Some, however, argue that the international bureaucracy is itself a pluralistic whole of actors. Four major themes surface in the literature about international secretariats: the leadership that can be exercised in forging agreement between member states, the organization's ability to affect the policy agenda, the impact of intra- and inter-organizational turf wars and the loyalty conflicts experienced by individual international civil servants.

Because organizations are ruled by coalitions of interests depending on mutual accommodation, international consensus, according to Haas, can come about as the result of continuous bargaining between governmental delegates, the international organization's bureaucracy and also independent experts, in which the organization's leadership may take the lead and persuade member states to move beyond the lowest-common-denominator outcome by 'splitting the difference' or even 'upgrading the common interests' (Haas 1968: 111). Displays of leadership may even go beyond acting as a mere broker. This is evident from several studies of the role various secretaries-general played in UN organizations. Individual leadership, then, means that an international civil servant is able to affect decision making on the basis of his or her own policy agenda. The prime example is UN secretary-general Dag Hammarskjøld, but similar claims can be made for others, such as the chairman of the European Commission Walter Hallstein (Knight 1970; Rosenthal 1975; Meyers 1976). Similarly, the UNCTAD secretariat created by Raul Prebisch had a substantive impact on UNCTAD's actual policies for a generalized system of trading preferences (Bhattacharya 1976).

A small number of studies pays attention to bureaucratic battles and coalitions within and across international organizations. In the wake of the bureaucratic-politics approach to foreign policy of the early 1970s, it was noted that international organizations compete with each other in trying to sell policies to member states. This was the case with the Food and Agricultural Organization (FAO), which saw its existence threatened by the advent of the World Food Program (WFP) (Weiss and Jordan 1976). Following the wave of transnationalism, other studies pointed to transnational coalitions of (subunits of) international bureaucracies and (subunits of) national bureaucracies in powerful member states (Hopkins 1976). Appreciating the conflict international civil servants have perceived between loyalty to their international organization and to their country of origin, several studies focused on socialization processes within international bureaucracies. Their findings suggest that the development of an 'internationalist outlook' depends on the length of time one serves within an organization, on whether one is paid by one's country of origin or by the organization, and on the extent to which the international organization is characterized by conflict (Scheinman and Feld 1972; Wolf 1973; Ernst 1978; Michelmann 1978; Peck 1979).

Some of the studies of decision making within international organizations, focusing on the so-called participant subsystem, demonstrated that international bureaucracies can have an individual impact on the policies adopted. These studies thus preceded later investigations into the relative policy autonomy of international organizations. Moreover, those with a focus on the relationship between an organization and its member states in the representative subsystem anticipated the portrayal of that relationship as one between an agent and its principals. Most studies are poorly informed by general theories of decision making, despite the sporadic use of middle-range theories, such as bureaucratic politics from foreign policy analysis and socialization theory from sociology. Furthermore, important elements of decision making remain absent. These include the role of non-state actors such as NGOs and international businesses (Gordenker and Weiss 1995; Arts *et al.* 2001), the connection between international policy making and domestic politics, the nature of the preferences put forward by the international bureaucracy, and the independent role of norms and of international and European law.

How to re-launch and improve the study of decision making within international organizations?

A re-launch of the study of decision making within international organizations would profit from the three crucial points of departure mentioned above: the recognition that the policy autonomy of an international organization is embedded in a tense relationship between international organizations and their member states, that a pragmatic attitude towards the rationalist/constructivist divide in international relations may be fruitful in producing empirical studies, and that the study of decision making within international organizations is best served by modest theoretical claims regarding contingent empirical phenomena. What is the rationale behind these considerations?

Principals and agents

Principal–agent theory aims at analysing the relationship between an actor – the principal – who delegates, but does not surrender, authority to a certain body – the agent – specifically designed to perform certain tasks (see Bendor *et al.* 1987; Bendor 1990). The relationship between member states and the bureaucracy of an international organization can be described as a principal–agent relationship. International organizations are part of institutional arrangements that serve to increase the predictability of the behaviour of states and thus to mitigate the negative consequences of international anarchy (see Lake 1996: 10, 14). Even from a strictly neo-realist perspective, therefore, states have an interest in setting up intergovernmental organizations, as long as the latter will further their interests. Whether states do create them also depends on the costs they will incur (see Lake 1996: 15). With the growth of globalization states have concluded many more international treaties and have founded quite a few additional international organizations to deal with some of its consequences (see Shanks *et al.* 1996). States and international organizations are now caught up in a principal–agent relationship more than ever.

When states create international organizations, they delegate authority in certain areas to them and engage in a principal–agent relationship in which they are the principals. The main analytical problem is to determine and explain the agent's leeway (see Meunier 2000). Although formally a principal can withdraw the delegated authority, this is a drastic measure, which may not outweigh its costs (see Frey 1997: 116–17). This is all the more so in the case of international organizations, because these have not one, but many principals. One state's withdrawal is not likely to be very effective. An agent's freedom of manoeuvre stems mainly from an asymmetrical distribution of information favouring the agent. This asymmetry then produces 'shirking' – also called 'bureaucratic drift': agents pursuing interests of their own (see Pollack 1997: 108–9).[3] In order to curb the potential for an agent's freedom, principals develop various oversight procedures or construct situations in which one agent is set against another, expecting them to hold each other in check. Oversight procedures and their enforcement, however, involve additional costs for principals and their application is dependent on a cost–benefit analysis by the principals (Pollack 1997: 111). Some academics argue that an agent's independence is more apparent than real, because of such oversight procedures and because agents will anticipate the principals' preferences and thus will seldom propose actions that will not gain majority agreement (e.g. Bendor *et al.* 1987: 888; Pollack 1997: 108–11). Others argue, however, that several conditions weaken these checks on agents. If a principal–agent relationship is characterized by the presence of many principals, an agent may exploit the differences between them. This capacity is enlarged if the decision rules governing the principals' decisions allow the agent to exploit such differences. For instance, if unanimity between principals is required, an agent needs to form a coalition with one principal only. Furthermore, if no agreement between principals is reached, the status quo may well be to the advantage of the agent (Pollack 1997: 111–12).

The principal–agent characterization helps in investigating decision-making processes taking place within international organizations. It provides what we would like to call the *baseline*. International organizations and member states are caught up in a structural relationship of mutual dependency. States have founded international organizations because they benefit from them. International organizations physically exist because they receive funding from their member states. This relationship implies that at all times a scenario is possible in which it is more beneficial for principals to rein in their agents, despite the costs involved. This threat, for instance, is permanently felt at the United Nations, an organization which has been in financial trouble for decades and which is often pressured by its main financial supporter, the US, to adjust its policies at the risk of not receiving American membership dues. This inherent tense relationship between principal and agent is even felt in the highly legalized EU (see Van Kersbergen *et al.* 2000). In the 1990s EU member states attempted to, and sometimes succeeded in, curbing the policy autonomy of the European Commission. For example, regarding the EU's external economic relations, in 1997 the member states determined that on certain, crucial, trade issues, such as services and intellectual property, the Commission was to share negotiating authority with the Council, while before that the Commission held exclusive negotiating competence (Meunier 2000). Many contributions to this volume recognize that decision making within international organizations develops against this realist background of the principal–agent baseline, without denying alternatives.

Principal–agent analysis also hints at the independent interests an international organization may be pursuing in exploiting the leeway granted to it by its principals. Here we touch the rationalist/constructivist divide in international relations. Principal–agent analyses assuming a rationalist perspective argue that agents (international organizations) tend to seek expansion of their missions or their budgets, or pursue a mixture of the two (see Bendor *et al.* 1987: 875). However, the concrete objectives of these agents may be hard to derive from such axiomatically ascribed motives (see Barnett and Finnemore 1999: 705–6). Often, the position of international organizations on international issues cannot simply be reduced to material interests alone. The United Nations Environmental Program (UNEP) has no immediate stake in specific solutions to environmental problems, but the organization's actual positions still need to be explained (Nicholson 1998). Adopting a more pragmatic attitude to the rationalist/constructivist divide implies that, in addition to taking rationalist propositions about the motives of an international organization into account, constructivist accounts of preferences help to explain an international organization's preferred policy and thus its behaviour during the decision-making process.

Furthermore, principal–agent analysis provides a first clue as to the sources of influence available to (organizational units within) international organizations and their member states. Three such sources surface in the principal–agent literature: (1) international organizations are more likely to affect decision making the more they have an information advantage over their member states; (2) international organizations are more likely to affect decision making the more principals they face, because the plurality of principals enables them to play off member states against each other; and (3) international organizations are more likely to affect decision making the more decision rules applied by member states work to the advantage of the organization. The closer decision rules resemble unanimity, the smaller the number of member states that have to ally with the organization in order to produce an outcome closer to the position of the international organization.

In summary, we recognize that international organizations and their member states are caught up in a structurally interdependent relationship. Rather than simply embracing the rationalist assumptions, we suggest that the study of decision making within international organizations would benefit from a moderate perspective in two ways. First, by recognizing that decision making within international organizations always takes place against the background of the potential conflict between principals and agent, a conflict that occasionally can emerge and affect the decision-making process. Second, by recognizing that a moderate perspective offers important suggestions regarding preferences and sources of influence of an international organization.

Rationalists and constructivists

Officially labelled as such in the 50th-anniversary issue of *International Organization* (Katzenstein *et al.* 1998), the rationalist/constructivist divide in international relations now constitutes the third 'big debate' in the discipline,[4] which has reduced the differences between neo-realism and neo-liberalism to a gentle conversation between like-minded rationalists (Ruggie 1998). Constructivism, however, is an umbrella term for many different theoretical and epistemological positions. Nevertheless, all constructivists oppose rationalism's dominance of the international relations discipline. Rationalism strives to formulate theories about the behaviour of nation states, which are considered to be the main actors in world politics. These theories conceive of states as rational, utility-maximizing and unitary actors. Neo-realist and neo-liberal theories focus on patterns of conflict and cooperation between states acting under the conditions of international anarchy. At the very least, international anarchy renders international cooperation difficult, because it prevents states from trusting one another. In its worst form, it makes conflict endemic to the system because states permanently have to take into account shifts in their relative power positions. International organizations are of limited significance in these accounts. Neo-realists see them essentially as a vehicle for the interests of the major states. Neo-liberals consider them as part of international institutions that may help improve international cooperation by lowering transaction costs, for instance through the provision of information about other states' intentions (Keohane 1984). Generally, however, international organizations are considered incapable of playing an independent role. The only exception is rationalist principal–agent theory, which argues that international organizations may dominate decision making because they have carved out policy autonomy for themselves. Yet this policy discretion ultimately depends on member states, which believe it rational to delegate certain tasks to international civil servants and are aware that the costs of reining them in mostly outweigh the benefits.

Constructivists agree that the rationalists' account of international relations is restricted, because they take interests or preferences as given and have an inapt view of the role of norms and ideas in international relations. Constructivists offer a different account on various grounds. They allow for the possibility that behaviour in international relations is not interest-driven, but rather motivated by identity and related beliefs, norms and values (Price and Reus-Smit 1998; Ruggie 1998; Weldes 1999). This is rooted in their central notion that actors in world politics socially construct their environment. Anarchy and the security dilemma are not an everlasting objective condition, but a situation created by states themselves and reproduced in their language (sovereignty), symbols, rules of conduct (diplomacy) and corresponding interactions. States, however, are able to change the conditions of anarchy and develop a new system of interaction (see Wendt 1999). Nevertheless, even under conditions of anarchy, actors may be motivated by concerns other than power and material interests alone. Normative concerns, such as human rights, the environment or poverty, may be part of the equation of what constitutes an actor's preference in international relations and in international decision making.

Furthermore, once normative concerns have acquired legitimacy in the international arena, for instance through the adoption of a resolution or the creation of an international organization in order to deal with the problems being addressed, these concerns produce a constitutive effect (Klotz 1995; Ruggie 1998), that is to say they almost take on a life of their own. Once a norm has been formally accepted, it becomes more difficult for those states whose interests are not served by the norm to simply ignore its existence, even if they only pay lip service to it. In general, its formal acceptance means that it is possible that it starts affecting the behaviour of nation states. Monitoring mechanisms, such as prescribed by international conventions, contribute to the general awareness of the extent to which states abide by the accepted norm, and thus affect the reputation of states in international relations. The constitutive effect of norms may thus produce a change in preferences of interest-driven actors that should be taken into account when analysing multilateral decision making.

Finally, normative concerns have an empowering effect. They not only affect international and domestic public agendas, but they also legitimize new, often non-state, actors and offer them windows of opportunity to take part in the policy-making process (Klotz 1995; Keck and Sikkink 1998). International organizations are a major beneficiary of the discussion and acceptance of international norms. They often provide a podium for actors expressing such concerns and are regularly charged with the tasks of monitoring international agreements and of playing a part in their implementation in national political systems. International organizations thus acquire authority and leeway. NGOs, both international and domestic, often benefit from international norms in a similar fashion. Very often this happens through their formal incorporation into international negotiations, either within the organization or as members of national delegations. It comes as no surprise that the constructivist emphasis on the constitutive and empowering effects of norms entails the recognition that international relations and decision making involve many more relevant actors than states alone and that the separation of the international and domestic spheres is rather unhelpful.[5]

Due to its different viewpoint, constructivism adds to our understanding of decision making within international organizations. It suggests that an organization's independent preferences may stem from sources other than material interests and its inherent tendency to expand budgets and tasks alone. Rather, international organizations may develop original notions of preferred policy outcomes based on international civil servants' sharing of certain values, norms or bodies of knowledge. If one wishes to investigate the extent to which rationalism and constructivism are complementary, a next step would be to try and stipulate the conditions under which material and immaterial interests carry different weights. The baseline, adopted above from the principal–agent approach, suggests that the closer any threat is to the core business of an international organization, the more likely it is that the policy put forward by the organization reflects its narrow material interests.

Constructivism also suggests that international organizations pursuing policy objectives motivated by norms, ideas or identity are likely to form alliances with other like-minded actors in world politics. These might be member states, international NGOs, other international organizations or actors within the domestic society of member states. In the constructivist literature these like-minded actors are often depicted as a so-called epistemic community, although strictly speaking not all actors in the alliance need to be motivated by ideational concerns and some of them may act on the basis of material interests. The implication is that decision making within international organizations will be characterized by transnational coalitions consisting of domestic, transnational and state actors. Here the possible complementarity of rationalism and constructivism once more presents itself. Once having determined the extent to which a coalition of actors is motivated by ideational concerns, it will be necessary to investigate the actors' relative success in affecting decision-making processes within international organizations. This requires an analysis of their sources of power, for instance their technical information advantage, their ability to use shaming tactics or their ability to mobilize domestic actors in order to put pressure on member states' national governments (a good example is Klotz 1995).

Finally, constructivism suggests that through decision making within international organizations normative concerns may have an empowering effect. Four such effects can be distinguished. First, the arenas of international organizations have offered ample opportunities for allowing a seat at the conference table to ideational actors. International organizations have the authority to give formal accreditation or observer status to actors other than member states, such as NGOs and other intergovernmental organizations. These thus suddenly find themselves able to affect the international conference's agenda or debates. Second, because decision making within international organizations consist of a regular pattern of (bi-) annual conferences, ideational concerns, once tabled, remain a legitimate topic of discussion. States acting on the basis of narrow material interests will find it difficult to remove these concerns from the agenda and, at the very least, are forced to pay lip service to them. Third, decision making within international organizations often ends with a decision to entrust the international secretariat or a special committee with monitoring compliance with adopted policies. International organizations are thus empowered to let ideational concerns affect their assessment of their member states' policy performance and are given an instrument to apply shaming tactics if compliance is deficient. Finally, if decision making within an international organization results in policies that are motivated by normative concerns, it may have a constitutive effect on the baseline itself. That is, the boundaries of the playing field of the international organization may have been pushed outwards because new norms allow the organization to do more than before. Eventually, these dynamics may change the rules of the game between the principals and the agent.

To sum up, we argue in favour of an approach that stresses the complementary elements of the rationalist/constructivist divide. We are of the opinion that international organizations may be motivated by a combination of material and ideational motives. Moreover, normative concerns may have important constitutive and empowering effects. At the same time, we recognize that power politics remain part of the game that is being played within international organizations. Explaining the outcomes of decision-making processes within international organizations thus not only requires an adequate account of actors' preferences, but also of their tools of influence.

Middle-range theories

The discussion between rationalists and constructivists is not limited to substantive issues such as the origin of preferences and the impact of ideational factors. It also extends to the question of the role theory should play in social science. Some constructivists would go as far as to reject the rationalist position completely on epistemological grounds. They consider the starting point of individual actors giving meaning to, or constructing, their environment as inherently irreconcilable with the behaviouralism of many rationalists and see the latters' interest in sweeping generalizations (see, for a discussion of this position, Price and Reus-Smit 1998; Zehfuss 2002: 5–6, 38–9). We take a so-called middle-ground position (see Adler 1997). In our attempt to account for processes of decision making within international organizations and their outcomes, the optimal strategy may be to look for contingent generalizations for particular phenomena, or what has been called 'small-t[heory]-claims' (Price and Reus-Smit 1998: 275). With regard to decision making within international organizations, these contingent generalizations may pertain to process characteristics such as agenda setting and organizational learning, the impact of actors, such as bureaucratic agencies within an international organization and NGOs, on particular policies, or specific tools of influence such as expert knowledge, shaming or the power of the purse. Explicit research questions regarding particular phenomena will resolve the problem of the extent to which insights from rationalism should take precedence over insights from constructivism (see Verbeek 2000).

This 'small-t-claim' approach has already been practised extensively in the subdiscipline of comparative foreign policy analysis (see Neack *et al.* 1995: 4–5). Over the years scholars in foreign policy analysis have accumulated a toolbox of theoretical approaches, some better refined than others, that aim at accounting for classes of particular phenomena, rather than attempting to formulate a general theory of foreign policy (see Hermann and Sundelius 2004). Research informed by these theories often is conducted through single or multiple comparative case studies (see George and McKeown 1985; George 1993). Interestingly, many of these so-called middle-range theories deal with decision making, albeit within the nation state. They include, amongst others, theories of national role conceptions, bureaucratic politics, group decision making and the impact of individual cognitive beliefs. Apart from in a small wave of studies in the 1970s (see the section above), these theories have barely been applied to decision making within international organizations. We believe that a renewed interest in using them is warranted, all the more so because some of the recent debates surrounding these theories echo the debates between rationalists and constructivists. For instance, students of bureaucratic politics discuss the limits of the simple notion that bureaucracies have an a priori interest in budget expansion and the possibilities of a theory that bureaucracies develop policy preferences on the basis of substantive and normative considerations (Welch 1998; Weldes 1998).

Many of the contributions to this volume are informed by these middle-range theories. Most of them consist of single case studies. Only Schemeil, Woods and Dratwa (Chapters 4, 6 and 13) deal with two organizations. Middle-range theories applied in this volume are garbage can theory (Joachim, Chapter 11), bureaucratic politics (Freitas, Chapter 7), two-level game (Kerremans, Chapter 2; Bayne, Chapter 8), role conflict theory (Trondal, Chapter 9), groupthink (Woods, Chapter 6), epistemic communities (Bayne, Chapter 8; Schemeil, Chapter 4) and the role of institutions (Lovecy, Chapter 3; Hazelzet, Chapter 10). Most contributors operate in the middle ground between constructivism and rationalism. They present their analysis against the background of the baseline of member states (principals) and international organizations (agents). We thus hope that this volume will demonstrate that a more pragmatic attitude towards current debates within the international relations discipline will improve the study of decision making within international organizations.

Research questions

In general this volume seeks to investigate the conditions under which an international organization will make use of its room for policy manoeuvre and, equally importantly, to account for the policies it will try to promote. The examination of these questions requires a more in-depth analysis of the decision-making processes within international organizations. Contributors to this volume will first describe the extent to which the international organization they analyse is enjoying a significant degree of policy freedom. A next question is how to account for the organization's (more specifically, its secretariat's) attempts, or lack thereof, to exploit that freedom to promote its own policy preferences. This requires an analysis of the origin and nature of its preferences as well as of the attempts to make these preferences prevail in the decision-making process within the organization.

Within that framework this volume looks to address the following general questions: (1) to what extent is decision making within international organizations restricted by the baseline defined by the principal–agent setting characteristic of the relationship between international organizations and their member states?; (2) to what extent do insights from rationalist and constructivist perspectives contribute to accounting for an international organization's preferences and its relative success in promoting them?; (3) to what extent do middle-range theories contribute to accounting for the outcomes of decision-making processes within international organizations?

Overview of the volume

The authors in this volume present their contributions under six headings, all of which clarify major elements of decision making within international organizations. These are leadership, consensus building, organizational dynamics, conflicts of loyalty, policy windows and learning processes. These themes have been chosen because they allow for an assessment in the concluding chapter of the pragmatism we advocate with regard to the principal–agent approach and the rationalist/constructivist divide, as well as the application of middle-range theories.

Leadership

Leadership refers to the ability of international organizations and their subunits to exploit their relative policy freedom to initiate policies that go beyond the baseline set by their member states and to make the latter accept these further-reaching policies. Leadership thus presents an important clue in investigating the importance of the borderline as suggested by the principal–agent approach.

In Chapter 2 Bart Kerremans explores successful leadership in a supranational policy domain of the European Union. He combines Putnam's two-level game with principal–agent theory to analyse the dynamic nature of the relationship between EU institutions in the context of multilateral trade negotiations. Within the WTO multilateral trade rounds the European Commission, negotiating on behalf of the EU, has to find the right balance between the member states' concerns and the requests made by its negotiating partners in the WTO. This specific context provides the Commission, fulfilling the role of agent, with opportunities to act independently of its principals. The Commission itself, however, clearly restricts this autonomy. Instead of using its opportunities extensively, the Commission involves member states' representatives in such a way that pressures from these representatives are being transmitted to their domestic political systems, in order to secure the member states' approval of the agreements the Commission is negotiating within the WTO. Internal EU decision making about this external negotiating process is definitely controlled by the Commission, in particular by its dominance over the leeway given to member states' representatives within the WTO and its ensuring that member states understand the rationale for concessions made by the Commission within the WTO.

In Chapter 3 Jill Lovecy investigates the possibilities of leadership of a highly intergovernmental organization, the Council of Europe. She departs from a neo-institutionalist approach that conceives of institutions as encompassing formal rules, policy structures and social norms. In order to analyse the Council of Europe as an arena of decision making with a relatively large degree of autonomy, she derives the concept of a dominant policy framework from historical and sociological institutionalism, in this case as a project centred on marrying democratic institutions with enforceable human rights. The core values of this framework are sustained by organizational arrangements, in which the main site of governmental representation (the Committee of Ministers) is unable to control the organization's agenda. Instead, the Parliamentary Assembly emerges as an unexpected leader. In order to explore the terms on which the member states have delegated specific powers to the Committee and the Assembly Lovecy applies the rational-institutionalist concept of institutional decision rules (an important independent variable in principal–agent theory). The crux of this arrangement is the Assembly's right of policy initiative in conjunction with practices of differentiated and deferred implementation, as was further developed and institutionalized in the Council of Europe's regional human rights regime.

Consensus building

The chapters discussing consensus building analyse how international civil servants contribute to achieving consensus among member states. Two different types of consensus building are presented: within an international organization with the aim of reaching a decision, and between an international organization and (one of) its member states over policy implementation.

Yves Schemeil, in Chapter 4, discusses the first type. He depicts the often informal procedures contributing to consensus building within the World Meteorological Organization (WMO) and the World Trade

Organization. He propounds that experts and bureaucrats within an international organization have more power the less fixed the issues are. Drawing attention to the revision of not-fully-identified issues by an internal 'bureaucracy' of experts and secretariat members, he argues that the technical nature of issues within the WMO and WTO often compels member states' representatives to include external and internal experts more closely than originally specified in both organizations' charters or assumed by theories predicting that governments control multilateral regimes. He questions the underlying dichotomization of 'expert networks' and 'political agents' and their alleged involvement at successive stages of the negotiating process, in which experts first indulge in truth-seeking consensus and politicians afterwards vote in order to know the distribution of power. Schemeil shows on the basis of both formal and informal procedures within the two organizations that this dichotomization is not an accurate description of the WTO and WMO decision-making processes. He instead discerns a strong inclination towards consensual statements, contractual settlements and political compromise, related to a process in which decisions are made through a delicate balance of power between three parties and their subcomponents: external and internal consultants, members of the international secretariat, and governmental representatives. The outcomes of their negotiations depend on the ways expertise and political competence are combined at various stages of the whole decision-making process by people who display both kinds of skill, and who frequently switch from positions where expertise is required to positions where diplomacy is needed.

In Chapter 5 Martin Marcussen focuses on the second type of consensus building, that between an international organization, the Organization for Economic Cooperation and Development (OECD), and a member state that has to reach agreement on the implementation of an internationally accepted policy. In this case member states do not comply with international norms because of sanctions or self-interest, but because of an ongoing common procedure based on the collection, elaboration and diffusion of data, analyses, perspectives and ideas that eventually results in consensus-based 'soft' regulation. This procedure enables learning processes to occur in a closed, deliberative forum where national civil servants and the OECD secretariat meet on a very frequent basis. National civil servants are thus socialized into OECD norms. The OECD secretariat plays a role of its own, because the multilateral surveillance process is an interplay between national central administrations and various OECD organs in which the secretariat takes the lead, whereas other, potentially more critical, actors are not included. Marcussen regards the OECD secretariat as an ideational artist and arbitrator. It tries to shape and fashion the political agenda in the surveyed countries through the creation of a common vocabulary between experts across national boundaries and a regular monitoring procedure (cyclical peer review) based on this common vocabulary. States comply with this soft regulation because they have gradually learned to accept and respect its international norms during the decision-making process within the OECD.

Organizational dynamics

The next two chapters explore the organizational dynamics within an international bureaucracy. A better understanding of decision making requires us to abandon the idea that international bureaucracies can best be described as unitary actors with clear policy preferences. Rather, international bureaucracies consist of many organizational subunits which may develop their own perspectives on policy problems. In addition, unusual circumstances, such as crisis situations, may have a decisive impact on their performance.

In Chapter 6 Ngaire Woods considers the impact of a sudden currency crisis on small, but relevant, policy units within the IMF and the World Bank that are responsible for handling financial relations with the country in question. In particular, she discusses the possibility that small-group dynamics may account for the poor handling of these groups' policy discretion. Decision-making processes within international organizations may make it difficult for staff members of an international secretariat to challenge the organization's mainstream view. Woods applies groupthink theory to IMF and World Bank decision making during the 1994 Mexican financial crisis. She underlines that neither international financial institution has a formal right to interfere with policy making within member states. Once granted access, they must use information provided by national governments extremely carefully. The need to preserve access and confidentiality may lead to compromises, in which negative or adverse comments are suppressed. This can be regarded as an impediment to frank and impartial analyses of a country's economic situation. The effects of such an impediment may be aggravated by defects in decision making within the organizations, which mean that their personnel starts from the wrong assumptions and fails to consider alternative scenarios.

Raquel Freitas, in Chapter 7, demonstrates the impact of competence battles between organizational subunits within the United Nations High Commissioner for Refugees (UNHCR) with conflicting perspectives. She highlights another unexpected outcome. Like Kerremans, she argues that, although external changes may provide a window of opportunity for international organizations to attempt to increase their autonomy, they may not exploit that situation. In the 1990s the UNHCR had the opportunity to expand its mandate into assisting and protecting internally displaced persons (IDPs). In the event it did not do so, due to internal divisions between various departments with different organizational cultures and perspectives. Freitas expects the leadership of the organization to devise policies which are inclusive of a wide range of policy choices that will be acceptable to all relevant subunits and that take into account the external circumstances. Balancing between pressures from the external and the internal environments, organizational leadership is expected to exploit the differences between external actors and to promote an outcome closer to the preferences of the internal actors. This mechanism occurred within the UNHCR. Thanks to political brokerage by the high commissioner the final decision making about IDPs resulted in an expansion of assistance, but without a formal expansion of UNHCR's mandate.

Conflicts of loyalty

Conflicts of loyalty present a clue to understanding the behaviour of individual international civil servants. It also is a subject at the crossroads of rationalist and constructivist perspectives, juxtaposing member states' interests and identification with an international organization. On the one hand, international bureaucrats are expected to feel allegiance to their organization, its ideals and interests, while on the other hand they continue to feel close bonds with their country of origin. The more supranational the international organization, the more likely it is that conflicts of loyalty are resolved in favour of the organization.

In Chapter 8 Nicholas Bayne investigates the loyalty of the G7/G8 sherpas to their national states. What happens when national civil servants are repeatedly involved in multilateral decision making? Bayne focuses on the personal representatives of the heads of governments, who operate at the heart of the G7/G8 summit process. These so-called sherpas are members of the personal staff of the heads of government or belong to the top section of the national bureaucracy. Bayne argues that the sherpas neither have agenda-setting power, nor constitute an epistemic community. They owe their influence to their position as the fulcrum between the political reflexes of their patrons and the bureaucratic pressures of the national government machine. Sherpas prepare decision making by playing two-level games with their patrons, usually trying to harness their innovative instincts so as to promote workable agreements, and with the government machine, where they seek to overcome bureaucratic inertia. At both levels they use their close links with their fellow sherpas to increase the possibilities of reverberation, whereby international pressures help to produce policy decisions domestically. Although sherpas are the most influential figures in determining what issues go to the summit and what agreements are concluded there, their role has become more demanding and their power has been eroding due to challenges from the heads themselves, from the extension of the G8 apparatus and from outside forces. There is, however, no conflict of loyalty because the sherpas remain national civil servants, be it that they are able to use international pressures domestically.

Jarle Trondal, in Chapter 9, explores several types of conflict of loyalty at various administrative layers within the European Union. He analyses a specific segment of the bureaucracy: EU committees composed of national and EU civil servants. He investigates what happens to civil servants' identities and role orientations during decision-making processes: to what extent do national civil servants invoke intergovernmental, supranational or functional loyalties, roles, identities and allegiances when attending EU committees? Drawing from sociological and cognitive perspectives on decision making, he assumes that the identities and roles are moulded institutionally, through processes of matching perceptions of appropriateness to particular situations and through systematic and routinized allocation of attention. Trondal concludes that national government officials interacting in EU committees are multiply embedded with multiple roles and identities. Functional roles and identities are called upon, amongst others, in expert committees that prepare decisions for the Commissioners, whereas supranational roles and allegiances are assumed at the permanent representation in Brussels, owing to the intensity of participation in EU committees. His main finding is that national civil servants tend to become empathetic towards the EU's perspective. This is particularly true for civil servants from functional ministries and for those participating in functional committees in Brussels.

Policy windows

Whether and how international organizations make use of their freedom of manoeuvre depends on the extent to which opportunities, or policy windows, to table certain topics occur or can be created. When successfully put on the agenda, the issue may lead to a redefinition of actors' preferences, constructivists argue. It might even lead to a change in the baseline. At the same time, resistant member states may use the agenda-setting process to keep such issues out, rationalists would claim. In this agenda-setting game, international organizations can create policy windows by striking alliances with actors, especially NGOs, for instance by allowing them consultative status at international conferences (see Reinalda and Verbeek 2001).

In Chapter 10 Hadewych Hazelzet discusses the conditions under which non-state actors influence EU reactions to human rights violations. She argues that the influence of non-state actors depends on the type of decision they want to influence and, consequently, on which actor they gain access to, and at which stage of the decision-making process. She expects non-state actors to be able to lobby the Commission with more ease than the Council, since the Commission speaks with one voice whereas the Council consists of 15 member states. Although non-state actors seldom had a decisive role in EU decision making with regard to sanctions for specific countries, they contributed through fact finding and raising awareness. Their greatest influence was found, contrary to expectation, during the initial stages of the decision-making process, when the EU contemplates whether to react (a Council decision) rather than later when the EU decides on how to react (a Commission decision). She explains this finding by showing the strengths of non-state actors and the nature of EU decision making.

Jutta Joachim, in Chapter 11, demonstrates how NGOs operating within the United Nations affected the outcomes of multilateral negotiating processes. Her case is the issue of reproductive rights and health, which women NGOs successfully placed on the UN agenda and which, due to continued NGO influence within the UN, resulted in an officially adopted platform for action. Joachim applies theories of both agenda setting, in particular the garbage can model, and social movements. These suggest that NGOs are able to mobilize governmental support for their issue by framing problems and solutions strategically, by exploiting the political opportunity structure in which they are embedded and by drawing on the mobilizing structures which they have at their disposal. The Women's Alliance that played the crucial role in this case went through a learning process itself. During the early stages of the agenda-setting process its framing activities still had an inchoate quality and seemed more determined by changing political opportunities. But by the time the final decisions were made at the official population conference the Women's Alliance was operating in a strategic way and was able to use institutional rules and procedures as well as its own mobilizing structures to its advantage.

Learning processes

Every decision-making process entails a feedback mechanism. The outcomes of decision making serve as an input into the next round. This is certainly true for international conference diplomacy. The regular pattern of (bi-)annual conferences ensures that the game is never really over. Feedback mechanisms enable actors to learn from past experience and to change their attitude. Rationalists as well as constructivists have discussed learning. Rationalists basically argue that actors learn to adapt their behaviour to the conditions of international politics. International competition socializes them into imitating successful behaviour. From a rationalist perspective, the interests or preferences of actors remain the same (Waltz 1979). Constructivists, however, claim that social learning may lead actors to acquire new interests or preferences (Checkel 1999: 548–9). The final two contributions to this volume take on the issue of learning, focusing on two different types of institutional setting. Dirks in Chapter 12 investigates social learning by an international organization after a first round of decision making. Dratwa in Chapter 13, however, points to the possibility that decision making within an international organization on a specific norm or regulatory principle may not end with a formal decision on its precise contents. Rather, small incremental steps on related issues may slowly narrow down the precise meaning of the norm. The social-learning effect of these small steps may be that actors gradually change their preferences regarding the contents of the norm.

Jan Dirks explains the adoption of a far-reaching convention by the International Maritime Organization (IMO) in 1995 in two steps. He begins with a rational-choice perspective, which explains why the seafarers' and ship owners' organizations supported the formulation and implementation of the new convention, and why the IMO member states adopted it. A win-win situation emerged as a result of bargaining processes between governmental and non-governmental actors that took place within the IMO arena. In order to explain the specific outcome of the debates, however, a second step is necessary. A social-constructivist perspective is required in order to view the IMO as a bureaucratic learning actor that has induced its member states as well as the NGOs to redefine their interests. The IMO started to question its own activity-guiding theories-in-use and its own understanding of its role. With regard to the new convention, the IMO acted as an idea-generating centre that allowed the various actors to identify new activity options for solving the qualification of seafarers' issues under discussion. The adoption of the convention hence was the result of a combination of two factors. First, a favourable actor constellation, which allowed the development of overlapping interests during the bargaining process. Second, ongoing organizational learning processes, which allowed the international bureaucracy to act as an innovator of ideas acceptable to the various parties.

Jim Dratwa investigates the evolution of a specific norm, the precautionary principle. He argues that one must pay attention to how this evolving norm structures international decision making. He analyses the principle's development within the EU and the Codex Alimentarius, an expert wing of the WTO in matters related to food. Dratwa argues that the advent of a common understanding of this fundamental but difficult-to-grasp principle is the result of three types of social learning: learning by individuals in international organizations, by international organizations themselves, and by states, polities or societies (hence coined 'societal learning'). What happens within the EU and Codex Alimentarius is a process of boundary definitions and integration of issues, actors and domains. This gradual process structures decision making on the basis of the principle. There is no such thing as a final decision about a general or a universal principle, but rather a series of decision acts, also in different policy sectors and different polities.

Conclusion

This volume seeks to revitalize the study of decision making within international organizations. The short-lived blossoming of the subject in the

1970s on the basis of Cox and Jacobson's seminal work should be the basis for a fresh start. Their *Anatomy of Influence* taught us that an organization's apparatus can crucially influence decision making. At the same time, Cox and Jacobson rightly warned against an underestimation of the power and interests of the organization's member states. We believe that the adoption of the principal–agent framework can help in further mapping out the boundaries between an organization's freedom of manoeuvre and the limits set by its member states. Adopting this approach should not imply the mistake of blindly taking up its rationalist premises. Furthermore, this volume is pleading in favour of a pragmatic attitude to the rationalist/constructivist debate. If the substantive claims of both sides are paid due attention, it will become possible not only to account for an organization's policy discretion, but also for the contents of the specific policies it is advocating. Moreover, it allows for the possibility that the fundamental dependency relationship between an international organization as agent and its member states as principals – what we dubbed the baseline – may be transformed because decision making produces changes in preferences. Finally, previous studies of decision making suggest that the development of modest theoretical claims may be the best way forward to a better understanding of what happens within large organizations. This volume thus proposes that a renewed interest in decision making within international organizations calls for a return to and further development of what constructivists would call 'small-t', and others would call middle-range, theories. We expect the individual chapters of this volume to contribute to that fresh start.

Notes

1 This volume is explicitly aimed at analysing decision making within *intergovernmental* organizations. The term *international* organization is used here as synonymous with intergovernmental organization.
2 The UN Security Council is an exception. Rather than convening once a year, it can be called into session in case of a threat to international peace and security.
3 Another consequence may be 'slippage'. This is not the concern of this volume.
4 The first debate was between idealists and realists, the second between traditionalists and behaviouralists.
5 Note, however, that for constructivists it is not necessarily the case that actors other than states are relevant in the international system. As a matter of fact, Wendt formulates a constructivist theory of state behaviour. The salience of non-state actors in international relations has its roots in transnationalism and pluralism. Obviously, non-state actors can be analysed from both rationalist and constructivist perspectives.

References

Abbott, K.W. and Snidal, D. (1998) 'Why States Act Through Formal International Organizations', *Journal of Conflict Resolution*, 42(1): 3–32.

Adler, E. (1997) 'Seizing the Middle Ground: Constructivism in World Politics', *European Journal of International Relations*, 3(3): 319–63.

Arts, B., Noortmann, M. and Reinalda, B. (eds) (2001) *Non-State Actors in International Relations*, Aldershot: Ashgate.

Barnett, M.N. and Finnemore, M. (1999) 'The Politics, Power, and Pathologies of International Organizations', *International Organization*, 53(4): 699–732.

Baylis, J. and Smith, S. (eds) (2001) *The Globalization of World Politics. An Introduction to International Relations*, Oxford: Oxford University Press.

Bendor, J. (1990) 'Formal Models of Bureaucracy: A Review', in N. Lynn and A. Wildavsky (eds) *Public Administration. The State of the Discipline*, Chatham: Chatham House, 373–417.

Bendor, J., Taylor, S. and Van Gaalen, R. (1987) 'Stacking the Deck: Bureaucratic Missions and the Search for Alternatives', *American Political Science Review*, 81(4): 873–96.

Bhattacharya, A.K. (1976) 'The Influence of the International Secretariat: UNCTAD and Generalized Tariff Preferences', *International Organization*, 30(1): 75–90.

Bowett, D.W. (1982) *The Law of International Institutions*, London: Stevens & Sons.

Checkel, J.T. (1999) 'Social Construction and Integration', *Journal of European Public Policy*, 6(4): 528–44.

Codding Jr, G.A. (1981) 'Influence in International Conferences', *International Organization*, 35(4): 715–24.

Cox, R.W. and Jacobson, H.K. (eds) (1973) *The Anatomy of Influence. Decision Making in International Organization*, New Haven: Yale University Press.

Dubin, M.D. (1983) 'Transgovernmental Processes in the League of Nations', *International Organization*, 37(3): 469–93.

Easton, D.E. (1965) *A Systems Analysis of Political Life*. New York: Wiley.

Ernst, M. (1978) 'Attitudes of Diplomats at the United Nations: The Effects of Organizational Participation on the Evaluation of the Organization', *International Organization*, 32(4): 1037–44.

Frey, B.S. (1997) 'The public choice of international organizations', in D.C. Mueller (ed.) *Perspectives on Public Choice. A Handbook*, Cambridge: Cambridge University Press, 106–23.

George, A.L. (1993) *Bridging the Gap. Theory and Practice in Foreign Policy*, Washington: United States Institute of Peace Press.

George, A.L. and McKeown, T.J. (1985) 'Case Studies and Theories of Organizational Decision Making', *Advances in Information Processing in Organizations*, 2(1): 21–58.

Goldstein, J., Kahler, M., Keohane, R.O. and Slaughter, A.-M. (2000) 'Introduction: Legalization and World Politics', *International Organization*, 54(3): 385–99.

Golub, J. (1999) 'In the Shadow of the Vote? Decision Making in the European Community', *International Organization*, 53(4): 733–64.

Gordenker, L. and Weiss, T.G. (1995) 'Pluralising Global Governance: Analytical Approaches and Dimensions', *Third World Quarterly*, 16(3): 357–87.

Haas, E.B. (1958) *The Uniting of Europe*, London: Stevens.

—— (1968) *Beyond the Nation-State. Functionalism and International Organization*, Stanford: Stanford University Press.

Hermann, M.G. and Sundelius, B. (eds) (2004) *Comparative Foreign Policy Analysis*, Englewood Cliffs: Prentice Hall.

Hopkins, R.F. (1976) 'The International Role of "Domestic" Bureaucracy', *International Organization*, 30(3): 405–32.
Jacobson, H.K. (1979) *Networks of Interdependence. International Organizations and the Global Political System*, New York: Alfred A. Knopf.
Judge, A.J.N. (1985) 'International Organizations: An Overview', in: *Yearbook of International Organizations 1985/86*, Muenchen: K.G. Saur, 1591–1606.
Katzenstein, P.J., Keohane, R.O. and Krasner, S.D. (1998) '*International Organization* and the Study of World Politics', *International Organization*, 52(4): 645–85.
Kaufmann, J. (1996) *Conference Diplomacy. Third Revised Edition*, Houndmills: Macmillan Press.
Keck, M.E. and Sikkink, K. (1998) *Activists Beyond Borders. Advocacy Networks in International Politics*, Ithaca: Cornell University Press.
Keohane, R.O. (1984) *After Hegemony. Cooperation and Discord in the World Political Economy*, Princeton: Princeton University Press.
Keohane, R.O. and Nye, J.S. (eds) (1972) *Transnational Relations and World Politics*, Cambridge: Harvard University Press.
—— (1977) *Power and Interdependence. World Politics in Transition*, Boston: Little, Brown.
Kim, S.Y. and Russett, B.M. (1996) 'The New Politics of Voting Alignments in the United Nations General Assembly', *International Organization*, 50(4): 629–52.
Klotz, A. (1995) *Norms in International Relations. The Struggle against Apartheid*, Ithaca: Cornell University Press.
Knight, J. (1970) 'On the Influence of the Secretary-General: Can We Know What It Is?', *International Organization*, 24(3): 594–600.
Kratochwil, F. and Ruggie, J.G. (1986) 'International Organization: A State of the Art on an Art of the State', *International Organization*, 40(4): 753–75.
Krause, L.B. and Nye, J.S. (1975) 'Reflections on the Economics and Politics of International Organizations', *International Organization*, 29(1): 324–42.
Lake, D.A. (1996) 'Anarchy, Hierarchy and the Variety of International Relations', *International Organization*, 50(1): 1–33.
Malanczuk, P. (1997) *Akehurst's Modern Introduction to International Law. Seventh Revised Edition*, London: Routledge.
March, J.G. and Olsen, J.P. (1989) *Rediscovering Institutions. The Organizational Basis of Politics*, New York: The Free Press and Collier Macmillan.
—— (1998) 'The Institutional Dynamics of International Politics', *International Organization*, 52(4): 943–69.
Meunier, S. (2000) 'What Single Voice? European Institutions and EU–U.S. Trade Negotiations', *International Organization*, 54(1): 103–35.
Meyers, D.B. (1976) 'The OAU's Administrative Secretary-General', *International Organization*, 30(3): 509–20.
Michelmann, H.J. (1978) 'Multinational Staffing and Organizational Functioning in the Commission of the European Communities', *International Organization*, 32(2): 477–96.
Morgenthau, H.J. (1978) *Politics Among Nations. The Struggle for Power and Peace. Fifth Revised Edition*, New York: Alfred Knopf.
Murphy, C.N. (1994) *International Organization and Industrial Change. Global Governance Since 1850*, Cambridge: Polity Press.
Neack, L., Hey, J.A.K. and Haney, P.J. (1995) 'Generational Change in Foreign

Policy Analysis' in L. Neack, J.A.K. Hey and P.J. Haney, *Foreign Policy Analysis. Continuity and Change in its Second Generation*, Englewood Cliffs: Prentice Hall, 1–15.

Newcombe, A.G., Young, C. and Sinaiko, E. (1977) 'Alternative Pasts: A Study of Weighted Voting at the United Nations', *International Organization*, 31(3): 579–86.

Newcombe, H., Ross, M. and Newcombe, A.G. (1970) 'United Nations Voting Patterns', *International Organization*, 24(1): 100–21.

Nicholson, M. (1998) 'A Rational Choice Analysis of International Organizations. How UNEP Helped to Bring About the Mediterranean Action Plan' in B. Reinalda and B. Verbeek (eds) *Autonomous Policy Making by International Organizations*, London: Routledge, 79–90.

Peck, R. (1979) 'Socialization of Permanent Representatives in the United Nations', *International Organization*, 33(3): 365–90.

Peters, B.G. (1999) *Institutional Theory in Political Science. The 'New Institutionalism'*, London: Pinter.

Pollack, M.A. (1997) 'Delegation, Agency, and Agenda Setting in the European Community', *International Organiztion*, 51(1): 99–134.

Price, R. and Reus-Smit, C. (1998) 'Dangerous Liaisons? Critical International Theory and Constructivism', *European Journal of International Relations*, 4(3): 259–94.

Rai, K.B. (1972) 'Foreign Policy and Voting in the UN General Assembly', *International Organization*, 26(3): 589–94.

Reinalda, B. (1998) 'Organization Theory and the Autonomy of the International Labour Organization' in B. Reinalda and B. Verbeek (eds) *Autonomous Policy Making by International Organizations*, London: Routledge, 42–61.

Reinalda, B. and Verbeek, B. (eds) (1998) *Autonomous Policy Making by International Organizations*, London: Routledge.

—— (2001) 'Theorising Power Relations Between NGOs, Inter-Governmental Organisations and States' in B. Arts, M. Noortmann and B. Reinalda (eds) *Non-State Actors in International Relations*, Aldershot: Ashgate, 145–58.

Rosenthal, G. (1975) *The Men Behind the Decisions*, Farnborough: Lexington Books.

Ruggie, J.G. (1998) *Constructing the World Polity. Essays on International Institutionalization*. London: Routledge.

Scheinman, L. and Feld, W. (1972) 'The European Economic Community and National Civil Servants of the Member States', *International Organization*, 26(1): 121–35.

Shanks, C., Jacobson, H.K. and Kaplan, J.H. (1996) 'Inertia and Change in the Constellation of International Governmental Organizations, 1981–1992', *International Organization*, 50(4): 593–627.

Snyder, R.C., Bruck, H.W. and Sapin, B. (1962) *Foreign Policy Decision-Making. An Approach to the Study of International Politics*, New York: Free Press.

Van Kersbergen, K., Lieshout, R.H. and Verbeek, B. (2000) 'Institutional Change in the Emerging European Polity' in O. Van Heffen (ed.) *Governance in Modern Society*, Dordrecht: Kluwer, 35–60.

Verbeek, B. (1998) 'International Organizations. The Ugly Duckling of International Relations Theory?' in B. Reinalda and B. Verbeek (eds) *Autonomous Policy Making by International Organizations*, London: Routledge, 11–26.

—— (2000) 'Criticizing US Method and Thought in International Relations: Why a Trans-Atlantic Divide Narrows IR's Research Subject' in T.C. Lawton, J.N. Rosenau and A.C. Verdun (eds) *Strange Power. Shaping the Parameters of International Relations and International Political Economy*, Aldershot: Ashgate, 139–57.

Vincent, J.E. (1972) 'An Application of Attribute Theory to General Assembly Voting Patterns, and Some Implications', *International Organization*, 26(3): 551–82.

Voeten, E. (2000) 'Clashes in the Assembly', *International Organization*, 54(2): 185–215.

Waltz, K.N. (1979) *Theory of International Politics*, New York: McGraw-Hill.

Weiss, T.G. and Jordan, R.S. (1976) 'Bureaucratic Politics and the World Food Conference: The International Policy Process', *World Politics*, 28(July): 422–39.

Welch, D. (1998) 'A Positive Science of Bureaucratic Politics?', *Mershon International Studies Review*, 42(Supplement 2): 210–16.

Weldes, J. (1998) 'Bureaucratic Politics: A Critical Constructivist Assessment', *Mershon International Studies Review*, 42(Supplement 2): 216–25.

—— (1999) *Constructing National Interests. The United States and the Cuban Missile Crisis*, Minneapolis: University of Minnesota Press.

Wendt, A. (1999) *Social Theory of International Politics*, Cambridge: Cambridge University Press.

Wolf, P. (1973) 'International Organization and Attitude Change: A Re-Examination of the Functionalist Approach', *International Organization*, 27(3): 347–71.

Zehfuss, M. (2002) *Constructivism in International Relations*, Cambridge: Cambridge University Press.

Part II
Leadership

2 The European Commission and the EU member states as actors in the WTO negotiating process

Decision making between Scylla and Charibdis?

Bart Kerremans

Introduction

Since the end of the Uruguay Round, the role of the European Commission as negotiator on behalf of the European Union (EU) in multilateral trade negotiations has increasingly come under attack. Questions have been asked about the exact powers of the Commission and about the way in which it has wielded these. Related to these questions, concerns have been raised – especially among the EU's external negotiating partners (see Barchefsky 2001) – on the authoritative nature of the deals the Commission agrees to and about its authority and accountability inside the EU (see Paemen and Bensch 1995: 95). Indeed, the question of authority, accountability and relative powers remains a daunting one when it concerns the EU's conduct of external trade negotiations.

It is perhaps no coincidence that this question comes up in the context of negotiations conducted within the framework of the World Trade Organization (WTO). This framework provides both opportunities for the European Commission to act independently of the EU member states, and incentives to do so. It is a framework that has too large a membership to allow the EU to completely control it. It is equally a framework that creates a negotiating agenda which also contains issues on which the EU prefers not to have any multilateral negotiations at all. Consequently, internal EU decision making on WTO negotiations takes place under the pressure engendered by an external (WTO) negotiating process. It pushes the EU to consider concessions, even if these are unattractive, and it puts pressure on the EU negotiators – and thus, the Commission – to strike the right balance between the concerns of the EU member states and the requests made by the EU's negotiating partners in the WTO. Striking this balance is often a difficult exercise. As the member states' reactions to the November 1992 Blair House Agreement have shown, it may even backfire on the Commission's role as a negotiator. It is important therefore to ask how the Commission strikes this balance, what the effect of the WTO negotiating context is (if any), and how it affects the relationship between the Commission as negotiator on behalf of the EU and the EU member states. That is the subject of this chapter. I will show that although the WTO framework may provide the Commission with opportunities to act autonomously, it is not in the Commission's interest to use these opportunities extensively. On the contrary, the Commission must use the WTO system, and the EU system itself, to involve the member states' representatives sufficiently in the WTO negotiations for pressures from the member states to be transmitted to their domestic political systems. Only by doing so can the Commission secure the member states' approval of the agreements that it negotiates in the WTO.

The analysis itself is based on two pieces of empirical research. The first and most extensive part consists of interviews with both Commission officials and officials of the member states in charge of the negotiations on the Uruguay Round.[1] The aim of these interviews was not to conduct research on the substantive issues of the cases, but rather to help the interviewees focus their answers on concrete cases and not on the abstract notion of negotiations in general. This was necessary, because the questions themselves dealt with the way in which respondents perceived their role and the opportunities of their role in both internal EU decision making and external negotiations, as well as the limits of that role and its opportunities, given the involvement of other actors (external partners, member state representatives, Commission representatives), and the impact of certain factors (the institutional context of external negotiations, stages in the negotiating process, politicization of negotiating issues, constraints of the mandate, etc.).[2]

The second part of the empirical research was conducted through interviews with European Commission negotiators, officials from the Belgian trade administration (February–April 2001) and British trade officials (May–July 2002). Due to time constraints, this part only encompasses seven Commission officials, three Belgian officials and seven British officials directly involved in the operation of Committee 133. The interviews focused on the preparations for the (failed) attempts to start the Millennium Round (1998–9) and the subsequent attempts by the Commission to revive the idea of a round of multilateral trade negotiations in 2001 (Everything but Arms Initiative).

External trade negotiations and principal–agent analysis

When analysing international trade negotiations, it seems obvious to do so from the perspective of Putnam's two-level game. In this game, the chief of government (COG) negotiates agreements with other countries while taking into account that these agreements have to be ratified domestically. Part of the COG's role is to anticipate the reactions of the domestic ratifiers by trying to conclude an agreement that is within their win-set. But in doing so, the COG has opportunities to affect the agreement by influencing the domestic actors' win-set itself. In addition, due to her/his double-edged position – as an actor at both international and domestic level – (s)he can determine to a certain extent where an international agreement will be located within the win-set of the domestic actors. This combination of dependence (on the subsequent ratification process) and autonomy (due to her/his double-edged position) means that the COG's actions can be analysed from a principal–agent perspective, in which the agent has to face several domestic principals.

In external trade negotiations conducted by the European Union, it is the Commission that fulfils the role of agent, while the member states take on the role of principals (see Meunier and Nicolaïdis 1999: 480; 2000: 327–8). Central to the principal–agent analysis is the autonomy acquired by the agent and the restrictions the principals experience in preventing this (see Schmidt 2000: 41). Different explanations can be put forward for why principals delegate, why agents are interested in being autonomous, and how they achieve this (see Majone 1996; Pollack 1997). Whatever these explanations, the agent's attempts to be autonomous are important in the principal–agent analysis. These attempts involve the use of formal and informal devices by the agent to safeguard her/his own interests and to escape from the principals' control. Even if most authors discussing the principal–agent theory stress the agent's desire to gain autonomy, it remains an empirical question whether this is always the case. There are situations in which an agent may have an interest in restricting her/his own autonomy and in allowing the principals to provide legitimacy and the concomitant authority (see Nicolaïdis 1999; also Majone 2001: 109–14).

Most importantly, principal–agent theory points the researcher to the fact that the relationship between the agent and her/his principals can only be fully understood by analysing the formal and informal interactions between the two. This means that in order to fully grasp the governance regime of the EU's external trade policy, one has to look at the informal and formal aspects of the relationship between the different actors involved, and raise the question of whether, and if so how, the principals try to impact upon the agent, and *vice versa*. The system can be fluid therefore, because the principals may be prepared to invest in efforts to monitor the agent at certain points in time, but not at others. Likewise, the system's fluidity can be exposed by the agent's concern to escape from the principals' control at one moment and to seek such control at others. In other words, the relationship between the principal and the agent is a dynamic one, where concerns about autonomy, authority and control may lead to different outcomes at different points in time; outcomes that are affected by the use of both formal and informal devices. As such, principal–agent theory forms an attractive perspective – complementary to Putnam's two-level game – for analysing the dynamic nature of the relationship between the EU institutions in the context of multilateral trade negotiations. The specifics of this relationship, and the context in which it is being analysed, are that one agent has to deal with several principals (see Majone 1996: 38–9; Stone Sweet and Sandholtz 1997: 313; Hooghe and Marks 2001: 76–7), and that this agent has a double-headed position: one inside the EU itself, and one in the external trade negotiations (in this case the WTO).

Negotiating in practice

The Treaty of the European Community (TEC) provides several legal bases for the conduct of external trade negotiations. As far as trade in goods is concerned, Article 133 TEC applies. Under certain conditions, paragraph 3 of Article 300 TEC and Article 310 TEC (on association agreements) are also used.

The third paragraph of Article 133 TEC[3] distinguishes three consecutive stages in trade negotiations (on goods): initiation, negotiation and ratification. Following this article (and the text of Article 300 TEC), the initiation stage starts with recommendations made by the Commission to the Council and ends with the Council authorizing the Commission to open negotiations. The negotiation stage consists of negotiations conducted by the Commission and followed closely by a committee consisting of member states' representatives. This committee – which is in reality a structure of committees – is better known as Committee 133. At the end of the negotiation stage the Commission concludes the agreement, if any, on an *ad referendum* basis, after which the Council decides on its approval, i.e. ratification (Article 300 par. 2 TEC).

The Council may issue directives that determine 'the framework' within which the Commission has to negotiate. In the literature, these directives are quite often referred to as the mandate given by the Council to the Commission. From a principal–agent perspective, both the committee of member states' representatives and the mandate provide the tools with which the principals (i.e. the member states) can exert control over the agent (i.e. the Commission). However, treaty provisions in Articles 133 TEC and 300 TEC equally grant the agent – i.e. the Commission – veto power. This power is granted twice, first at the start of the initiation stage and then again at the start of the ratification stage. In the former case, the Commission can withdraw any proposal if it feels that negotiations among the member states will result in directives that it cannot accept. In the latter case, the Commission simply does not conclude an agreement with its external partners.

The system described above suggests a more or less adversarial model of the EU's conduct of external trade negotiations, where the Commission negotiates and the Council disposes. The Commission may have a double right of veto, but during the negotiations it has to consult with Committee 133. This committee's influence is guaranteed by the fact that on the one hand, the member states can hold a Sword of Damocles in the threat of not approving the agreement and, on the other hand, a mandate already exists during the negotiations that clearly sets the confines of what the member states will be prepared to accept at the end of the process.

But the Commission needs to negotiate, and in order to be able to do so it needs some autonomy. Given this combination of the need for autonomy and the member states' ability to control, Articles 133 and 300 seem to provide an 'invitation to struggle', an invitation to adversarial relations. The picture as outlined by practitioners, however, is partly different. 'Partly', because some conflict indeed arises, at times fairly strongly. But cooperation, sometimes quite intense, seems to be a word that captures the situation as much as conflict does. Two elements play an important role in this. First, the way in which the mandate is approached and, second, the fact that the member states exert a large part of their control through authoritative representatives.

The relative role of the negotiating mandate

When talking to Commission trade officials and their member state counterparts, one is struck by the discrepancy between the prominent place of the negotiating mandate in the literature and its more equivocal role in reality. This seems to be a consequence of the fact that the mandate is a double-edged sword in a twofold sense. On the one hand, mandates are inherently contrary to the adaptive capacity of the EU in external trade negotiations, and this creates its own risks for the principals. On the other hand, mandates define the parameters, not just for the Commission but also for the member states themselves. They allow the principals to tie the hands of the agent, but at the price of mutually tying their own hands as well.

As far as the former is concerned, it is important to point out – as several interviewees did – that the Treaty does not *require* the Council to define a mandate or to issue negotiating directives. It only *allows* the Council to do so. Besides that and contrary to what one can find in the literature, the Treaty does not refer to a mandate but to directives. Most of the interviewees emphasized this. The term 'mandate' sounds more compelling than 'directive'; even if the Council has issued a directive, it remains the political responsibility of the Commission to assess its precise binding nature.

Whereas the Treaty does not require a mandate, not even a directive, it requires an authorization. Indeed, the Commission cannot formally start external trade negotiations without being authorized by the Council to do so. Based on information derived from interviews, however, one can conclude that in many cases such authorization is granted without the immediate issuance of negotiating directives, let alone a formal mandate. Directives are created during the negotiating process and regularly adapted in piecemeal fashion. And even then, the precise status of these directives is unclear. Examples are the 'mandates' the Commission received during the Uruguay Round and immediately before the Seattle Ministerial Conference.

Although some have claimed that the Commission took part in the Uruguay Round negotiations on the basis of a mandate, Commission officials themselves and their counterparts in the member states paint a more confused picture. First, the claim that 'the EU negotiated the conclusion of the Uruguay Round in 1993 under a mandate written in 1985!' (Nicolaïdis 1999: 102) cannot be confirmed, because many doubt that there even was a mandate. There was a text, the 1986 'conception d'ensemble', but all the way through the seven-year cycle of the Uruguay Round the status of this text remained unclear. In addition, this text was formulated in such vague terms that its usefulness declined the more detailed and focused the negotiations became. Finally, the text was never formally adopted by the Council (Paemen and Bensch 1995: 96).

Second, during the cycle itself, the Council and Committee 133 regularly discussed the negotiations and took decisions on the issues at stake. But once again, the precise nature of most of these decisions was unclear, and they can certainly not be interpreted as a formal mandate. A few exceptions occur, however, the most prominent of them over agriculture. There the Council adopted several texts that were meant to be clear and strict negotiating directives, to the extent that in these cases one can indeed define them as mandates.

Equally, in the preparatory stage of what was meant to become the Millennium Round the Council authorized the Commission to negotiate without issuing a formal mandate. The Council did adopt a position on the agenda of the Millennium Round, but relatively late in the process – in October 1999 – and in a way that can not be interpreted as laying down negotiating directives, let alone a mandate. The model that the EU (both the Commission and the member states) had in mind was quite similar to the model used during the Uruguay Round. During the WTO Seattle Ministerial Conference the Council would adopt a text formally authorizing the Commission to take part in a new cycle of multilateral trade negotiations, including a list of objectives to be achieved. As a matter of fact, on their way to Seattle the Commission officials already had a draft text for this authorization, which could be adapted depending on the negotiations the EU and its external partners would have in Seattle on the agenda of the Millennium Round. The text of the authorization was meant to closely reflect the WTO Ministerial Declaration to be adopted in Seattle. As such, it can hardly be considered a mandate in the strict sense of the word.

This authorization without a formal mandate is – according to the interviewees – the rule rather than the exception, even if member state representatives stressed that this does not mean that the member states do not provide any guidance on how the Commission should conduct the external negotiations. But there is a reluctance to do this through a strictly defined mandate. In explaining this, two arguments have been put forward. First, that if a mandate is determined at the start of the process, the EU's adaptive capacity is affected negatively. Indeed, as Commission officials have stressed, if the Council engages in the process of determining a mandate, the most conservative member states (those fearing concessions in the external negotiations) are able to pin the EU down to a minimalist position, with the result that later in the process – when external negotiations are taking place – the question will arise to what extent this position can be maintained. This lowest common denominator is the price member states in favour of the negotiations have to pay to those preferring the status quo.

Member state respondents stressed that from the point of view of the member states such a situation is dysfunctional. Given a minimalist mandate and strong external pressure on the EU to give in, the inability to adapt the mandate later in the process will inevitably lead to a situation where the Commission is going to weigh the pros and the cons of exceeding its mandate. The point here is that if the Commission decides to do so, it can do so in an uncontrolled way. What direction is the Commission going to take when exceeding the mandate? Will the Commission create a *fait accompli*, which will put the pressure directly onto the member states to decide whether or not to reject an agreement in excess of the mandate reached between the Commission and its external partners? In short, the negative effect on the EU's adaptive capacity translates into two problems: the difficulty of strategically adapting to the external negotiations, and the risk of a *de facto* loss of control by the member states over the Commission.

Apart from this argument about the effect on the EU's adaptive capacity, however, another argument is important as well. Contrary to what one can conclude from the Treaty, negotiating directives, or even a mandate, commit not only the Commission but also the member states. Taking away flexibility from the Commission means taking away flexibility from themselves. Conceding on issues in a compromise on the text of a mandate entails accepting all those parts of the mandate that one does not like. The Commission – and the other member states – could refer to these concessions if later on a member state declared itself unhappy with the concessions made in negotiations. This makes the member states reluctant to pin themselves down on clear positions, especially early in the process. Later on, when the external bargaining context is much clearer and the consequences of different options are much more predictable, this reluctance may decline, depending on where one stands compared with the other member states.

Because of the absence of a clear negotiating mandate at the start of, and even during, the external negotiating process, the emphasis is much more on an *interactive* determination of negotiating guidelines within the EU. In this process, the relationship between the Commission and the member states, or rather between the Commission and the members of Committee 133, is not by definition adversarial. It is a relationship that consists of a mixture of cooperation and opposition. In this sense, the approach adopted regarding the mandate and the negotiating directives directly affects the negotiation process between the Commission and the member states on the one hand, and the Commission and its WTO partners on the other.

Interaction rather than confrontation during the negotiating stage

The mixture of opposition and cooperation is a consequence of two factors. First, one of the important tasks of Committee 133 is to control the Commission, which suggests that some kind of conflict exists, or may emerge, between them. And Committee 133 is organized in such a way that it is able to control the Commission at all stages of the negotiating process. It convenes regularly at senior level and weekly (on Fridays) at deputy level. Whenever technical issues are on the agenda, the committee meetings can also be attended by national experts, or *ad hoc* Committees 133 can be created, as happened during the Uruguay Round. The resulting system of committees allows the member states to keep maximum control over the Commission's activities in the external negotiations. Thus, there is a form of opposition. Whereas up to a certain extent (and as we will see, it is indeed 'up to a certain extent') the Commission has an interest in negotiating without too much control by the member states, the member states want to keep as much control as possible over the Commission.

The second factor, the one that affects the 'cooperation side' of the mixture, is that ultimately the member states will have to approve the agreement through their representation on the Council. Commission officials stressed therefore that they have an interest in keeping the member states' representatives involved in the external negotiations. First, because this provides the Commission with an additional instrument to measure the member states' sensitivities. Second, because if necessary the latter have to feel 'the heat' of the external negotiations as much as the Commission does. It is only if this happens that they will understand why the Commission acted as it did, even if this meant that it had to interpret the negotiating guidelines 'flexibly'. But Commission officials stressed that in the process of defining the guidelines, too, they have an interest in involving the members of Committee 133 as much as possible. If these members know the external negotiating environment sufficiently well, there will be less risk that they will tie the hands of the Commission – through strictly defined directives – in a way that would jeopardize the external negotiations themselves.

The fact that the Commission has an interest in cooperation on the one hand, and in opposition on the other, affects the way in which it approaches its relationship with Committee 133. On the whole, most Commission negotiators prefer not to negotiate in the presence of the member states' representatives, unless such negotiations give the Commission the opportunity to show these representatives that it is working hard to defend their interests. Otherwise, when major concessions have to be made, the Commission negotiators tend to prefer more private negotiating sessions and the strategy of the accomplished fact. The external negotiating environment, especially in a setting such as the WTO, allows for variation in the extent to which the member states can attend – without being able to speak themselves – the negotiating sessions. The formal sessions – like the Trade Negotiating Committee (TNC) and the different Negotiating Groups during the Uruguay Round – provided the member states with the opportunity to attend. But most negotiations took place in more informal settings. The green room meetings are the first example, although there the tendency has emerged to allow at least the EU Council Presidency in alongside the Commission negotiators, and for the last few years most member states have been able to attend some of these meetings as well.

But apart from the green room meetings – where the 1994 Code of Conduct applies[4] – major breakthroughs tend to be achieved in private meetings between Commission negotiators and their main counterparts. Sometimes other forums, such as the 'Quad' meetings (the US, EU, Canada and Japan), are used, or private meetings behind the scenes of OECD ministerial meetings or G7 meetings. However, this does not imply that final agreements are drawn up in these kinds of private meetings. Yet it is significant that the outlines of final agreements are negotiated in such a way that a major opportunity emerges for the member states to completely reject them and, in doing so, jeopardize the possibility of achieving a final agreement.

In this whole system of *de facto* autonomy – whatever the terms of the mandate – there are two 'lubricants' that make the process less adversarial than it seems. First, the assumption of trust and, second, the carefully considered involvement of the member states. These two are largely intertwined.

Trust is of course an important facet of the delegation of negotiating authority to the Commission, although some respondents – both from the Commission and from the member states – stressed that there is no such thing as trust (Braithwaite 1998: 47; Levi 1998: 78;).[5] As one observed: 'Everybody knows, even expects, that the Commission will cheat or will have to cheat one way or the other. It is more a question, therefore, of limiting distrust, rather than granting trust' (Interview 27 February 2001). It is only because the member states assume that the Commission will cheat only when necessary, i.e. will fight as much as possible for a European interest that is sufficiently close to their own and will not give in unless really necessary, that they grant or leave it a certain amount of leeway. In the absence of this assumption the member states would not grant this latitude.[6] The acrimonious conflict that surrounded the Blair House Agreement of November 1992 led to a situation where some member states – notably France – believed that this assumption did not hold true any longer (see Meunier and Nicolaïdis 1999: 483–4). It partly explains why the provisions of Article 133 became an issue at the 1996–7 Intergovernmental Conference, and again at the 2000 IGC.

Second, it helps if the member states feel the heat of the external negotiations as well. Their involvement, which is partly a consequence of the Code of Conduct and partly the result of the Commission's willingness to properly expose them to the dynamics of the external negotiations, leads to a situation where Committee 133 transmits the pressures from the external negotiations through the EU system to the member states. Commission officials stressed that they perceive Committee 133 partly in this role. The transmitters are therefore both the Commission – which explains its actions to Committee 133 – and the member states' *representatives* on this committee.

As Committee 133 is also meant to be the arena where the member states express their concerns and their sensitivities to the Commission, it basically functions as a forum in which the pressure of the external negotiations and the pressure of internal concerns over these negotiations meet. Ultimately, the Commission officials – the people who negotiate externally – will have to decide what to do about these pressures, but more often than not they do not like to take that decision in a vacuum. They want to know the political parameters set by each of the member states and they want the member states to reassess these in the light of the political parameters of the external negotiating environment. In this sense, the Commission may take risks, but they are calculated risks.[7] The member states – as their representatives have witnessed – expect the Commission to take such risks, knowing (or expecting) however that in the first place these risks will be calculated, and in the second place that the arithmetic to calculate them will be based on the member states' interests and concerns.[8]

A cooperative system?

The picture painted above may give the impression that the EU's system of external trade negotiations is based on cooperation only, that the Commission has an interest in exposing Committee 133 to all information it has about the external negotiations. The reality, however, is more complex. First of all, the member states know perfectly well that the Commission's privilege as the external negotiator provides it with the opportunity to impact on the internal decision-making process in ways that would not exist in the absence of such a privilege. As one Commission official observed: 'Although the member states accept that the Commission is the sole negotiator, sometimes the concomitant privileges or the issues it proposes are difficult to swallow. Indeed, it means surrendering part of your control over the talks' (Interview 22 February 2001).

To a certain extent of course – due to the rules and the Code of Conduct – the Commission has to involve the member states through their representatives on Committee 133. Moreover, the Commission has an interest in doing so. But this still leaves the Commission some leeway to carefully meet out the member states' involvement in the external negotiations. The fact that an important part of the negotiations takes place in informal settings – such as the green rooms in the GATT/WTO – and through private contacts, provides the Commission with opportunities to strategically increase or limit Committee 133 members' access to the external negotiating process. When the Commission works towards a package deal for instance, which it is going to present as a *fait accompli* to the member states, it has an interest in restricting the transfer of information about that deal to the member states for as long as it has not been finalized with its external partners. There are two reasons for this. First, because constructing a package deal means that the Commission tries to give each of the member states sufficient reasons not to reject the agreement, and therefore the extent to which the Commission has succeeded in this can only be assessed when the agreement has been finalized and accepted by its external partners. Second, because exposing all its 'trump cards' to the member states early on in the process would mean that it would expose them to its external partners also. As recognized by both Commission officials and members states' representatives, the EU system is a 'leaking sieve' in which it is difficult, if not impossible, to keep a secret.

Once again, and up to a certain extent, the respondents from the member states indicated that *faits accomplis* are an inevitable part of the process, and that they accept that the Commission needs to do this – albeit within clear parameters – in order to be able to do what they expect it to do: fulfil its responsibilities by working towards an agreement. After all, the member states possess the ultimate sanction in case they are dissatisfied with the outcome: they – jointly – have the ability to veto it.[9]

Conclusion

Based on the above, how can one assess the Commission's autonomy as a negotiator in the WTO on behalf of the EU? It is clear that the external negotiations – those in the WTO – create opportunities for the Commission to act autonomously. This is certainly the case, because informal talks play such an important role in the WTO.

The WTO also provides incentives for the Commission to act autonomously. The construction of package deals on the one hand, and the pressure to negotiate on issues that are extremely controversial for some EU member states on the other, requires that the Commission shields its activities from continuous member state scrutiny. But the Commission has no interest at all in closing the WTO process completely to direct member state involvement. In order to ensure that the member states will understand the rationale for concessions made, the Commission needs to expose their representatives directly to the WTO negotiating process. Due to its central position between the external WTO process and the internal EU process (see Figure 2.1), and due to the opportunities the WTO process provides to engage in informal negotiations without member state attendance, the Commission can control the member state representatives' involvement (see dotted arrows in Figure 2.1) to a certain extent so as to strike the right balance between its negotiating autonomy and the need to get member states' backing for its activities. The WTO may thus provide opportunities for Commission autonomy, but this may serve the Commission's authority only up to a point. Rather than choosing between Scylla and Charibdis therefore, the Commission can avoid both by adjusting the interaction between the WTO negotiations and the EU's internal decision making on them. At the end of the day, it will be the latter which determines whether the Commission can remain a credible representative of the EU in the WTO.

Notes

1 The interviews on the Uruguay Round focused on the negotiations that took place between September 1986 (Punta Del Este) and December 1990 (Heysel Conference in Brussels).

2 The respondents were Commission officials who acted as negotiators in the external trade negotiations, and two groups of national officials: one group

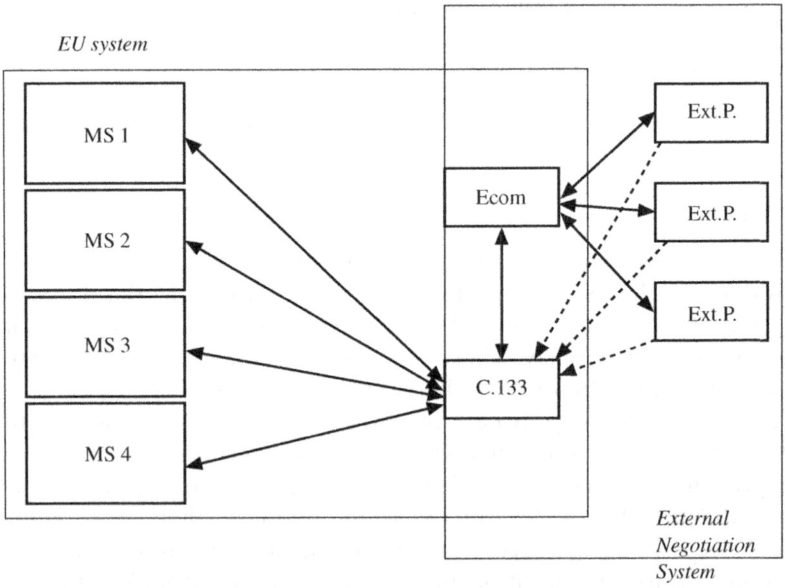

Figure 2.1 Interactions between the Commission, Committee 133 and the EU's WTO partners (C. 133 = Commission 133; Ecom = European Commission; Ext.P. = External partner; MS = member state).

directly involved in controlling the Commission, and a second group to which the first group was directly accountable. All these officials were selected on the basis of the snowball method. The national officials were – for reasons of time and finance – restricted to Belgium, the Netherlands, France, Germany and Britain. For the latter two, interviews were limited to the permanent representations in Brussels. For the former, interviews were conducted with officials both in the permanent representations and in the respective national administrations.

3 Version as amended by the 1997 Amsterdam Treaty (see Kerremans 1998, and Meunier and Nicolaïdis 1999).

4 The (informal) Code of Conduct of 1994 provides that all member states are entitled to attend the informal external negotiations, unless Committee 133 decides otherwise (interviews with Commission officials, March 2001).

5 Trust refers to an attitude 'involving a willingness to place the fate of one's interests under the control of others' (Hoffman 2002: 376–7). That is particularly important in the context of this chapter.

6 As Hoffman (2002: 377) observes, 'there are always limits on trust, but these limits are not necessarily obvious'.

7 The mirror of this calculated risk is the calculated risk taken by the member state that the Commission will not abuse their trust (see Hoffman 2002: 378).

8 Obviously, this means that it is unclear whether the member states' trust is predictive – based on the prediction that the Commission will defend their interests because the cost of not doing so would be too high – or fiduciary, where they expect the Commission to act loyally, scrupulously, uprightly and truthfully. Trusting relationships of a fiduciary nature are, therefore, special forms of cooperation 'involving discretion-granting policies and leaders that view one another as trustworthy' (Hoffman 2002: 384; also Majone 2001: 113).

9 As one Commission official phrased it: 'Losers can run away. Institutions cannot. If you abuse them, they will turn against you' (Interview 20 February 2001). And in the same vein, Hoffman (2002: 381) observes: 'Trustors create trusting relationships; trustees determine the success of these relationships.'

References

Barchefsky, C. (2001) *Reflections at a Moment of Transition: The Transatlantic Relationship and its Future*, Speech given at the European–American Business Council, 17 January 2001, Washington DC: EABC.

Braithwaite, V. (1998) 'Communal and Exchange Trust Norms: Their Value Base and Relevance to Institutional Trust', in V. Braithwaite and M. Levi (eds) *Trust and Governance*, New York: Russell Sage Foundation: 46–74.

Hoffman, A.M. (2002) 'A Conceptualising of Trust in International Relations', *European Journal of International Relations*, 8(3): 375–401.

Hooghe, L. and Marks, G. (2001) *Multi-Level Governance and European Integration*, Lanham: Roman & Littlefield.

Kerremans, B. (1998) 'Le systéme économique international et l'Union européenne après Amsterdam: vers une politique commerciale extérieure plus cohérente', in F. Dehousse, J. Vandamme and L. Hardy De Beaulieu (eds) *L'Europe et les grands défis de l'an 2000*, Bruxelles: Presses Interuniversitaires Europeennes: 175–97.

Levi, M. (1998) 'A State of Trust', in V. Braithwaite and M. Levi (eds) *Trust and Governance*, New York: Russell Sage Foundation: 77–101.

Majone, G. (1996) 'Theories of Regulation', in G. Majone (ed.) *Regulating Europe*, London: Routledge: 28–46.

—— (2001) 'Two Logics of Delegation. Agency and Fiduciary Relations in EU Governance', *European Union Politics*, 2(1): 103–22.

Meunier, S. and Nicolaïdis, K. (1999) 'Who Speaks for Europe? The Delegation of Trade Authority in the EU', *Journal of Common Market Studies*, 37(3): 477–501.

—— (2000) 'EU Trade Policy: The "Exclusive" versus Shared Competence Debate', in M. Green Cowles and M. Smith (eds) *The State of the European Union. Vol. 5: Risks, Reform, Resistance, and Revival*, Oxford: Oxford University Press, 325–46.

Nicolaïdis, K. (1999) 'Minimising Agency Costs in Two-Level Games: Lessons From the Trade Authority Controversies in the United States and the European Union', in R.H. Mnookin and L.E. Susskind (eds) *Negotiating on Behalf of Others*, London: Sage, 87–126.

Paemen, H. and Bensch, A. (1995) *From the GATT to the WTO. The European Community in the Uruguay Round*, Leuven: Leuven University Press.

Pollack, M.A. (1997) 'Delegation, Agency, and Agenda Setting in the European Community', *International Organization*, 51(1): 99–134.

Schmidt, S.K. (2000) 'Only an Agenda Setter? The European Commission's Power over the Council of Ministers', *European Union Politics*, 1(1): 37–61.

Stone Sweet, A. and Sandholtz, W. (1997) 'European Integration and Supranational Governance', *Journal of European Public Policy*, 4(5): 297–317.

3 Framing decisions in the Council of Europe

An institutionalist analysis

Jill Lovecy

Introduction

This case study of decision making in international organizations focuses on a regional European organization, the Council of Europe, which, it will be argued here, from its establishment in 1949 operated with an important element of *relative autonomy as an arena of decision making*. It thus presents an intriguing exception to the predominant mode of decision making within international organizations set out in the introduction to this volume, and to the general thesis presented there concerning the timing and causality of change in this 'hierarchical' model of dominance by member governments.

The Council of Europe is one of a cluster of organizations that were established in a first phase of postwar regional institution building in Europe.[1] Under its founding treaty, the London Statute of May 1949, the Council was entrusted with the broad task of pursuing 'peace based on justice and international co-operation' through the promotion of 'closer unity . . . and association' between European states (HMSO 1949: Preamble). More specifically it was designed, with its Committee of Ministers, Assembly,[2] and supporting Secretariat, to serve as a broad, collaborative policy forum through which its member states could 'reaffirm their devotion . . . to individual freedom, political liberty and the rule of law, the principles which form the basis of all genuine democracy' (HMSO 1949: Preamble) and promote 'agreements and common action in economic, social, cultural, scientific, legal and administrative matters and in the maintenance and furtherance of human rights and fundamental freedoms' (HMSO 1949: Article 1b).

Today, with more than 170 Conventions and 500 Recommendations to its credit (Council of Europe 1999a; 1999b), the Council has become a sizeable organization. Its Strasbourg headquarters employs 1,300 permanent staff, with an annual budget of 169 million Euros in 2002, whilst some 370 non-governmental organizations, formally accredited with consultative status, contribute to its work (www.coe.int). In its first 40 years the Council succeeded in doubling its initial nucleus of ten West European high-contracting parties to 22. Since 1990 that number has doubled again, encompassing all of Central and Eastern Europe and the Baltic rim, along with parts of the Balkans and six states in the former Soviet Union, including Russia. With a membership of 44 nations (Appendix 3.1), the Council has thus now acquired a pre-eminently pan-European vocation (Huber 1999).

For much of the last half-century the Council of Europe has been portrayed as occupying a relatively low-profile position within Europe's new regional architecture, as a site of 'unspectacular functional co-operation' (Laffan 1992: 29). Nevertheless, shortly after its foundation, through its November 1950 European Convention on Human Rights and Fundamental Freedoms, it was responsible for launching and has subsequently been responsible for managing what has proved over the last 50 years to be an extraordinarily radical and far-reaching challenge to the sovereignty claims of European states. The unprecedented delegation of authority to a supranational jurisdiction that this regime has entailed for its signatory states remains without parallel in the world to this day (Keohane *et al.* 2000).

New Instititutionalism

In making a case for characterizing this regional European organization as a relatively autonomous decision-making arena, the present study adopts a broadly New Institutionalist approach, in which institutions are understood to encompass 'formal rules, policy structures and social norms' (Pierson 1996: 125). It therefore draws on the burgeoning literature on the governance of the European Union (EU) that has sought over the last decade to investigate and theorize issues of relative autonomy (Schneider and Aspinwall 2001), challenging intergovernmentalist accounts in which policy outcomes are ultimately explicable by reference to patterns of exogenously given – or, in the case of liberal intergovernmentalism, domestically driven – member state preferences (Moravcsik 1993). This literature on the EU has reflected the wider field of New Institutionalist studies in being comprised of three divergent theoretical strands: historical, rationalist and sociological institutionalism (Hall and Taylor 1996). The analysis developed in this case study will draw on conceptual and analytical tools that are derived from all three strands of this literature.[3]

This case study focuses on the early years of the Council and on the conditions that initially promoted and then consolidated a degree of autonomy in the operation of this regional decision-making arena. The main body of the chapter is divided into two sections, dealing respectively with the London Statute, and with the adoption of the European Convention on Human Rights and Fundamental Freedoms (ECHR) and the regional human rights regime founded by this. The analysis is organized around three linked propositions: (1) that a dominant policy frame informed the Council's work at its founding, centred on subordinating the majoritarian institutional practices and normative discourses of liberal democracy to an activist commitment to individual human rights; (2) that the core values of this dominant policy frame were sustained by key features of the Council's organizational arrangements; and (3) that, as a result, the Council's main site of member government representation, its Committee of Ministers, was not itself able to control the setting of the organization's agenda in a way that would align the Council with the 'hierarchical' model of decision making in international organizations. Instead this body largely functioned as a gatekeeper, responding to and caught up in processes of normative construction driven forward by a mix of other non-state and state actors. Two of the conceptual tools used in analysing this material deserve some preliminary commentary.

The concept of a dominant policy frame derives from the work of both historical and sociological institutionalists. Drawing on historical institutionalism's concern with the path-dependency of international organizations and of their embedded legitimizing values founded in a historically-specific bargain struck between states (Steinmo *et al.* 1992; Armstrong and Bulmer 1998), the concept will be employed here primarily to refer to the enduring integration of the Council's core values into a project centred on combining democratic institutions with enforceable human rights. In considering the origins and construction of this dominant policy frame in the third section, and its subsequent renewal and institutionalization in the fourth section, the work of sociological institutionalists points us both to the potential role of non-state as well as state actors in the communicative and discursive practices that drive forward such framing processes (Christiansen *et al.* 1999) and to the underpinning of such processes by mechanisms of shaming, emulation and rhetorical entrapment (Schimmelfennig 2001).

If this part of the case study's argument is located within the constructivist terrain of international relations, a second part is concerned with identifying the organizational factors that contributed to operationalizing and sustaining this dominant policy frame. Here the study focuses in particular on the relationship between this policy frame and the unusual rules governing the Council's decisional process, and turns to the rationalist institutionalist literature that has employed principal–agent theory to investigate the inherently problematic relationship between states and the international bodies to which they delegate specific powers as their agents (Tsebelis 1994; Pollack 1997; Tallberg 2000). The concept of institutional decisional rules, which serves as a main independent variable in principal–agent theory, will be used to explore the terms on which the member states of the Council of Europe have delegated specific policy-making powers to the Council's Committee of Ministers and Assembly. The third section identifies two sets of rules incorporated in the London Statute that reflect the Council's core values as established in that text and that mark a significant departure from the classical intergovernmental model of 'hierarchical' decision making in international organizations. The fourth section investigates the role these rules then played in structuring the intergovernmental negotiations that led to the adoption of the ECHR and in shaping the Convention's substantive terms.

Constructing a dominant policy frame: the Council of Europe and the London Statute

As noted at the beginning of this chapter, the terms of the London Statute set out what is effectively a dual remit for the Council of Europe. Alongside its role in developing policy collaboration between European states across a whole range of policy sectors, the Statute identifies a loftier task for the Council. This is the promotion and safeguarding of individual freedom, political liberty and the rule of law, values 'which form the basis of all genuine democracy' (Preamble) and which the Statute presents as deriving from a shared heritage and being constitutive of a specifically 'European' identity. If the sustaining of democracy is therefore placed at the heart of this new enterprise, what Article 3 spells out is a more specific, and solemn, commitment: 'Every Member of the Council of Europe must accept the principles of the rule of law and of the enjoyment by all persons within their jurisdiction of human rights and fundamental freedoms.' Moreover, violation of the terms of Article 3 is cited in Article 8 as the sole grounds for excluding a member state from the organization. The special status that these two articles in combination accord to marrying democratic politics and the enforcement of human rights, as a collective goal to be organized and pursued at the regional European level, can thus be identified as establishing a dominant policy frame for the new regional organization. This presents the safeguarding of individual human rights as entailing the subordination of political processes and democratic elective mandates to the rule of law at national level. But the Statute remains silent on the need for some supranational mechanism to enforce the member states' collective commitment to human rights at European level.

The Council's dominant policy frame is thus informed by a quite specific reading of democracy. One that is shaped by lessons drawn from European experiences of the 1930s and the Second World War and sensitized to the dangers inherent in the majoritarian features of elective representation, and to the nationalistic and xenophobic excesses which these may facilitate especially – but not only – in 'bad times': internal aggression against minorities and external aggression against neighbouring states. In order to understand how this came to be projected into the London Statute, we need to give due weight to the role of wider ideational processes and non-state actors in structuring the discursive context in which the multilateral negotiations around this Statute took place.

In the period 1947–8 this reading of democracy had emerged as a shared ground on which an extraordinary array of leading political figures from across Europe temporarily coalesced in what would come to be known as the European Movement (Lipgens 1982).[4] This movement was very much a product of the unusual pattern of regional opportunity structures of postwar Europe, as the emergent Cold War led to the division of Germany into two states and at the same time endowed the reference to individual rights with a new ideological resonance, as the litmus test of regime acceptability in the West. In this context, although lacking a clearly agreed vision of the new regional order it sought to create, the European Movement established itself as a novel kind of transnational non-state actor through its May 1948 Congress in The Hague, enabling it to play a crucial agenda-setting role in framing the initial terms on which these negotiations got under way (Bitsch 1986: 165–8; Gerbet 1987). The 'Message to Europeans', adopted at the Congress, proposed the establishment of a democratically representative body of the peoples of Europe enjoying some significant transfer of powers from the states of Europe, and called for the collective guaranteeing and enforcement of human rights through the creation of a supranational jurisdiction (Congress of Europe 1949; Robertson 1956: 3–4).

Accounts of the London Statute negotiations emphasize that the final text embodied what was, effectively, a Franco-British compromise: with the French, as the proponents of a project with supranational elements, largely ceding to Britain's preference for relying on more limited, piecemeal intergovernmental collaboration (Bitsch 1986: 173–98; Gerbet 1987). The willingness of the parties to the negotiations, and in particular the French, to adopt this compromise reflected their recognition of the urgency of developing a regional organization into which the German Federal Republic could, once constituted, be rapidly integrated and their awareness of the strength of American support for such a project. And it was West Germany's intended membership that underpinned the new organization's dominant policy frame with its concern to entrench the values of democracy and individual human rights. However, the commitment to human rights inscribed in Article 3 is couched in declaratory terms without explicit reference, of the kind made in the The Hague resolutions, to the establishment of a supranational jurisdiction. The latter project would instead be the focus of the first substantive Convention adopted by the new Council of Europe.

In organizational terms, too, the sovereignty-transference language of the The Hague resolutions is notably absent from the London Statute (Robertson 1956: 12–15). But the compromise embodied in the London Statute created an unusual institutional mix (Archer 1990: 45–52), establishing an Assembly as 'the deliberative organ of the Council' (Article 22) alongside the Council's intergovernmental executive body, its Committee of Ministers (Article 13), comprised of the member governments' foreign ministers. This compromise between breaking with and shoring up the normal practices of intergovernmental cooperation is also reproduced in the rules incorporated in the text which govern the power to initiate policy proposals and the power to decide policies proposed for implementation by the member governments. In both cases the signatory states' solemn commitment to the upholding and furtherance of democratic values in Europe is reflected in innovative features of significance. This case study focuses on the ways in which these rules, as subsequently operationalized, allowed the workings of this regional decision-making arena to be characterized by a degree of autonomy.

Undoubtedly where the institutional decisional rules set out in the Statute are most innovative, in terms of their relative autonomy potential, is in Article 22's provision for the Assembly, as a body more broadly representative of the peoples of Europe, to share the Committee of Ministers' right to initiate policy proposals (Article 15). The Assembly's exercise of this (joint) power of policy initiative was, however, hedged around in the Statute with a series of procedural and other constraints. The way was nevertheless opened for a complex process of path-dependency stretching back to the The Hague Congress's resolutions to come to fruition, with the Assembly developing in the following period as a policy entrepreneur in its own right and proposing common actions across the whole range of policy fields enumerated under Article 1b. This outcome was critically mediated by the fact that a high proportion of the Assembly's early members was drawn from the ranks of the European Movement (Robertson 1956: 86; Bitsch 1997: 5–6). But this study in the following section will focus more specifically on the institutional incentives that were put in place for the Assembly to operate as the carrier of the Council's dominant policy frame.

Another innovative set of rules is to be found in Article 20's complex provisions for the policy deliberations of the Committee of Ministers. These establish varying forms of majority voting (De Vel 1994: 58–61), breaking with the classical means for shoring up member government control in international organizations and safeguarding their sovereignty claims: the unanimity rule. However, the innovation of majority voting was tempered by its being combined with the signatory states' avoidance, under the terms of Article 15, of any clear-cut delegation to the Committee of a policy-making competence that would be binding, in the case of Conventions, on the member governments (Robertson 1956: 30–1).[5] In the event the member governments from the outset deliberately eschewed any resort to majority decision making; instead the Committee's members rapidly established an informal norm of consensus building and unanimity (Robertson 1956: 40; De Vel 1994: 60). The path-dependency that imposed itself here was therefore one deriving from traditional practices and conventions of diplomacy within international organizations that the foreign ministers brought with them into this new regional arena.

Arguably, however, the real centre of gravity of this second set of decisional rules, in the form in which they were operationalized by combining unanimity in the Committee's deliberations with the non-binding character of its decisions, resides in the system of variable geometry or, the term that will be used here, differentiated[6] and deferred *implementation*, that they provide for. The non-binding rule itself facilitated the securing of unanimity in the Committee's deliberations, since the member states' representatives were not committing their governments to subsequently ratifying a Convention adopted there. But it also enabled new European norms and standards to be established that would be implemented in the first place by only some of the member states. 'Closer association' through 'agreements and common action' was thus promoted (and the informally agreed norm of unanimity protected) precisely by allowing agreements to proceed in the name of the Council even though they did not command the support of all. These practices of differentiated and deferred implementation thus shifted the locus of decision making to the ratification process at national level. But they exposed the non-ratifying states, in both their domestic politics and their international diplomacy, to the presence of norms and standards that had been accorded a specifically European status. These practices therefore opened the way for such states to be drawn into longer-term accretive processes of normative socialization through emulation, shaming and rhetorical entrapment (Schimmelfennig 2001).

It is this combination of the Assembly's right of initiative with a decision-making process encapsulating this mechanism of differentiated and deferred implementation that we now need to examine in the founding of Europe's regional human rights regime.

Renewing and institutionalizing the Council's dominant policy frame: the ECHR and Europe's regional human rights regime

The new regional human rights regime founded under the November 1950 ECHR was itself to give permanent – and, over time, increasingly prestigious – institutional expression to the dominant policy frame embedded in the London Statute. But it is difficult to make sense of key features of this regime unless we place the intergovernmental negotiations leading up to the Convention's adoption within the very distinctive framework provided by the Council of Europe's policy structures, decisional rules and normative ethos. The analysis developed here, emphasizing the mediating role of the Council's institutions, therefore contrasts with Moravcsik's recent account of the founding of the ECHR as a case of democratic delegation in postwar Europe conforming to a liberal-republican model of multilateral negotiations between state actors (Moravcsik 2000). Of critical importance here was the Assembly's (joint) right of policy initiative. This was immediately brought centre-stage at the Assembly's first plenary meeting in the summer of 1949, when a draft proposal for what would become the ECHR was tabled. This landmark text inaugurated what was to become a common pattern of policy making in the following period. With key conventions and other formal agreements originating as Assembly-initiated proposals (Robertson 1956: 34, 60–2; Bitsch 1997: 9), the subsequent negotiations under the aegis of the Committee of Ministers would be based on, and thus to some degree framed by, proposals initially formulated by the Assembly.

In the case of the ECHR, what was controversial in the Assembly's Recommendation to the Committee was not so much the human rights principles it proposed, which were largely based on the 1948 United Nations' Declaration of Human Rights, as the four linked mechanisms through which the draft text sought to enforce these rights at European level (Robertson 1956: 146–9). These were, first, the establishment of a European Commission for Human Rights to receive complaints concerning alleged breaches of the Convention and secure, where possible, a friendly settlement of the matter. Second, the establishment of a full European Court to consider cases where the Commission's mediation had failed to secure a settlement acceptable to all the parties involved. Third, the principle of interstate petition to the Commission and the Court. And fourth, the right of individual petition to the Commission and the Court. Clearly the second and fourth of these mechanisms were of greatest importance, in terms of their threatening to erode the member states' established sovereignty prerogatives, and here again the role played by those who had been active in the European Movement in incorporating these elements into the text and securing their adoption by the Assembly needs to be emphasized.

Faced with this Assembly initiative and the desirability of establishing a regional framework entrenching human rights principles for the new West German state, the Committee of Ministers' adoption of some form of human rights convention was not in doubt. But the terms finally incorporated into the text and their longer-term dynamics are ultimately only explicable by reference to the Council's practices of differentiated and deferred decision making. This latter mechanism was now drawn into the heart of the Council's work and embodied in the complex terms of the Convention. The variable geometry and sheer ingenuity which went into its construction are themselves testimony to the uphill nature of the task, which involved securing agreement from states jealous of their national sovereignty and whose domestic institutions, moreover, organized the relationship between law and politics on widely varying bases. Everything, it seems, was therefore done to build in maximum flexibility, in order to enable the member states to support the Convention's adoption in the Committee of Ministers and to then allow sufficient states to ratify it, even if only, initially, on the most limited and *à la carte* basis.

The Convention itself, under Article 66, required ratification by ten states, that is two-thirds of the Council of Europe's fifteen high-contracting parties at the time of the signing of the Convention by the Committee of Ministers in November 1950. This was achieved in September 1953. Its core provisions included interstate petition (Article 24) and the establishment of an independent international organ, the Commission of Human Rights (Articles 20–21 and 29–33), and of a Court (Articles 38–42), but these two bodies could only be brought into play once all domestic procedures had been exhausted. The main remit of the Commission, meeting *in camera*, was to achieve where possible a friendly settlement of disputes. But Article 32 provided for unresolved disputes to be forwarded to the Committee of Ministers for final arbitration and rulings there, made by a two-thirds majority of the Committee's membership, were to be binding (Robertson 1956: 150–2). Despite the flexibilities permitted and the modest profile of the new Commission, signing the Convention therefore entailed a real and unprecedented element of extraterritorial adjudication in interstate disputes.

Nevertheless, ratification of the Convention itself was not made a condition of membership of the Council; indeed, the Convention set out procedures for a signatory state to freely denounce the Convention (Article 65). Moreover, signatory states were permitted to opt out, on a temporary or permanent basis, from any of the Convention's provisions by entering a formal, written reservation to that effect (Article 64). But the two most critical provisions of the Convention were given a quite distinctive status, since both required a specific 'opt-in'. Thus any signatory state could choose, by declaration at the time of ratifying the Convention or at any later date, to recognize either or both of the main sovereignty-ceding provisions: the right of individual petition for all persons subject to that state's jurisdiction (Article 25); and the jurisdiction of a full European Court of Human Rights, either for a specific case only, or as a general principle (Article 46). Perhaps in compensation, the minimum ratification thresholds for these provisions to take effect were set at significantly lower levels: six for individual petition and eight for the full Court (Robertson 1956: Appendix 2). Moreover, in contrast to all the other piecemeal concessions to the sovereignty prerogatives of the member states, the new European Court of Human Rights, as the crucial symbol of the signatories' ceding of their own state authority, was to be set up without any threshold number of 'opt-ins' being required to trigger this. It is true that cases could only be forwarded to it once eight states had agreed to accept its authority. But the Court was nevertheless to be established prior to this, with its membership designated indirectly on the basis of one judge per member state. The Court was thus to be the collective creation of all the member states, whether or not they accepted the Court's authority in respect of persons within their own jurisdiction; and members of the judiciary of each member state were to be drawn into the common experience of serving on this supranational instance. In this critical respect, a firm limit was set to what in other respects was an extraordinarily differentiated architecture of implementation.

The sequel to these modest beginnings of Europe's new human rights regime is well known. Five years after the Convention's original adoption by the Committee of Ministers, seven of the Council's 15 members had agreed to accept the right of individual petition but only five the jurisdiction of the court, so that only the former provision at this stage came into force. In 1959 the Court was established and, although not a formal condition of membership, it became increasingly difficult for new member states not to ratify the Convention at the time of their accession to membership of the Council and to opt into both these provisions. By the mid-1960s the number of states opting into both provisions had crept up to 11 out of 18, including the UK as of January 1966 (Palmer and Lambert 1968). However at this stage France, a founding member of the Council, had still not ratified the Convention itself. Nevertheless, by the mid-1970s all of the Council's 21 member states had ratified the Convention, only one (Turkey) had not accepted the Court's jurisdiction and nearly all had accepted the right of individual petition (Robertson and Merrills 1989: 114; Burban 1996: 58). By the end of 1990, when well over five hundred cases had been declared admissible with the overwhelming majority of them stemming from individual petitions, nearly all the signatory states had seen cases brought against them and a majority had had cases against them referred to the Court. The Court had heard 244 cases and produced 129 judgements against member states (Forsythe 1994: 182).

The ECHR's adoption also set in train an additional element of path-dependency that is of importance to the central argument of this case study. For this new regional human rights regime was effectively dependent, for the subsequent extension and updating of the range of human rights enforceable through its court system, on formal amendments to its founding Convention. This brought into play new institutional incentives for the Assembly's role as an activist carrier of the Council's dominant policy frame. This body proceeded to initiate a stream of additional protocols that have over time substantively expanded the parameters of Europe's regional human rights regime. The first of these was adopted in March 1952, with Protocols II–V following between 1963 and 1966, a further three (Protocols VI–VIII) between 1983 and 1985 and two more (Protocols IX–X) in the early 1990s. Protocol I established rights to property, religious pluralism in education and free elections, whilst later ones have covered such diverse issues as: freedom of movement (Protocol IV, Article 2); equality between spouses (Protocol VII, Article 5); prohibition of the expulsion of nationals (Protocol IV, Article 3); prohibition of the collective expulsion of aliens (Protocol IV, Article 4) and procedural safeguards relating to such expulsions (Protocol VII, Article 1); the abolition of the death penalty (Protocol VI); and the right of appeal in criminal matters, compensation for wrongful conviction, and the right not to be tried twice for the same crime (Protocol VII, Articles 2, 3 and 4) (Spielman 1999: 758).

Moreover, whilst attempts by the federalist-minded members of the Assembly to secure a more far-reaching reform of the Council's institutions in this early period failed, the Assembly's policy-initiating role was strengthened by its success in unpicking some of the limitations imposed under the London Statute, enhancing its autonomy and claims to democratic legitimacy (Council of Europe 1951: 6–7; Robertson 1956: 47–50, 59–62, 84–98). The formal Statute revisions adopted by the Committee of Ministers in May and August 1951 notably gave the Assembly the right to control its own agenda (Article 23), and replaced member government with parliamentary appointment of the national delegations to the Assembly (Article 25). The Committee had previously also agreed to an expansive interpretation of Article 24, allowing the Assembly's committees and commissions to operate on a permanent basis, meeting between the Assembly's two limited formal sessions (Robertson 1956: 60). In addition, there were growing opportunities for the Assembly to develop its role of policy entrepreneur in the early 1950s, as its main interlocuteur, the Committee of Ministers, acquired a more bureaucratized character. In effect the bulk of the work of the Committee of Ministers was now devolved from politicians to career diplomats, as the twice-yearly full meetings of the Committee were supplemented from 1952 by a dozen or more Meetings of Ministers' Deputies, these latter comprised of the member governments' permanent representatives based in Strasbourg (Robertson 1956: 37–8; De Vel 1994: 19–20).

Conclusion

Adopting a broadly New Institutionalist approach, this study has focused on the early years of the Council of Europe and investigated the conditions that from its founding enabled this regional decision-making arena to operate, unusually, with a degree of relative autonomy. The analysis has centred on exploring the combination of two distinctive features of the Council of Europe as an organization that contributed to this outcome: its dominant policy frame, centred on marrying democratic institutions and enforceable human rights; and the Assembly's exercise of its right of policy initiative, operating in conjunction with practices of differentiated and deferred implementation.

The Council's unusual status as a regional organization exclusively comprised until 1989 of 'Western' states is also clearly important. In this it is unlike the other organizations studied in this volume, where the ideological tensions of the Cold War promoted an enhanced concern with sovereignty prerogatives. In contrast, in the case of the Council of Europe Western critiques of the Soviet bloc served to reinforce the credibility and moral weight of the Council's dominant policy frame.

It seems likely that in later years the key early role played by the Assembly's policy initiative in sustaining a degree of relative autonomy in the operation of this regional decision-making arena has been supplemented, notably by the expanding influence of the Secretariat (Archer 1990: 52). As its permanent staff grew from 300 in the mid-1950s to 950 in the mid-1990s (Burban 1996: 48–53), there is some evidence of it too becoming a more proactive carrier of the Council's commitment to promoting democracy in tandem with human rights (Lovecy 2002: 276–7). And Checkel's work on the Council's dual nationality conventions has identified expert committees operating under the aegis of the Committee of Ministers as providing a key mechanism for drawing member governments into complex processes of normative socialization, in which small-group dynamics and the persuasive advocacy skills of key individuals may effect crucial shifts in member governments' established policy preferences (Checkel 1999).

In the more recent period, the fall of the Berlin Wall and the implosion of the Soviet bloc have served to reinforce the salience of the Council of Europe's vision of marrying liberal democracy and the collective enforcement of human rights at European level, catalysing a further consolidation of Europe's human rights regime from November 1998 when a single permanent Court and core set of substantive provisions came into force for all member states under Protocol XI (www.coe.int). But in other respects the end of the Cold War would seem to have undercut the conditions that previously favoured this regional decision-making arena operating with a degree of relative autonomy, as the Council was now caught up in coping with a large wave of applicant states and with managing substantial new cooperation programmes in Central, Eastern and South-Eastern Europe (De Vel 1994: 45–7). This has led to a strengthening of its intergovernmental machinery, with much more frequent meetings of the Committee of Ministers and Ministers' Deputies, and to new procedures for coordinating the Council's activities and decision making with those of the EU (De Vel 1994: 21, 76–8). The 1990s also saw the launching of the Council of Europe Summit of Heads of State and Government, with the Commission President of the EU in attendance. The first summit was held in Vienna in October 1993 (De Vel 1994: 50–5). However, although this was followed by a second one in Strasbourg in October 1997, none has been held since, so the status of this new organ of intergovernmental leadership now seems uncertain.

Appendix: Chronological listing of the Council of Europe's membership, as of April 2002

5.5.1949	Belgium	5.5.1989	Finland
	Denmark	6.11.1990	Hungary
	France	29.11.1991	Poland
	Ireland	7.5.1992	Bulgaria
	Italy	14.5.1993	Slovenia
	Luxembourg		Estonia
	Netherlands		Lithuania
	Norway	30.6.1993	Czech Republic
	Sweden		Slovakia
	United Kingdom	7.10.1993	Romania
9.8.1949	Greece	10.10.1994	Andorra
	Turkey	10.2.1995	Latvia
9.3.1950	Iceland	13.7.1995	Albania
13.7.1950	Germany		Moldavia
16.4.1956	Austria	9.11.1995	Macedonia
24.5.1961	Cyprus		Ukraine
6.5.1963	Switzerland	28.2.1996	Russian Federation
29.4.1965	Malta	6.11.1996	Croatia
22.9.1976	Portugal	27.4.1999	Georgia
24.11.1977	Spain	25.1.2001	Armenia
23.11.1978	Liechtenstein		Azerbaijan
16.11.1988	San Marino	24.4.2002	Bosnia-Herzegovenia

Notes

1 Its founding was preceded by the Brussels Treaty Organization in March 1948 and the Organization for European Economic Cooperation in April 1948.
2 Initially termed the Consultative Assembly, the title of Parliamentary Assembly acquired common usage but was not officially adopted by the Committee of Ministers until 1994 (De Vel 1994: 16). Here it will be referred to simply as the Assembly.
3 The case for applying these theoretical approaches to institutional autonomy to the Council of Europe is discussed more fully in Lovecy 2003.
4 This title was adopted in October 1948. Previously it was known as the International Committee of Movements for European Unity.
5 In contrast to the position in the OEEC, a point emphasized by Robertson (Robertson 1956: 30).
6 The term is adopted from Ehlermann's analysis of the new 'flexibility' provisions of the EU's Amsterdam Treaty (Ehlermann 1998).

References

Archer, C. (1990) *Organizing Western Europe*, London: Edward Arnold.
Armstrong, K. and Bulmer, S. (1998) *The Governance of the Single European Market*, Manchester: Manchester University Press.

Bitsch, M.-T. (1986) 'Le rôle de la France dans la naissance du Conseil de l'Europe', in R. Poidevin (ed.) *Histoire des débuts de la construction européenne (Mars 1948–Mai 1950)*, Bruxelles: Bruylant, 65–198.

—— (1997) 'Introduction' in M.-T. Bitsch (ed.) *Jalons pour une histoire du Conseil de l'Europe*, Berne: Lang, 3–13.

Burban, J.-L. (1996) *Le Conseil de l'Europe*, Paris: Presses Universitaires de France.

Checkel, J. (1999) 'Social construction and integration', *Journal of European Public Policy*, 6(4): 545–60.

Christiansen, T., Joergensen, K.E. and Wiener, A. (eds) (1999) 'Constructivism in European Studies', *Journal of European Public Policy*, 6(4), Special Issue.

Congress of Europe (1949) *Verbatim Report of the Congress of Europe 1948*, The Hague: Congress of Europe.

Council of Europe (1951) *Concise Handbook of the Council of Europe*, Strasbourg: Directorate of Information.

—— (1999a) *Conventions and Agreements*, Strasbourg: Directorate of Legal Affairs Treaty Section.

—— (1999b) *European Conventions and Agreements. Volume VII 1995–98*, Strasbourg: Council of Europe.

De Vel, G. (1994) *Le Comité des Ministres du Conseil de l'Europe*, Strasbourg: Council of Europe.

Ehlermann, C.D. (1998) 'Differentiation, Flexibility and Closer Co-operation: The New Provisions of the Amsterdam Treaty', *European Law Journal*, 4(3): 246–70.

Forsythe, D.P. (ed.) (1994) *Human Rights in the New Europe. Problems and Progress*, Lincoln: University of Nebraska Press.

Gerbet, P. (1987) 'The Origins: Early Attempts and the Emergence of the Six (1945-52)', in R. Pryce (ed.) The Dynamics of European Union, London: Croom Helm, 39–45.

Hall, P.A. and Taylor, R.C.R. (1996) 'Political Science and the Three New Institutionalisms', Political Studies, 44(5): 936–58.

HMSO (1949) *The Statute of the Council of Europe*, Command 7686, London: Her Majesty's Stationery Office.

Huber, D. (1999) A Decade That Made History – The Council of Europe 1989–99, Strasbourg: Council of Europe.

Keohane, R., Moravcsik, A. and Slaughter, A.-M. (2000) 'Legalised Dispute Resolution: Interstate and Transnational', International Organization, 54(3): 457–88.

Laffan, B. (1992) *Integration and Co-operation in Europe*, London: Routledge.

Lipgens, W. (1982) A History of European Integration. The Formation of the European Unity Movement, 1945–7, London: Oxford University Press.

Lovecy, J. (2002) 'Gender Mainstreaming and the Framing of Women's Rights in Europe: The Contribution of the Council of Europe', *Feminist Legal Studies*, 10(3): 271–83.

—— (2003) 'European Integration and the Conditions for Institutional Autonomy: The Case of the Council of Europe', University of Manchester: *European Policy Research Unit Working Paper.*

Moravcsik, A. (1993) 'Preferences and Power in the European Community: A Liberal Intergovernmentalist Approach', *Journal of Common Market Studies*, 31(4): 473–524.

—— (2000) 'The Origins of International Human Rights Regimes: Democratic Delegation in Post-war Europe', *International Organization*, 54(2): 217–52.

Palmer, M. and Lambert, J. (1968) *European Unity. A Survey of the European Organisations*, London: George, Allen and Unwin.

Pierson, P. (1996) 'The Path to European Integration: A Historical Institutionalist Analysis', *Comparative Political Studies*, 29(2): 123–63.

Pollack, M. (1997) 'Delegation, Agency and Agenda Setting in the European Community', International Organization, 51(1): 99–134.

Robertson. A.H. (1956) *The Council of Europe: Its Structure, Functions and Achievements*, 2nd edn, London: Stevens, 1961.

Robertson, A.H. and Merrills, J.G. (1989) *Human Rights in the World. An Introduction to the Study of the International Protection of Human Rights*, 3rd edn, Manchester: Manchester University Press.

Schimmelfennig, F. (2001) 'The Community Trap: Liberal Norms, Rhetorical Action and the Eastern Enlargement of the European Union', *International Organization*, 55(1): 47–80.

Schneider, G. and Aspinwall, M. (eds) (2001) *The Rules of Integration. Institutionalist Approaches to the Study of Europe*, Manchester: Manchester University Press.

Spielman, D. (1999) 'Human Rights Case Law in the Strasbourg and Luxembourg Courts: Conflicts, Inconsistencies, and Complementarities' in P. Alston (ed.) *The EU and Human Rights*, Oxford: Oxford University Press: 757–80.

Steinmo, S., Thelen, K. and Longstreth, F. (1992) *Structuring Politics. Historical Institutionalism in Comparative Analysis*, Cambridge: Cambridge University Press.

Tallberg, J. (2000) 'The Anatomy of Autonomy: An Institutional Account of Variation in Supranational Influence', *Journal of Common Market Studies*, 38(5): 843–64.

Tsebelis, G. (1994) 'The Power of the European Parliament as a Conditional Agenda-Setter', American Political Science Review, 88(1): 128–42.

Part III
Consensus building

4 Expertise and political competence

Consensus making within the World Trade Organization and the World Meteorological Organization

Yves Schemeil

Introduction[1]

Trade, weather and climate are specific fields of knowledge entrusted to intergovernmental institutions where experts (academics, advisers, bureaucrats) engage in dialogue with politicians (permanent representatives, ministers, rulers). Expertise and political competence may nevertheless conflict. An established reputation in a scientific and technical field does not entail political vision and solid skills in consensus making, confidence building, bargaining and logrolling. When experts call for urgent policy making, politicians expect scientific matters to be handled at minimum cost. The opacity of the decision-making process gives economists, legal specialists, custom experts (in the World Trade Organization, WTO), or meteorologists, hydrologists, mathematicians and engineers (in the World Meteorological Organization, WMO) an opportunity to prevail over state representatives, who use publicity to frame or reflect the views of the public.

The resilience of sound expertise in an increasingly politicized context explains why such organizations must reach decisions by consensus, even though voting procedures are detailed in their constitutions. How and why do expert networks and political leadership contribute to such arrangements? In trade and environment there is no simple answer to this question. In contrast to other institutions where experts indulge in truth-seeking consensus while politicians vote in order to discover the distribution of power, the WTO and the WMO mix 'cosmopolitan academics' with humanitarian concerns, 'transnational technocrats' dedicated to their intergovernmental organization, and 'official representatives' buttressing the 'national interest' of their home government. Many agents are both knowledgeable people and civil servants who will switch during their professional lifetime from science and engineering to diplomacy and bureaucracy, as well as from their home capital to Geneva, Brussels, New York or Vienna. They often 'tend to forget their national origins' (WTO commonsensical analyses, explaining why three-quarters of the problems are solved by experts without any political intervention), or are required to do so (WMO constitution, applying to permanent representatives freshly elected to the Executive Council).[2]

Another difficulty in answering the research question within these two contexts is the blurred distinction between groups and individuals. The scholarly literature dichotomizes 'expert networks' and 'political agents', allegedly involved at successive stages of the negotiation process; empirical studies tell the real story, of influential people moving from expertise to politics and eventually changing the views of world leaders (as in Haas 1992b). These findings fit into the agent-structure debate, questioning the role of individuals in international relations compared to collective bodies such as epistemic communities, advocacy coalitions and public policy networks. Both contrast leadership with political culture. Whatever the relevance of these distinctions in other cases, contrasting individual with collective actors and real characters with ideal types is not so easy within the WTO and the WMO, where governments are dedicated to stability. This does not fit in with the contradictory concerns about citizens demanding more accountability (Rosenau 1994) in a complex and unstable world. Such concerns are welcomed because they challenge more 'rationalized' views of international relations (Allan 1994). Rather than focusing on agents, cultures and structures, I shall therefore discuss how issues are identified, situations defined, statements tabled, agendas set and opportunities taken.

Finally, such debates are framed by the canonical political power/economic interest, realism/institutionalism and rational choice/constructivism divisions. It is not my purpose here to probe these epistemological issues with my empirical findings.[3] Lack of space leads me to tackle the research question as follows. To what extent does the originality of the procedure depend upon the substance discussed in the two organizations (first section)? Is their conciliatory stance due to the individuals' organizational learning or is it prompted by the homogeneity of 'epistemic communities' (second section)? What does 'consensus' mean and how is it arrived at (third section)? What is the role of 'leadership' (fourth section)? The last section will sum up the findings of this study. First, intergovernmental organizations (IGOs) operating in a single sector with a global impact, and dealing with private as well as public goods, combine expertise and politics, with the effect that national negotiators frame their statements in a cosmopolitan language and academics eventually become leaders. Second, such organizations accommodate two different types of competence (scientific or technical knowledge and organizational or diplomatic skills) better than others. Third, leadership matters because talents such as academic and political authority are often embodied in the same people: heads of organizations, chairs and judges.[4]

Procedure and substance

Within the WTO and the WMO, it is not so easy to make a clear-cut distinction between compelling decisions and voluntary quests for consistency:[5] type of knowledge, styles of behaviour, verbal commitments and actual policy measures. Moreover, some decisions are real and many others are virtual: decisions to postpone decisions; decisions to stick to former decisions.

WMO and WTO decisions are very much understated. Most of the time, they are mere agreements 'binding only for those Members which accept them'. Courts do not have 'verdicts', they issue 'reports'. 'Rules' are provisional. In the WTO, there have been no less than three attempts to modify the 'Dispute Settlement Understanding' since 1994, and Committees' participants often express discontent by not adopting the minutes of their proceedings (*Annual Report*, 2000: 59, 91). Governments are not bound by 'resolutions', they make 'offers' – if there is no phasing-out offer there is no commitment, hence no sanction for non-compliance with a 'rule'. Once made, offers can be withdrawn before a deadline; after that members cannot contest the schedule of the negotiation, although they keep the right to challenge its content (Croome 1999).

Such fluidity in decision making contrasts with the established international hierarchy. Assuming that outcomes are less pre-determined than in other IGOs, 'small' or 'remote' states such as Norway, Belgium, Egypt, Pakistan, New Zealand and Australia invest in their Geneva base. Part of the comparative advantage these peripheral powers have is explained by the fact that the WTO and WMO act as providers of information and producers of alternatives, rather than by immediate gains.[6] To protect their interests in future negotiations, major decision makers behave with restraint and with respect for the established standards of interaction. Pretending to be patient and tolerant, they are more open to expertise than in institutions where power politics prevail. This is not to say that experts are involved in 'low' and politicians in 'high' politics: 'soft' and 'hard' politics would be more accurate. The more scientific and technical the issues under discussion are, the longer and the more pluralistic the decision-making process should be. In specialized IGOs, 'committees' should prevail over 'assemblies'. Committees are conducive to discreet mediation and integrative or deliberative bargaining, while assemblies lead to open confrontation and strategic or positional bargaining (Young 1991: 283; Majone 1997). In New York, the General Assembly of the United Nations is the seat of an unending and public political dispute over redistributive decisions, in Geneva (or Brussels) experts work behind closed doors on regulatory agreements.

The main goals of the two organizations are not redistributive but regulatory, because they are common to mankind: they meet the standards of Kant (perpetual peace) and the UN Development Program UNDP (common goods). While free-traders place 'peacekeeping' at the top of the list of the ten 'benefits' expected from their activity, meteorologists succeed in keeping the tools of weather forecasting and climate watching intact even in time of war. Other goals are 'global public goods' such as a stable environment for all, or free access to every resource. However, WTO and WMO are also addressing diverse issues relating to the marketing of private goods, such as trade in services, intellectual property, desertification, depletion of the ozone layer and climate change. It is therefore difficult to classify issues as of concern to experts or as problems for diplomats: the two fields are as intertwined as trade and the environment, or as the trading in weather forecasts. In meteorology, for instance, a heated debate led in 1995 to 'Resolution 40'. A United States-led group claimed the right for each national meteorological service to provide any corporation with free data collected through the WMO world network. A European Union-led coalition opposed this claim, on the grounds that corporations operating abroad would be in competition with a local service intending to sell its own data. Both arguments were disputable: 40 per cent of national meteorological information is already paid for, either by airlines and airports, or by the media; taxpayers certainly 'buy' national meteorological data through their taxes, but they do not 'buy' data freely sent by foreign institutions. Addressing this very controversial issue in an appropriate way was crucial, since the whole system depended on free access for all members to meteorological information and fair budgeting for the activities coordinated by the WMO through each national service. The solution found was a compromise between experts' demands and political initiatives: 'basic' data (meaning: 'essential data and products which are necessary for the provision of services in support of the protection of life and property and the well-being of nations') were declared 'free and unrestricted' (meaning 'non-discriminatory and without charge – at no more than the cost of reproduction and delivery'); but 'conditions' could be placed by the meteorological services 'on their re-export for commercial purposes' of 'additional data and products . . . which are required to sustain WMO Programmes . . . for reasons such as national laws or costs of production'. At the May 2000 EC meeting, the chair had to 'remind the participants that WMO is built on the concept of cooperation among nations and a commitment to mutual assistance in the interests of the entire global community' (WMO, EC-LII/PINK1, Appendix, 1.1.6). In the WTO, the 'safeguards' issue seems to be the best approximation of the same dilemma. Designed to help members enhance their 'offers' to phase out tariffs (and other public obstacles to commerce) without unnecessary injury to their national economies and to private industries, safeguards provide for the waiving of some commitments for a limited period of time – in particular, during transitional phases. Although there are numerous examples, they are considered 'exceptions to the rules' and members are allowed not to implement an agreement provided their claim is 'WTO consistent'.

As evidenced by such cases, both specialists and generalists have good cards to play in the two organizations. On the one hand, scientists have deliberative skills enabling them to propose consensual solutions to debated issues which cannot easily be handled by politicians: in complex situations, being able to identify a chain of causes and effects 'can in fact lead to the redefinition of preconceived interests or to the identification of new interests' (Haas 1992a: 15). On the other hand, politicians have the last say: agreement between experts still has to be shaped into a treaty by politicians and interpreted by them:[7] epistemic networks and political leaders must be equally combined to make organizations work.

Experts' autonomy or organizational learning?

The WTO needs state support to deal with anti-globalization movements. The WMO relies on states for weather observation and data. For example, while 'strongly' supporting the idea of a 'Third World Climate Conference' sponsored by the United Nations Conference on Environment and Development, a WMO Executive Council Advisory Group 'recognized the considerable constraints that the ... review would place on the convening of a fully independent event'. Consequently, it recommended keeping it at expert level, 'leaving open the option of attracting ministerial representation' (WMO, EC-LII/WP 4.2.(1), Appendix, 4.2.6). This did not prevent the WMO from feeling 'the need for enhanced promotion of the status and visibility of National Meteorological Services, particularly through a better appreciation of their roles by governments' (WMO, EC-LII/PINK 11.1, appendix, 11.2.11).

Actually, the two organizations currently give technical or scientific advice to governments and fight hard to defend their 'authoritative' status against a trend towards politicization (EC-LII/Doc 3.1. Appendix; WMO, *Annual report*, 2000). Pledging 'to provide recommendation and guidance', both are ruled by principles of distributive justice emanating from political philosophers, development economists and legal advisers. Their epistemic community repeatedly expresses two concerns. One is fairness ('capacity-building in the developing countries', WMO; 'technical assistance to LDC [Least Developed Countries]', WTO), the other is equality ('policy-neutrality', WMO; 'Most-Favoured Nation principle', WTO).

Reviewing major issues facing the WMO, the Executive Council noted 'the widening gap between the level of Meteorological and Hydrological services provided in the developed countries on the one hand, and the developing countries and those with economies in transition', on the other. It 'recognized the importance of [their] participation in the relevant constituent body sessions' (WMO, EC-LII/PINK 11.1, Appendix, 11.1.4). When regional associations suggest setting up too many committees at the same time, applications from some regions are turned down to avoid imbalance between the funds accruing to each region. In the WTO, poor countries can obtain more safeguards for a longer period of time. They are entitled to special funds to assist their bureaucrats in dealing with existing trade agreements or in negotiating new ones.

Both organizations spend large amounts of money on training programmes. Supported by the UNDP's assistance department, the WMO also receives donations from rich states for the 'Voluntary Cooperation Programme'. Some of these states tend to spend their money on 'trust-fund projects', i.e. special programmes for particular members. In members' capital cities, WTO training seminars invite participants to work out the ultimate effects of their commitments, which allows room for second thoughts (OMC [WTO], *Manuel de coopération technique et de formation*). In Geneva, simulation games are designed to integrate newcomers into small groups long before real negotiations begin among 140 participants.

New WTO and WMO members are now ready to join a network of experts going back and forth between 'Geneva' and other diplomatic posts. Because diplomatic services usually welcome careers in various UN-type organizations, diplomats who specialize in trade are quite misunderstood by their peers, which might lead them to trust delegates from other countries more than they do their own national colleagues in other fields (Adamantopoulos 1997; Petersmann 1997; Croome 1999). Members of this 'invisible college' are not only cemented by a 'specialized knowledge', but also linked by 'everyday intersocial skills' (E. Haas 1990: 42–3) as in Peter Haas's 'transnational epistemic community', which shares a core set of normative principles, practical know-how, scientific beliefs and ability to assess the real impact of the common knowledge on policy making (P. Haas 1992a and b). His concept is a refined version of Ernst Haas's depiction of such communities as 'composed of professionals (usually recruited from several disciplines) who share a commitment to a common causal model and a common set of political values ... united by a belief in the truth of their model and by a commitment to translate this truth into public policy, in the conviction that human welfare will be enhanced as a result' (E. Haas 1990: 41). This is not to say that epistemic community members indulge in political activism. They are separate from the more instrumental 'policy networks' that include key political leaders, and should not be confused with the more expressive 'advocacy coalitions' pushed by non-governmental organizations. Moreover, they are less active at the macro (political) level of the whole organization than they are at the micro (social) and meso (technocratic) levels of decision making, where they 'shape' policies rather than 'set' them. They do not 'make history', they cannot make strategic decisions, they simply choose 'between alternative courses of action' (Peterson 1995: 71–9).

All this is clearly shown in meteorology and commerce, two fields where specialists in law and economics are numerous (Drake and Nicolaïdis 1992). Competence in trade affairs will also include learning specific terminology embodying the idiom of consensus. Experts and diplomats must have a good understanding of the requisite wording, such as 'providing much insight', 'giving comprehensive information', 'frank and comprehensive responses', or conducting 'a positive and open debate'. They will make extensive use of understatements. Disappointed members 'express concerns' or possibly 'serious concerns' about unfriendly measures. Dissatisfied parties congratulate others on their 'creative way', 'cooperative spirit' and 'tremendous amount of goodwill', even though negotiations end up in a deadlock.[8]

Reaching consensus

Once trained in the idioms and mores of their organization, WMO and WTO members are definitely prejudiced against voting.[9] In the WTO, there is good reason for preferring informal conciliation to formal counting. Out of exasperation with developing countries that delayed the launching of the Uruguay Round, the United States once asked for a formal vote, to press the minority which blocked the whole process to come out into the open. Opponents to the Round had no alternative but to fall in with the majority: voting against the launching of a new negotiating cycle would amount to their self-exclusion from the General Agreement on Tariffs and Trade, GATT (Croome 1999). Even when unavoidable, voting has little meaning. In the WTO admission requires a majority vote, but new members are always unanimously welcomed through postal ballots. Waivers are submitted to a vote, but abstentions are presumed to be supportive of the measure. When and if Amendments to the Marrakech Agreements are demanded they will constitutionally require a two-thirds majority.

The old GATT had already invented the '*consensus of all Members but one*'. The WTO went further with its '*reverse consensus*'. According to the Marrakech Agreements, 'thirty days after it is issued, the Appellate Body's report will be adopted by the Dispute Settlement Body, and unconditionally accepted by the parties to the dispute, *unless there is a consensus against its adoption*' (*WTO Press Release*, 32, 29 November 1995). When the chair raises the gavel to declare that an agreement is reached, voters not raising their country card or not sitting in the room are counted in as in favour. The disadvantage of this procedure is that a 'premature consensus' may be reached at the expense of committee-wide support. On the other hand, accommodating abstentions and absentees risks a long-lasting process of consensus reaching with no foreseeable conclusion.[10]

Consensus seeking includes *agreements on not disagreeing openly*. This may explain why some people in the Secretariat blame problems on a growing increase in precision in writing the minutes. Each time some members vote against a motion and their arguments are recorded, they have no choice but to refrain from supporting the final agreement at the last minute. A dramatic move such as voting against a motion is easier to make if it is not minuted ('negotiators don't speak for the records'). Being discreetly committed to consensus allows members to know with certainty at which stage of the discussions agreement is reached. At that moment the chair has to switch from informal methods of debating to formal IGO procedures for registering the outcome ('agreed?' – if no objection is raised: 'it is so agreed').

Since in both organizations a self-enforcing consensus is sought among a growing number of members, the decision-making process must be split into several phases. In the WMO, the successive meetings of the Congress take the shape of plenary 'Committees' (A, B, C), each specializing in some issues. In the WTO, the General Council frequently gathers informally under the guise of a 'HOD' (Head of Delegations) meeting, before convening a formal session as a 'Plenary GC', a 'Trade Policy Review Board', or a 'Dispute Settlement Body'. Most WTO meetings are kept informal, albeit formally announced and followed up: permanent representatives entering the William Rappard Centre in Geneva must join a 'Working Party', a 'Committee', a 'Seminar', a 'Workshop', etc.

Because it takes time and resources, the informal process of consensus seeking is eventually formalized. In the WMO, coordination of the various positions is delegated to a subcommittee of the Executive Council, although its constitution does not mention this practice, which was inaugurated at the Second World Congress in 1955. More exclusive than the 'Committee of the Whole', it includes the President, Vice-President, Secretary General, the Presidents of the six Regional Associations, the Russian and the American representatives (a legacy of the Cold War), plus a few guest members selected each year from among the most influential heads of meteorological services. The most adamant opponents of a proposal are always included in this group, which meets twice a year, in January and immediately before an Executive or a Congress meeting (to prevent or settle last-minute crises). Moreover, at the first Executive Council meeting of the year and on Congress day, members of this group appoint the chairs of every committee and subcommittee, and of the Financial Advisory Committee.

In the WTO, 'blocks and alliances' are numerous: GATT 'Founding Parties'; US–EU dialogue; G7; G77; the Cairns Group. The most important one is the 'Quad'; however, the US, EU, Canada and Japan are losing influence. Membership is expanding and their share of world trade is shrinking. They tend to be succeeded in the 'hegemonic coalition' by regional groupings, be they formed from the top (as in the WMO, with its six official geographical zones), from the bottom (as in the WTO, with its numerous informal–formal factions more or less tied to a cultural area) or from the outside (the North American Free Trade Area NAFTA, the Southern Common Market MERCOSUR, the Asia Pacific Economic

Cooperation APEC, the Association of South East Asian Countries ASEAN).

There are also committees named after their purpose – for example helping the Director General and the chair – or according to the number of representatives attending the first of their meetings. 'The Eighteen', for instance, was an advisory group officially formed in July 1975 to help launch the Uruguay Round. Originally convening on a temporary basis, it remained active until 1990 (*WTO Official Documents*, MTG/GNG MG 14 W5, 9/6/1987). Its main purpose was to reconcile conflicting demands from developed and developing countries about the timing of phasing-out policy measures in agriculture as well as their contents, and to assist in launching GATS (General Agreement on Trade in Services). Another group, 'the Twenty-Five', met in Singapore during the Ministerial Conference of 1996 to settle diverse views about trade-related social rights measures. It included hardliners from both sides, acting as proxy for other members, ready to contribute to the drafting of the final statement. As successor to the GATT, the WTO is also the seat of 'Friends'-type groups. Such groups are named after the first 'Friends of the Chair' – those who supported the GATT Chairman in 1984–5 – which still meets today (Croome 1999: 317). 'Friends' often meet outside the conference room, with no formal assistance from the Secretariat (however, the Director General may be present). When convening, any informal group can draw on the same logistics as more formal bodies (except for translation services). People from the Secretariat know how to behave in each context, when to become involved, and when to remain discreetly in the background at meetings to which they have been informally invited although they are not on duty (Croome 1999). There are no minutes of such informal proceedings, although a 'memorandum of understanding' may circulate afterwards among Directors.

Expert networks and political leadership

WTO members may also be invited to meetings convened by the heads of the organization. During the 1960s, a single 'green room' held about half of the organization's membership. There are about 35 seats in this main floor room, with its American colonial-style furniture and its portraits hanging on beige walls. When such brainstorming moments were invented, people talked, drank and smoked freely for hours on end in what was like an exclusive gentlemen's club, to which they felt privileged to be admitted. Now, drinking anything other than water is prohibited and it is a non-smoking area open to all, whether they have been asked to come or not. Large and bright, modernized or new lecture rooms accommodate up to a 150 people. Since consensus is really impossible to achieve with such numbers, large circles progressively make way for smaller meetings, until the 'old GATT green-room process' is discreetly reactivated by the chairpersons and the director.

Top-down processes are no less delicate than bottom-up dynamics. Officially, the WMO Secretary General and the WTO Director General have no power over the members – let alone over the outcomes.[11] The WMO relies on national meteorological and hydrological services, whose heads agree on scientific evidence and deliver 'authoritative' statements. The WTO is a member-driven, consensus-based organization which 'belongs to its members'. This said, the Secretary General and the Director General are not powerless. They are facilitators and arbiters backed by a solid structure. In the WTO, the Director General is assisted by several Directors. Strategic decisions about the agenda and the improvement of communication channels are taken by this 'core group'. As far as internal communication is concerned, great efforts are made to improve the way information is disseminated within the organization. In the WMO, 'recommendations' have to be conveyed to appropriate bodies (WMO, EC-LII/PINK1, Appendix, 1.1.7).

The chairperson is allegedly the most important individual in both organizations and is the most authoritative one in the WMO, with the privilege of giving the plenary some vision about strategy.[12] Nevertheless, the head of the bureaucracy works closely with the head of the political structure. This working in tandem is certainly conducive to consensus. Elected by the members (the only disputed vote in both organizations), the two heads hold a watching brief for any incident that may turn out to be a quagmire, and their joint efforts help to give full attention to every member's views. Through attentive observation at meetings, intense consultation, and a very active social life after work, the Secretariat identifies proponents and opponents of any controversial policy measure, as well as their respective 'friends'. Reports are made to the chairperson, who completes them before sending a joint text to the membership or suggesting further meetings to clarify some members' positions. At each stage and on each occasion administrators send written documents to each chair: such memos forecast difficulties to overcome and traps to avoid (WTO).

The consensus-oriented approach of the organization's top officials may create potential difficulties for experts in the WTO Secretariat. Experts are sensitive to a further blurring of 'neutrality' and to 'politicization'. They fear that unsettled 'technical' issues will be 'politicized' to such an extent that 'hot potatoes' will circulate from meeting to meeting, until plenary sessions tackle them.[13] In their view, expertise entails success, and politics implies failure. In the WMO, the World Watch Program Commission on Basic Systems was recently complimented by the Executive Council for having

> embarked on a trial of more flexible and cost-effective working arrangements, which involves more experts than before ... and addresses well defined tasks through several small expert teams ... The Council noted that the success of the new structure depended critically upon the dedication of experts to serve on the various teams.
>
> (WMO, EC-LII/Doc 3.1.3 and 4)

Conclusion

Since intergovernmental organizations in charge of freeing trade and protecting the environment deliver simple messages and operate on a single level of decision making (in contrast to the multi-layer methods of policy networks), they are more homogeneous than other international institutions. Homogeneity, in turn, inclines them towards consensual statements, contractual settlements, and political compromise. Hence, competent people to make these two organizations work are found in the very area where experts, diplomats, epistemic communities and charismatic leaders overlap.

This deliberative and bargaining mix is not only rooted in the very substance of WTO and WMO activity, it is also conducive to procedural, linguistic and behavioural consensus. That 'nobody wants to go the UN way' in these two organizations makes them different from other IGOs. To be influential, their politicians must become experts and their experts must learn politics. They learn a new organizational culture and find symbolic resources within the institution, instead of drawing on an exogenous asymmetric distribution of resources. Leaders are also learners. They are not selected according to the relative power of the country from which they come. What matters is their personal portfolio of capabilities, displayed in successive rounds of discussions. They must 'refine over time a negotiating text that serves as an organizing device for the sequence of discrete negotiating sessions', and combine 'bargaining leverage', 'negotiating skills' and 'intellectual innovation' (Young 1991: 283, 290, 306). Their influence lies in their ability to connect established procedures with new substance, and to reframe implicit theories and redefine problems when change of goals is required by scientific discovery, by evolving market conditions or by any transformation in the power structure. When 'science becomes a component of politics because the scientific way of grasping reality is used to define the interest that political actors articulate and defend' (Haas 1990: 3, 9, 11), expert political leaders are more influential and efficient than epistemic communities or diplomatic networks. Continuity and change in these IGOs is less due to scientific knowledge or political ideology disseminated throughout the whole organization than to 'consensual knowledge', concentrated in 'clusters of bureaucratic units' with a 'professional culture' which survives 'the process of social selection by demonstrating its ability to excel in solving problems' (Haas 1990: 21, 26, 36.).

Finally, there are no tangible differences between the two organizations. Although the scholarly literature contrasts epistemic communities with political leadership, private goods with global commons, functional IGOs with universal ones and cooperation with conflict, neither the bargaining WTO nor the deliberative WMO inclines towards either side. In international organization theory, it is definitely not legitimate to distinguish between trades-offs and weather reports.

Notes

1 A first draft of this chapter was presented at the Grenoble ECPR Joint Sessions, 6–11 April 2001. I thank participants in this session, the two organizers who are also editing this book, and my discussant, Jeffrey Checkel, for their enlightening comments and suggestions.
2 In contrast to the Council of Europe. There a 'cultural match' (consistency between the way agents construct their own identity within the intergovernmental organization, and the social environment from which they come, national culture or institutional structure) helps them to empower international norms (Checkel 1999: 83, 87).
3 For a similar epistemological mix of rational choice and constructivist paradigms see Hasenclaver *et al.* 1997; Risse 2000: 3, 4, 33.
4 The methodology is qualitative. I interviewed key people between 2000 and 2002 to compare organizational narratives from top users of the two institutions to the minutes of their proceedings.
5 Academics usually contrast behavioural compliance (a 'realist' assumption) with preference consistency (a 'constructivist' statement). They nevertheless agree on the importance of social and individual learning, whether through deliberation or through experience (Checkel 2001: 560–7; Haas 1990: 36–40).
6 'One way of investing in information is to create institutions that provide it … It is not only the information one receives, but the information one is able to provide to others that contributes to more efficient strategies' (Haftendorn *et al.* 1999: 3–4).
7 'Leaders are called to interpret and frame what is happening in the international arena for their constituencies and Governments … international constraints only have implications when they are perceived as such by the leaders whose positions count in dealing with a particular problem' (Hermann and Hagan 1998: 135).
8 'TPRB on Thailand', *Focus*, 44; 'TPRB on Iceland', *Focus*, 45.
9 'Decisions are made by the entire membership. This is typically by consensus. A majority of votes is also possible, but it has never been used in the WTO, and was extremely rare under the WTO's predecessor, GATT' (www.wto.org, June 2000).
10 'Group cohesion … can produce … premature closure around options preferred by the more powerful policymakers; bureaucratic interests generally only yield to compromise' (Hermann and Hagan 1998: 127).
11 The history of the Uruguay Round is full of dramatic statements by GATT Secretaries General (Croome 1999 *contra* Moravcsik 1999, who tends to minimize the explanatory power of leadership theories in international negotiations).
12 At the WMO 52nd Executive Council opening session, the Australian president of the organization mentioned 'the need to bring the experience and wisdom of all the members of the Council … not just on managing the daunting array of *issues, opportunities and threats* that confront the organization in the current inter-Congress period, but also, in many ways much more importantly, on laying out the early groundwork for the WMO's *strategy for the next decade* for *consideration* and *decision* by the Fourteenth Congress' (EC-LII/PINK.1, Appendix; my italics).
13 According to P. Haas (1992a: 11–12), 'even in cases involving what is regarded as a technical issue, policymaking decisions generally involve the weighing of a number of complex and non technical issues. Thus … outcomes in technical issues proved little different from those of more conventional high politics'.

References

Adamantopoulos, K. (ed.) (1997) *An Anatomy of the World Trade Organization*, London: Kluwer Law International.

Allan, P. (1994) 'La complexité, le hasard et l'individu dans la théorie politique internationale', in M. Girard (ed.) *Les individus dans les relations internationales*, Paris: Economica, 57–77.

Checkel, J.T. (1999) 'Norms, Institutions and National Identity in Contemporary Europe', *International Studies Quarterly*, 43(1): 83–114.

—— (2001) 'Why Comply? Social Learning and European Identity Change', *International Organization*, 55(3): 553–88.

Croome, J. (1999) *Reshaping the World Trading System. A History of the Uruguay Round*, London: Kluwer Law International.

Drake, W.J. and Nicolaïdis, K. (1992) 'Ideas, Interests and Institutionalization: "Trade in Services" and the Uruguay Round', *International Organization*, 46(1): 37–100.

Haas, E.B. (1990) *When Knowledge is Power: Three Models of Change in International Organizations*, Berkeley: University of California Press.

Haas, P.M. (1992a) 'Introduction: Epistemic Communities and International Policy Coordination', *International Organization*, 46(1): 1–35.

—— (1992b) 'Banning Chlorofluorocarbons: Epistemic Community Efforts to Protect Stratospheric Ozone', *International Organization*, 46(1): 187–224.

Haftendorn, H., Keohane, R. and Wallander, C. (eds) (1999) *Imperfect Unions: Security Institutions over Time and Space*, Oxford: Oxford University Press.

Hasenclaver, A., Mayer, P. and Rittberger, V. (1997) *Theories of International Regimes*, Cambridge: Cambridge University Press.

Hermann, M. and Hagan, J.M. (1998) 'International Decision Making: Leadership Matters', *Foreign Policy*, no. 110: 124–37.

Majone, G. (ed.) (1997) *Regulating Europe*, London: Routledge.

Moravcsik, A. (1999) 'A New Statecraft? Supranational Entrepreneurs and International Cooperation', *International Organization*, 53(2): 267–306.

Petersmann, E. (1997) *The GATT/WTO Dispute Settlement System. International Law, International Organization and Dispute Settlement*, London: Kluwer Law International.

Peterson, J. (1995) 'Decision-Making in the European Union: Towards a Framework for Analysis', *Journal of European Public Policy*, 2(1): 69–93.

Risse, T. (2000) '"Let's argue!": Communicative Action in World Politics', *International Organization*, 54(1): 1–39.

Rosenau, J. (1994) 'Les individus en mouvement comme source de turbulence globale', in M. Girard (ed.) *Les individus dans les relations internationales*, Paris: Economica, 81–105.

Young, O.R. (1991) 'Political Leadership and Regime Formation: On the Development of Institutions in International Society', *International Organization*, 45(3): 281–308.

5 The Organization for Economic Cooperation and Development as ideational artist and arbitrator

Reality or dream?

Martin Marcussen

Introduction

The Organization for Economic Cooperation and Development (OECD) does not produce much 'hard' regulation. At best, it creates recommendations and 'good practice', and leaves it to the member states to enact these general guidelines in day-to-day policy making. Recently other international organizations have copied the OECD method. For instance, the much-discussed 'open method of coordination' of the European Union (EU) has been OECD practice for more than 40 years. It has been argued that the EU's old community method of decision making, as well as its various comitology procedures, are to an increasing extent slow, cumbersome and non-effective and have become democratically unsustainable (Bomberg and Peterson 2000), for which reason more flexible and decentralized procedures have been introduced. OECD analysts would argue that it is precisely because OECD transnational regulation is of the 'soft' kind that it has been so successful over the years (Sullivan 1997). Soft regulatory measures have allowed the OECD to deal explicitly with highly controversial issues (e.g. development economics and the paradigmatic shift from Keynesianism to monetarism) while maintaining its ideational authority in the member states. In full accordance with the principle of subsidiarity, the OECD has left it to the member states themselves to work out how their national models, routines, practices and ways of thinking fit into the conceptual framework developed within, and authorized by, the OECD. At no point has the OECD been able to rely on anything other than the 'good argument'. The organization has not, for instance, been able to back its recommendations with money and cheap loans (like the International Monetary Fund, IMF, and the World Bank), nor is OECD soft regulation watched over and enacted by an arbitration body (such as in the World Trade Organization) or an international judicial body (as in the United Nations and the Council of Europe). Despite this apparent weakness the OECD is often considered influential. The purpose of this chapter is, therefore, to come to a better understanding of OECD decision making on soft regulation. The guiding questions are: how is OECD 'soft' regulation produced, and which mechanisms does the OECD apply to enforce soft regulation?

The chapter is structured as follows. In the first section I will outline the main theoretical concepts applied to analyse transnational soft regulation, compliance and ideas. This discussion will end with a presentation of the concept of the 'idea game' and the various roles the OECD plays within that game. In the second section I will discuss a concrete mechanism used by the OECD to ensure that soft regulation is upheld in the member countries: multilateral surveillance. I will also discuss the challenges that have threatened OECD's ideational authority in recent years. Finally, in the third section I will summarize the chapter and discuss some directions the OECD idea game might take in the future.

Compliance and the idea game[1]

The main question asked in the so-called compliance literature is, of course, why states follow international norms and rules (Chayes and Chayes 1993; Koh 1997; Goldstein *et al.* 2000). A major research theme has been the extent to which international sanctions can be said (not) to work in practice (Morgan and Schweback 1997; Nossal 1999). Another major theme has been the social and economic impact of the IMF's (Bird 1996), World Bank's (Hopkins *et al.* 2000) and European Union's (Schimmelfennig *et al.* 2002) economic and political conditionality. However, recently our attention has turned to compliance mechanisms that cannot be placed within these two classical categories of 'sanctions' and 'self-interest'. The answers to the main question so far have been that states comply with international norms either because they fear the punishment of rule-enforcers (negative incentives), or because they want to benefit from the direct pay-offs involved in norm-conforming behaviour (positive incentives). More recent theorizing however suggests that states sometimes comply because they have learnt to accept and respect international norms. In other words, attention has been directed towards the issues of international persuasion, socialization and legitimacy (Hurd 1999; Risse *et al.* 1999; Risse 2000).

It is this last category of social-constructivist-rooted international relations theory that is best applied to analyse the roles and functions of the OECD in the production and diffusion of norms. We know that international organizations can take on a life of their own, and that some of them have international legitimacy and consequently also the authority that makes them powerful (McNeely 1995; Finnemore 1996; Barnett and Finnemore 1999). However, we still need to conceptualize the different ways in which an organization such as the OECD enacts its ideational authority.

One way of conceptualizing what an organization such as the OECD is actually doing, is to argue that it is playing an *idea game* through which it *collects and manipulates data, knowledge, visions and ideas and diffuses them* to its member countries and, to an even greater extent, to a number of non-member countries.[2]

In the idea game, the OECD was originally set up to play the roles of ideational artist and ideational arbitrator. For the organization's first Secretary General, Thorkil Kristensen, the OECD had a democratic obligation not only to inform national political and economic debates, but also to introduce entirely new political and economic themes onto the national agendas (Kristensen 1967). The OECD should act as an *ideational artist* in the international idea game; it should think the unthinkable, because the many existing national and international bodies (universities, ministries and Cold War organizations) somehow were too enmeshed with the establishment. Political and economic ties made these advisory and expert bodies accept standard policy discourses, as a result of which the national political debates became conservative and revolved around the main basic themes without ever really investigating new territory. In short, the OECD should care about its independence and should use it actively to say some of the things that national politicians did not want to hear – who else, Kristensen reasoned, was in a position to do this?

At the same time, Kristensen was well aware that think tanks could not make a difference if nobody listened to and learnt OECD lessons. The OECD, apart from being an ideational artist, should also act as an *ideational arbitrator* between national civil servants. By providing national civil servants with some breathing space in Paris, in the form of truly unconstrained and balanced technical discussions between experts, the OECD could create the right conditions for deliberation, socialization and norm-internalization. Enlightened and a great deal wiser through OECD ideational arbitration, national civil servants could be turned into reform entrepreneurs in their home countries. In this way, the OECD was no longer just a body in Paris, but also part of an increasing number of physical bodies and minds in the national capitals.

These two roles to some extent give an idea of the initial enthusiasm that prevailed in the OECD. Concrete manifestations of these roles in practice can be seen in the OECD's efforts in the 1960s to invent new ideas within the area of development economics, and its work in the 1970s with regard to the introduction of an anti-inflationary stability paradigm onto national agendas.

The idea game tells us something about the context in which decision making in international organizations takes place. It can help us understand which issues are on the *agenda* of the OECD's Council of Ministers, OECD ambassadors and the various committees. Both short-lived policy fashions and strongly consolidated policy paradigms can constrain or facilitate the introduction of some subjects, information and methods rather than others. The idea game can also help us understand that a *hierarchy* exists among OECD member states, as well as among OECD departments and among OECD committees. At the top we will find a group of theoretically- and politically-advanced member states, from which other member states learn. The flow of ideas on many occasions seems to be one-way, a trend that will be further strengthened as the OECD accepts new, less theoretically-advanced, states as members. A distinct hierarchy can also be seen among those committees and departments that do not belong to the OECD's economic core and those, such as the Economics Department and the Economic and Development Review Committee (EDRC), which in terms of prestige, reputation and resources are clearly right at the centre of decision making. Finally, the idea game can help us to focus on those decision-making processes which have been developed with the purpose of diffusing ideas through cyclical peer review. These processes, which are at the centre of this chapter, are very illustrative of *socialization processes* among national civil servants, a subject of which we have only scant empirical knowledge since it takes place behind closed doors.

In order to see how the OECD has been playing the roles of ideational artist and arbitrator, I will now take a closer look at one part of OECD's many activities: multilateral surveillance. This is a very specific choice, that can help shed light on the impact OECD civil servants have on the formulation and analysis of macro-economic problems in the member states. It tells a story about learning mechanisms in international organizations and about the many barriers the OECD is encountering in the idea game.

Acting as ideational artist and arbitrator through multilateral surveillance

One of the best-known activities of the OECD is its publication of regular country surveys, which on an almost annual basis critically analyse the macro-economic situation and performance of one of the member countries. The elaboration and publication of these surveys is the physical evidence that multilateral surveillance is taking place. To be better able to grasp the mechanisms and effects of OECD multilateral surveillance, it is necessary to also have a better understanding of the processes through which these country surveys are developed and of the institutional context in which OECD multilateral surveillance is embedded. In this section I will, first, sketch the relevant parts of the OECD structure involved in macro-economic surveillance and, second, take a closer look at the procedure through which multilateral surveillance takes place in practice, as the interplay between the national central administrations, the Economic and Development Review Committee and the Economics Department of the OECD Secretariat.

At the most general and simplified level, it makes sense to distinguish between two layers of organizational structure. One is the political, deliberative and consultative level, where national civil servants and, to a much lesser extent, national politicians meet in committees, working groups, expert groups and council meetings. The second layer is the administrative, analytical and data processing level, which is also known as the OECD Secretariat. Kristensen had this level of the organization in mind when describing the OECD as an ideational artist. Some parts of the Secretariat collect data, monitor trends and analyse and forecast economic developments, while others research social changes or evolving patterns in trade, the environment, agriculture, technology, taxation and many other areas.

The first layer of the OECD organizational structure relates more closely to OECD's role as an ideational arbitrator. This is where we find 42 committees and no less than 98 working parties and groups. Throughout the year, national experts and civil servants gather in these committees and working groups in order to discuss matters of common interest, most typically on the basis of data and analysis elaborated by either the OECD Secretariat or the member states. The OECD itself has described this level of its organization as a permanent intergovernmental conference (OECD 1998a: 12). Year by year, since the foundation of the organization in 1961, the committee structure has become increasingly complex. New groups, parties and committees have constantly been added to the original core (Chavranski 1997: 56). In order to better grasp OECD multilateral surveillance we will need to extract the relevant organizational elements on both of the above-mentioned levels.

At the level of the Secretariat, it becomes necessary to take a closer look at the Economics Department, which is the very essence of the OECD staff's self-definition (see Figure 5.1). At first glance, one can see that the OECD Secretariat has a five-tiered leadership. At the top, of course, is the Secretary General, who has overall administrative, financial and political responsibility. He delegates some of his responsibility to four Deputy Secretaries General. Below the Secretary General we find the Heads of Department, who take responsibility for the individual directorates and departments of the Secretariat. In the case of the Economics Department this person is referred to as the Chief Economist.

The Economics Department is functionally split into two branches – the Policy Studies Branch, which deals with macro-economic and structural issues in general, and the Country Studies Branch, dealing with these issues in relation to individual member and non-member countries. A Director and a Deputy Director head each branch. At the fourth level of management are the Heads of Division who, in the case of the Country Studies Branch, oversee a group of countries, usually six. Finally, at the lowest level of management, we find the Heads of Teams and Units (in the Policy Studies Branch) and Heads of Desks (in the Country Studies Branch). This person is normally a senior economist, who works with one or two administrators or economists. Each desk in the Country Studies Branch has the responsibility of writing country surveys for at least two

Figure 5.1 The structure of the economics department of the OECD.

countries every 18 months. Thus, the 20 desks in the Country Studies Branch cover on a regular basis the 30 OECD member countries and a number of non-member countries, such as the Baltic states, Russia, Brazil and China.

At the political level, the so-called Economic and Development Review Committee is central when studying the country-specific surveillance of the OECD. The EDRC is one of the OECD committees that convenes most frequently in Paris. Thirty delegates, typically the economic counsellors from the member states' permanent OECD delegations in Paris, make up the committee members. They convene four to six times a year in special sessions to discuss strategic, organizational and administrative issues among themselves and between 20 and 24 times a year to examine draft surveys produced by the country desks of the Secretariat. On the latter occasions, as we will see below, the permanent members of the committee, the chair, the two vice-chairs and a few OECD staff members are joined by a delegation from the relevant country, which travels to Paris to explain and defend the problematic issues raised by the draft country survey. The number of participants in these regular meetings can vary from around 45 to well over 100.

The EDRC multilateral surveillance process can roughly be split into five consecutive stages (OECD 1998b; Marcussen forthcoming). The entire process is shown in Figure 5.2.[3]

1 An idea stage, in which the desk economists collect impressions, ideas and plans from their immediate institutional environment. They typically end up with a plan which lists a series of topics that should be the object of investigation in the survey.
2 A data collection stage, which takes the form of both office work and missions in the field. Field missions directly involve a considerable number of national civil servants, representatives from interest organizations and country experts. They have all been asked to answer a set of questions in advance, with a view to steering the interview in the desired direction. Sometimes the country desk economists and their immediate superiors plan several field missions, covering both general macro-economic issues and the specific topic chosen for the so-called structural chapter of the country survey.
3 The drafting stage, in which the first complete draft of the survey is published on the OECD internal database to which all the permanent members of the EDRC have access. They and the relevant public authorities now have a chance to read the survey and consider their own interventions.
4 An EDRC meeting, at which representatives from the country in question come to Paris in order to be interrogated. The examiners are representatives from two other OECD member states, assisted and supported by the chair and the OECD staff. The meeting lasts all day and is structured by a so-called *Questions for Discussion Note* prepared by the OECD Secretariat. The chair ends the questioning by summarizing the main conclusions and underlining the aspects he or she expects to find in the introductory Assessment and Recommendations part of the survey
5 The publication stage, when the final survey, after unanimous adoption in the EDRC, is released to the public. Sometimes a release is followed by a press conference in the country concerned – on other occasions the release is without such publicity.

Multilateral surveillance as implemented in this way is an ongoing endeavour. The examination itself is but one stage in a much longer process, in

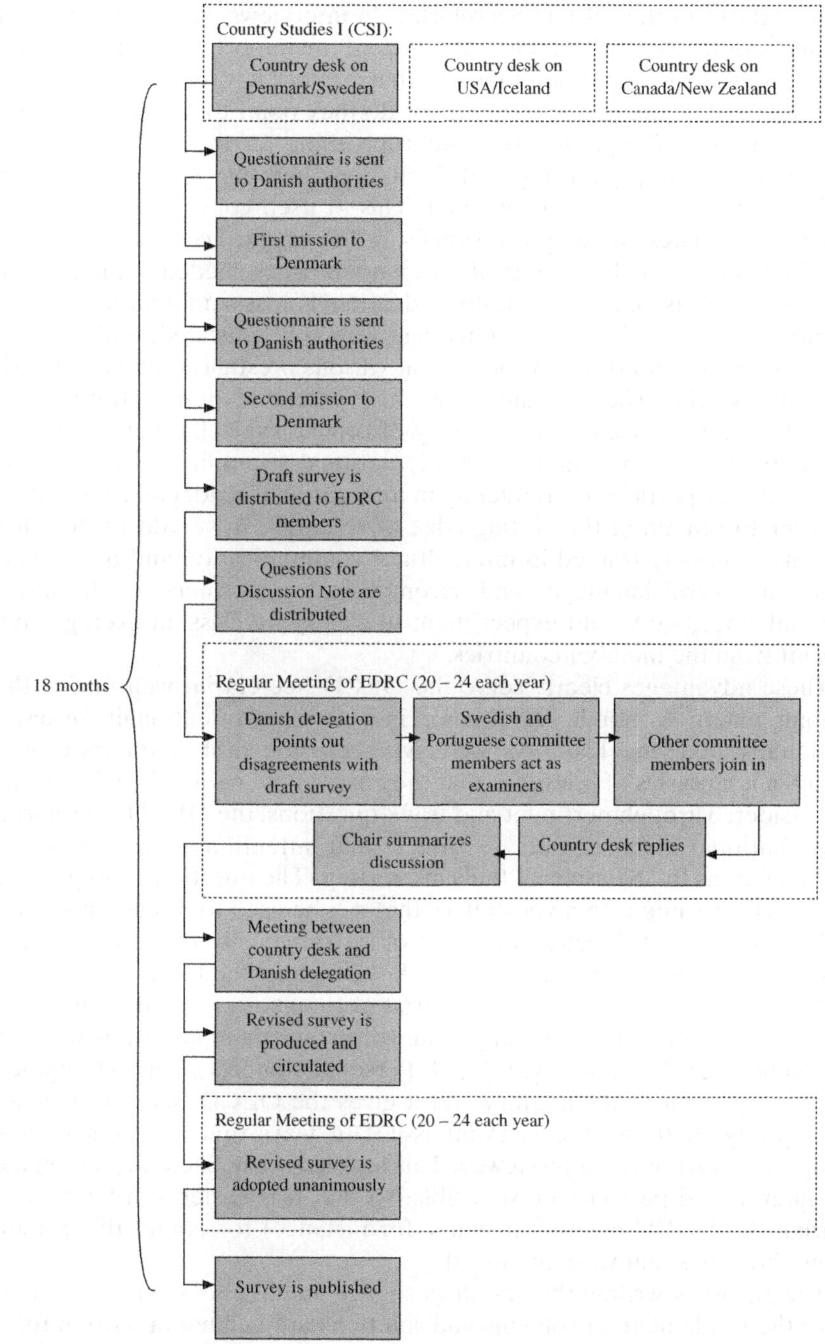

Figure 5.2 The EDRC multilateral surveillance process.

which national civil servants and experts communicate regularly with the country desks in the OECD Secretariat. In interviews, various permanent members of the committee have emphasized the importance of the process character of OECD multilateral surveillance. Very few look on the EDRC meeting itself as the decisive event, nor do they point to the actual release of the survey to the public. The important thing for them is the ongoing information sharing, learning and discussions between various parties in Paris and in the countries concerned. This in itself contributes to greater and better debates among professionals in the surveyed countries.

OECD personnel have most of the characteristics needed to make them efficient analysts and authoritative ideational artists in relation to the member countries. They are on average very well educated, both in their home countries and through sojourns at various prestigious universities all over the world. They usually have had extended administrative and leadership experience in their country of origin. Typically they have published extensively in national and international scientific and other journals, and they participate frequently in international academic conferences in order to remain at the cutting edge of research. If we add to that that they are generally trained in intercultural communication and diplomacy, fluent in several languages and accomplished performers on the international stage, we would expect them to clearly outclass an average civil servant from the member countries.

These advantages clearly serve the OECD Secretariat well during the ongoing macro-economic surveillance, in which they intentionally or unintentionally take the lead. As we have seen, the desk economists first launch a long series of *questions* that they expect the national civil servants to consider. Through pertinent and frank questions, the OECD Secretariat helps national civil servants to direct their attention to a number of problem areas the Secretariat finds interesting. The questions also provide these civil servants with a vocabulary that can be used to discuss the issues and, indirectly and directly, with a set of instruments to conceptualize the margin of manoeuvre when dealing with the highlighted topics in practice.

As mentioned, the OECD Secretariat also makes personal *visits* to the people most concerned, thereby again directing their attention towards the agenda developed by the OECD. Personal contacts clearly strengthen the message sent to the country and it gives the OECD ‘salespersons’ an opportunity to frame the relevant issues in ways that are immediately comprehensible to the interviewee. This also helps the Secretariat to make the interviewed person co-responsible, so that it is easier at a later stage (during the EDRC meeting in Paris, for instance) to remind this person about the issues that were discussed.

The power of writing the first *draft* survey should not be ignored either. Here the fundamental problems and solutions are defined in written form for the first time. Oral discussions can become confused in the minds of the involved parties over time. This is not so easy when it comes to texts, where – in the case of the surveys – the messages are increasingly straightforward and easy to understand.

The ability to set the agenda for the *meeting* itself is also important. By formulating the questions that ought to be discussed in Paris, the OECD Secretariat once again directs the participants' attention in one specific direction. The Secretariat itself participates in the meeting, and will always generously offer its assistance to anyone who needs expert advice.

Regular contacts with the national *media* provide the OECD country-desk economists with opportunities to place certain issues on the national political agenda. Typically, the native person at the OECD country desk is the international expert most referred to by the national media. It is not unusual for media statements from OECD experts to be answered by high-level politicians and central bankers in the relevant country, which illustrates that OECD expertise in some areas is highly valued and praised. This also applies to national civil servants who, to a greater or lesser extent, draw on their OECD contacts in their day-to-day business. The importance of regular professional contacts across national borders should not be ignored when it comes to analysing how far and fast ideas travel (Lerdell and Sahlin-Andersson 1997; Sahlin-Andersson 2001).

It would be too simplistic, however, to depict OECD civil servants as pure ideational artists who exist in a political vacuum. This is primarily because average OECD civil servants constantly find themselves faced with many different and mutually conflicting interests. At its narrowest, this means that the country desks in the OECD Secretariat cannot afford to ignore the political signals sent from higher up the secretarial hierarchy. The main policy guidelines are formulated from above, in the end by the Secretary General and the ministers at the annual Council of Ministers. These guidelines are, of course, political in nature and, consequently, the OECD Secretariat is far from able to act as a self-governed epistemic community on the ground.

Changes in the OECD's idea game

To add to that, typical OECD civil servants are far from completely detached from the country in which they were once professionally employed. The average tenure in the OECD is four to five years, after which they return home to their national civil service (OECD 2002: 11). That is an additional reason why we should not expect these people, during OECD multilateral surveillance, to think the unthinkable. After all, they will have to keep their options in the home country open for the future. To burn all bridges by acting as a pure and independent ideational artist would be brave, but also foolhardy.

Finally, yet another small consideration that must be kept in mind when evaluating the possibility and will of the OECD Secretariat to act as ideational artist is the question of time and money. The OECD was until the mid-1990s an international secretariat characterized by an abundance of resources. This is no longer the case. The new Secretary General who took office in 1996 had a clear mandate to cut down and streamline the OECD organization, while at the same time ensuring the Secretariat published more. The member states wanted more for less (Bayne 1998). Clearly, this has an impact on the ability of the Secretariat to invent new ideas and to explore untested ground. The average OECD civil servant is more likely to write what is expected of him or her, rather than to risk upsetting anyone.

This leads us to the somewhat wider circumstances that have changed the ways in which the OECD can play the idea game. More precisely, two developments made consecutive Secretaries General reconsider the roles the OECD is playing. The first concerns the multiplication of competing international organizations in the idea game. Originally the OECD had a secure monopoly with regard to inventing new ideas, but very soon a number of other organizations entered the field and provided competition. In contrast to the OECD, many of these organizations, in addition to participating actively in the idea game, were also in a position to enhance their international authority, because they had funds and certain regulatory competencies at their disposal. This forced the OECD to pay much more attention to the immediate needs of national policy makers in their day-to-day activities. It became important to convince national policy makers that the OECD was of direct importance to their work. Therefore the OECD started to constantly monitor the national and international political debates, in order to catch new trends at an early stage and then gain authority by cultivating these trends. In other words, the OECD started to become a trend follower rather than a trend setter – a fashion consumer rather than a fashion maker. It began to play the role of an *ideational agency* that was willing to sell whatever idea was in demand among its member states. Like an international consultancy, the OECD was continually trying to enlarge its markets and its repertoire of ready-to-sell ideas. New sections were added to the Secretariat and new working groups and committees to the organizational set-up, thereby making the OECD a complex web of bodies with varying membership, competencies and status (OECD 1998a). A series of popular ideas-of-the-day became part of the OECD cornucopia ('ethics in public administration' and 'international study assessment' are just two recent examples). The problem is, however, that these ideas had already been invented in other forums. OECD efforts, typically of an extremely high analytical quality, can be viewed as mere follow-ups and add-ons to trends that were already out there in the international market for ideas.

The second development that undermined the initial ideational roles of the OECD in the idea game came through the large member states. No Secretary General can afford to ignore the fact that just three member countries together pay 60 per cent of the OECD budget (the United

States, Japan and Germany). That is why strongly expressed requirements, from the United States in particular, concerning the OECD's organizational form and analytical activities have had direct consequences for the way in which the idea game is played. Apart from becoming an ideational agency that is always looking around for a good deal that can be done in the market for bright ideas, the OECD also in many respects began to function as an *ideational agent* for the United States. Having won the Cold War, the United States started to demand value for money from the various international organizations of which it was a member. It was no longer considered an objective in itself, and an essential element of the Cold War strategy, to be a member of as many international organizations as possible. International organizations, the OECD among them, were now considered integral parts of the central administration of the United States, and the main question became whether that country got what it wanted from international organizations' activities.

The present Secretary General, Donald J. Johnston, now talks about an identity crisis:

> Since my arrival as Secretary-General on June 1st, 1996, it has become clear to me that the OECD suffers from a lack of a distinct identity, with the breadth of its mission poorly understood.
>
> (OECD 1997: 3)

The core of the identity crisis is that the OECD is to a lesser and lesser extent playing the role of an *ideational authority* in the member states. Increasingly it is seen as just another international organization that does not distinguish itself from the crowd. Headlines are becoming rare. The OECD as an ideational agency and agent has begun to compete in a field where in all likelihood it will lose. It will not be able to compete for authority with international organizations such as the IMF and the European Union, which not only provide ideas, but also have money they can lend and hard regulation they can issue. Nor will it be able to act as a stand-in and spokesperson for the US and still be considered an intellectually free and inventive body.

The OECD and the idea game: Game over?

This chapter has promoted three arguments. First, it has been emphasized that there are other ways to make states comply with international norms than by just creating negative and positive incentive structures. Soft regulation through the collection, elaboration and diffusion of data, analyses, visions and ideas is just such an alternative. In this chapter, this alternative has been called the idea game and it has been argued that of the many international organizations in existence today, it is probably the OECD that has most experience in applying soft regulatory measures to member as well as non-member states. In recent years even supranational organizations such as the EU have contemplated engaging in the production of soft regulation and multilateral surveillance. The OECD method seems to succeed: (1) because it produces outcomes even in controversial policy areas where hard law would be difficult and (2) because the decentralist nature of soft law implementation is both flexible and considered legitimate.

Second, it has been argued that the multilateral surveillance of the OECD illustrates the ways in which its Secretariat is acting as ideational artist and arbitrator. The OECD Secretariat is constantly trying to shape and fashion the political agenda in the surveyed countries. Techniques, problems and solutions are conceptualized and discussed, and a common vocabulary is created between experts across national boundaries. In the literature this is referred to as gradual and simple learning, which eventually can lead to more complex patterns of norm-internalization (Checkel 2001). The decision-making processes studied in this chapter exemplify such learning processes in a closed, deliberative forum, where national civil servants and the OECD Secretariat meet on a frequent basis.

Third, the various constraints currently imposed on the OECD have been highlighted. It has been argued that it is difficult for the OECD to properly act as an ideational artist and arbitrator, because specific member states and competing international organizations force it to act as an ideational agent and agency. These macro-considerations, which relate to OECD's place in the global governance structure, are supplemented by micro-considerations relating to the situation of, and decisions made by, individual civil servants within the OECD. The short active career in the Secretariat and the close bonds of loyalty to the national capitals can be claimed to be factors that encourage OECD civil servants to auto-censure their analysis and thereby water down their roles as ideational artists.

It would be premature to declare 'Game Over' for the OECD's idea game. The OECD still has the extremely important function of innovating and developing the national political debates. One could argue, with Kristensen, that the OECD has a democratic obligation to dispel national myths, stereotypes and established world-views and to elevate itself above national strategic considerations and power structures. With that in mind, the statement of purpose and the basic structure of the OECD Secretariat and committees will have to be scrutinized and reconsidered. But what would such a reinvented OECD look like? How can we describe a learning organization that, through its decision-making processes, does not reproduce existing fashions and trends, does not mimic selected member states, and considers it a sacred obligation to think the unthinkable?

First, in a learning organization people really must have time to think. The publication rate of the OECD is impressive – but what difference does that make if the individual publications fail to attract attention? What about slowing down the publication and meeting frequency a bit, and valuing the 'inventiveness' and 'surprise effects' of publications and conferences a little more? Would it not be a sign of success if each average-sized unit in the OECD Secretariat could produce one decisive volume a year – a volume that constituted the reference point for a considerable period of time? The impact of one such volume and meeting could be much more decisive than a regular flow of reports, both in terms of turning the OECD into a veritable ideational authority, and with regard to making a difference in the real world.

Second, a learning organization does not deal with everything at the same time. The OECD should be one or two steps ahead of established fashions, so it needs to carefully, and at regular intervals, choose a series of strategic fields in which it wants to make progress. An explicit choice of themes is also an exercise in discarding other themes – but the strategic choices will have to be made. The important thing is that in selecting a small number of future-oriented themes, the ambitions with regard to newness and originality will have to be increased accordingly. That is only what one can expect from an ideational artist.

Third, a learning organization adapts its organizational structure and decision-making processes to the problem at hand. New strategic themes require new organizational forms and new configurations of employees which cooperate in new ways. Strategic thematic choices are individual, typically interdisciplinary, projects that can be carried forward by flexible teams of some of the world's finest analysts. The existing human capital of the OECD can be exploited to a much greater extent than it is today – to the benefit of OECD civil servants themselves, the member states and, in the end, deliberative democracy.

Notes

1 This section is based on data presented and discussed in Marcussen 2002.
2 For a related conceptualization, the OECD as an 'information-processing system', see Sjöstedt 1973.
3 The figure illustrates the development of an *OECD Economic Survey* of Denmark. The basic patterns, however, are the same for all countries.

References

Barnett, M.N. and Finnemore, M. (1999) 'The Politics, Power, and Pathologies of International Organizations', *International Organization*, 53(4): 699–732.

Bayne, N. (1998) 'International Economic Organizations – More Policy-Making, Less Autonomy', in B. Reinalda and B. Verbeek (eds) *Autonomous Policy Making by International Organizations*, London: Routledge: 195–210.

Bird, G. (1996) 'The International Monetary Fund and Developing Countries: A Review of the Evidence and Policy Options', *International Organization*, 50(3): 477–511.

Bomberg, E. and Peterson, J. (2000) 'Policy Transfer and Europeanization: Passing the Heineken Test'?, *Queen's Papers on Europeanization*, 2/2000.

Chavranski, H. (1997) *L'OECD – Au cœur des grands débat économiques*, Paris: Documentation Française.

Chayes, A. and Chayes, A.H. (1993) 'On Compliance', *International Organization*, 47(2): 175–205.

Checkel, J. (2001) 'Why Comply? Social Learning and European Identity Change', *International Organization*, 55(3): 553–88.

Finnemore, M. (1996) *National Interests in International Society*, Ithaca: Cornell University Press.

Goldstein, J., Kahler, M., Keohane, R.O. and Slaughter, A.-M. (2000) 'Introduction: Legalization and World Politics', *International Organization*, 54(3): 385–99.

Hopkins, R., Powell, A., Roy, A. and Gilbert, C.L. (2000) 'The World Bank, Conditionality and the Comprehensive Development Framework', in C.L. Gilbert and D. Vines (eds) *The World Bank: Structure and Policies*, Cambridge: Cambridge University Press, 282–98.

Hurd, I. (1999) 'Legitimacy and Authority in International Politics', *International Organization*, 53(2): 379–408.

Koh, H.H. (1997) 'Why do Nations Obey International Law?', *The Yale Law Journal*, 106(8): 2599–659.

Kristensen, T. (1967) 'Five Years of O.E.C.D.', *European Yearbook*, 13: 100–13.

Lerdell, D. and Sahlin-Andersson, K. (1997) *Att lära över gränser – En studie av OECD's förvaltningspolitiska samarbete. Rapport till förvaltningspolitiska kommissionen, SOU 1997:33*, Stockholm: Finansdepartementet.

Marcussen, M. (2002) *OECD og idéspillet – Game Over?* København: Hans Reitzels Forlag.

—— (forthcoming) 'Multilateral Surveillance and the OECD: Playing the Idea-Game', in K. Armingeon and M. Beyeler (eds) *OECD Surveillance and Welfare States in Western Europe*, Cheltenham: Edward Elgar Publishing.

McNeely, C.L. (1995) *Constructing the Nation-State. International Organization and Prescriptive Action*, London: Greenwood Press.

Morgan, T.C. and Schwebach, V.L. (1997) 'Fools Suffer Gladly: The Use of Economic Sanctions in International Crises', *International Studies Quarterly*, 41(1): 27–50.

Nossal, K.R. (1999) 'Liberal Democratic Regimes, International Sanctions, and Global Governance', in R. Väyrynen (ed.) *Globalization and Global Governance*, Lanham: Rowman and Littlefield, 127–50.

OECD (1997) *The OECD – Challenges and Strategic Objectives: 1997. Note by the Secretary General*, C(97)180, 10 September, Paris: OECD.

—— (1998a) *The OECD Committee Structure – A Review (The Vinde Report)*, CE(98)3, Paris: OECD.

—— (1998b) *EDRC Agreed Principles and Practices*, ECO/EDR/DIV(98)3/REV3, Paris: OECD.

—— (2002) *OECD Staff Profile Statistics, 2001*, C(2002)67, Paris: OECD.

Risse, T. (2000) '"Let's argue!": Communicative Action in World Politics', *International Organization*, 54(1): 1–40.

Risse, T., Ropp, S.C. and Sikkink, K. (1999) *The Power of Human Rights – International Norms and Domestic Change*, Cambridge: Cambridge University Press.

Sahlin-Andersson, K. (2001) 'National, International and Transnational Constructions of New Public Management Ideas', in T. Christensen and P. Lægreid (eds)

New Public Management – The Transformations of Ideas and Practice, Aldershot: Ashgate: 43–72.

Schimmelfennig, F., Engert, S. and Knobel, H. (2002) *The Conditions of Conditionality. The Impact of the EU on Democracy and Human Rights in European Non-Member States*, Paper prepared for the ECPR Joint Session of Workshops, Turin, 22–27 March.

Sjöstedt, G. (1973) *OECD-Samarbetet: Funktioner och Effekter, Stockholm Political Studies* 3, Stockholm: Statsvetenskapliga Institut.

Sullivan, S. (1997) *From War to Wealth – Fifty Years of Innovation*, Paris: OECD.

Part IV

Organizational dynamics

6 Groupthink

The IMF, the World Bank and decision making regarding the 1994 Mexican crisis

Ngaire Woods

Introduction

The International Monetary Fund (IMF) and the World Bank (International Bank for Reconstruction and Development) each have the responsibility to rigorously analyse and monitor economies across the world. For the IMF, 'surveillance' of countries making up the world economy, as well as the need to impose conditions on those using Fund resources, requires the institution to provide accurate and precise analyses. The World Bank has a mandate to finance investments and promote economic growth, and to provide expert advice to help governments make specific sectors of their economies more efficient and relevant to national development goals. These responsibilities equally require accurate research and the monitoring of members' economies.

To discharge their responsibilities, both the IMF and the World Bank are armed with first rate personnel and facilities. The two organizations have reputations as premier research institutions in economics and development. Yet in 1994 both the Fund and the Bank failed to see that their largest debtor was in dire economic trouble. As Mexico's exchange rate and economy went into free fall at the end of 1994, the organizations were accused of having their heads buried in the sand. In this chapter I investigate why this was so. The central argument is that several elements of the organizational structure of the two institutions favoured the occurrence of a small-group phenomenon called 'Groupthink' among staff members dealing with the Mexico crisis. Groupthink subsequently inhibited their attempts to clearly and precisely see the forthcoming crisis.

The first section of the chapter briefly outlines the 1994 crisis in Mexico and the warning signs of an impending crisis which the institutions should have noticed. The second section outlines the concept of Groupthink. The third section then analyses the experiences of the international financial institutions in their decision-making process with respect to Mexico throughout 1994. It highlights the extent to which so-called antecedent conditions of Groupthink, such as the homogeneity, insulation and cohesion among staff, favoured the occurrence of Groupthink and thus impeded rigorous and impartial analysis.

Mexico's 1994 crisis and the international financial institutions

In 1993 Mexico's economic future looked, to many onlookers, very promising. Under the tutelage of the IMF and the World Bank, the Mexican government had built steadily on a set of economic reforms begun a decade earlier. These reforms now seemed to be cemented in place by the completion of the North American Free Trade Agreement (NAFTA), Mexico's membership of the Organization for Economic Cooperation and Development (OECD), and the trailing of the Mexican case as a good example by the international financial community.

Yet in early 1995 NAFTA's promised capital movement became a nightmare for Mexico. In December 1994, after a period of economic policy difficulties, the Mexican government widened the exchange rate band by 15 per cent. Within weeks Mexico was on the verge of default as investors withdrew. From Washington, it looked as though this posed a risk to international financial stability, as Mexico's problems threatened to create a 'Tequila effect', spilling across Latin America and causing capital flight from the whole region. Extraordinarily, in spite of danger signs earlier in 1994 and even in 1993, neither the IMF nor the World Bank had sent out warnings about Mexico, nor indeed did either institution issue any kind of urgent advice to the Mexican government. Yet there were several warning signs which either institution could have picked up.[1] In early 1994 Mexico's current account deficit was exacerbated by the uprising in the Chiapas region (the government found this very difficult to deal with and it caused an adverse reaction in the markets), and the increase in US long-term interest rates, which was forcing down bond prices.[2] In international markets there was a significant rise in the risk premium being charged on Mexican debt. Yet in official documents neither the IMF nor the World Bank went beyond their usual states of 'concern' about the economy.

A couple of months later, in April 1994, the markets and the international financial institutions became aware that the Mexican government was substituting *tesobonos* (Mexican peso-denominated government bonds) for CETES (US dollar-denominated instruments). Yet IMF staff visiting in mid-1994 were not alarmed by the swiftly increasing stock of *tesobonos*, even while financial markets were reacting to the shift. Whilst foreign investment continued to flow into Mexico, a closer investigation into the nature of this investment would have revealed that it was creating new vulnerabilities for the Mexican economy. Certainly, once Mexico's monetary data up to April 1994 were released (in August 1994), the shifts should have been apparent to both the Fund and Bank. Later in 1994 the institutions should also have noted more carefully the shortening of maturity for new government security issues, the drop in foreign holdings of short-term public debt, and the drop in stock market prices.

Adding to this picture, figures released in early September 1994 revealed that Mexico's imports had grown by 25 per cent during the second quarter of 1993, and that the country's current account deficit had increased to 8 per cent of GDP on an annual basis. Furthermore, in the same month the government announced a policy package (the *Pacto*) which did nothing to correct the deteriorating trade balance or to tighten up the loosening of financial policies. At least this might have alarmed the IMF or the World Bank into action. Yet a senior World Bank official at the time was expressing a positive view (Edwards 1995), as were the IMF staff (see IMF, *Country Report* of January 1994, following 1993 Article IV consultations with Mexico).

Groupthink and the way decisions are made in international organizations

As in most international organizations, decision making in the IMF and the World Bank is perhaps affected first and foremost by the preferences of their most powerful members, who wield both formal and informal influence (Foot *et al.* 2003). Also significant are the senior management, the international context and the economic theories available to the institutions for use in resolving problems. Beyond these obvious kinds of influence, however, the way the agencies are organized and the way they make decisions result in more human and cognitive effects on their decisions (Ripley 1993; 't Hart *et al.* 1997).

Cognitive and psychological effects can be particularly important when decision makers work in small groups, which can become entrenched in a particular mindset in a way that detracts from impartial and rigorous analysis. The processes of decision making may make it difficult for staff to challenge the mainstream view, to criticize the general thrust of policy, or to offer alternatives. In some organizations the internal structure and management further exacerbate these effects. Such pathologies of decision making take us out of the realm of economics and into a realm of political psychology which has been extensively applied in foreign policy-making analysis (Lebow 1981; Roberts 1988). The concept of Groupthink is particularly pertinent to this.

Irving Janis formalized the concept of Groupthink after studying four disastrous episodes in American foreign policy making. After comparing the decisions with these from more successful episodes, Janis concluded that the failures were characterized by Groupthink – a term that describes and models an extreme 'concurrence-seeking tendency' displayed by decision-making groups (Janis 1982: 8). Seeking, and then clinging to, consensus as a group provides one way for its members to make a decision even where they have inadequate information about the situation and inadequate knowledge of the relevant cause-and-effect relationships, and lack a single utility criterion for dealing with the multiple competing values and interests involved (George 1997).

Groupthink is more likely to occur if the following conditions are present. First, when small groups of decision makers work under severe stress, often caused by an external threat (Turner *et al.* 1992). Psychologically, severe stress increases the need of each member of the group to reaffirm their affiliation, because 'participating in a unanimous consensus along with the respected fellow members of a congenial group will bolster ... [their] self-esteem' (Janis 1972: 203). Second, Groupthink pertains to particular groups in which members derive pride both from membership of the group and from its task. Third, a high degree of 'insulation' reinforces a group's tendency to rely on itself and not refer to or consult outside analysts or sources of information (McCauley 1989). Fourth, homogeneity among group members (e.g. shared backgrounds and training) may narrow the focus of the group and its ability to generate a range of solutions (Esser 1998). Fifth, a lack of methodological procedures requiring decision makers to examine alternatives, contingency plans and so forth before choosing a solution may hinder adequate decision making and promote early consensus (Callaway and Esser 1984). Finally, 'directive' or 'partial' leadership, where the group leader advocates a particular solution or approach, is likely to put a premium on early agreement by the hierarchically-inferior group members (Leana 1985).

Groupthink can be observed empirically through various symptoms. These can be summarized under three headings: (1) overestimation of the group by its members; (2) closed-mindedness; and (3) pressures for uniformity. *Overestimation of the group by its members* arises when a group has a strong belief in the rightness of its cause (belief in its inherent morality) and as a group becomes over-optimistic (illusion of invulnerability). *Closed-mindedness* occurs when a group indulges in collective rationalization of its position and in the stereotyping of 'out-groups'. *Pressures for uniformity* are exerted through demands on dissenters to conform, as well as through self-censorship. The group thus becomes increasingly entrenched through an illusion of unanimity, which pervades as it becomes more prone to screening out warnings and counter-information that might lead to a reconsideration of decisions.

The process described above is said to render groups vulnerable to defects in decision making, such as failing seriously to survey alternatives or to re-examine them; failing to examine the group's own objectives and preferred choices; selection bias and poor information gathering in the group's research; a failure to generate or to consider contingency plans; and a willingness to take greater risks than any member of the group would take individually. Small-group analysis and concepts such as Groupthink need to be seen as additional to the political power and institutional forces that drive policy within international organizations. Groupthink does not offer an alternative explanation, rather it amplifies our understanding of the way in which the decisions of the powerful can be transmitted through international institutions and lead to both intentional and unintentional outcomes. This will be examined in the following sections. First the structural context in which staff from Fund and Bank have to operate is given, then Groupthink is used as a framework to consider the nature of decision making in the Fund and Bank prior to the Mexican crisis.[3]

The structural context: Interdependency between IMF, World Bank and Mexico

A first important constraint on the ability of the international financial institutions to negatively interpret evidence from an economy is their relationship to governments they work with, which are not just their clients but also their principals. Both the Fund and the Bank can be conceived of as agents of sovereign governments which collectively delegate powers to the institutions. In their work with any one such government, both organizations rely heavily upon the cooperation and openness of that government, as well as on the influence of other principals acting both individually and collectively. Although the institutions have many authoritative instruments, they have no formal automatic right of entry into policy making within member states. They must persuade governments to give them access to confidential and sensitive statistics and policy questions. Once granted access, the institutions must use information extremely carefully – and in constant negotiation with government officials – so as to ensure continuing good relations. The need to preserve access leads to compromises, of which there are several historical examples. In 1981, prior to Mexico's 1982 debt crisis, when the World Bank was about to publish a report expressing some reservations about Mexican economic policy, the Mexican government despatched Carlos Salinas de Gortari (then a junior finance official) to Washington to ensure that any negative comments were suppressed. The final report put a more positive gloss on events (Interviews with officials involved). Of course, in such cases governments can remind the Fund and the Bank that any adverse comment or report will surely help to catalyse a crisis – even if there is little basis for one. There are clear and immediate costs to the Fund and the Bank if either one issues adverse analyses of an economy. Not only do they risk breaching the confidentiality which governments require in return for access to ministries of finance, planning and central banks, they also risk being shut out of subsequent negotiations: governments would simply close off access to the necessary information and this would prevent the institutions from performing most of their functions.

A second impediment to frank and impartial analyses of Mexico's situation in 1994 was the stake held by the two international financial institutions in the Mexican economy. This is best expressed in terms of reputation and credibility. Both organizations had given Mexico a 'stamp of approval'. Indeed, as we will see below, each had gone some way towards staking its reputation on Mexico. The reforms Mexico had undertaken during the late 1980s and early 1990s had been seen by many within the international financial community, including the World Bank and the IMF, as 'spectacular, lasting, and the envy of any reform economy' (Dornbusch and Werner 1994: 266). Mexico's special status as a role model for other developing countries is reflected in *Economic Transformation: The Mexican Way*, the former Mexican finance minister Pedro Aspe's account of how to reform *à la Mexico*. The involvement of the international financial institutions and their commitment of resources in Mexico were a sign of their confidence that the government had implemented, and would continue to liberalize, reforms and that these would lead, almost inevitably, to economic success. The figures reveal the extent of both international financial institutions' 'stake' in Mexico's ongoing success. The IMF's *International Financial Statistics* detail that by 1992 the Fund was lending Mexico some 401 per cent of that country's quota and would lend 442 per cent in 1995. The World Bank's *Annual Reports* show that institution's lending to Mexico to amount to nearly 12 per cent of the Bank's loan portfolio over the years 1990–4. Not only could a warning or a pessimistic note from the Bank or the Fund risk catalysing a crisis (through the markets' response to it), but it would also signal a failure of their more general project of persuading countries to liberalize and deregulate their economies. Indeed, very soon after the Mexican crisis, other countries, such as Brazil, India and South Korea, were arguing the case for slower or different types of reform with a note of triumphalism – pointing to Mexico as evidence of the failure of the international financial institutions' prescription.[4]

During the crisis of 1994 both the IMF and the World Bank had their reputations on the line and this, it is argued, influenced their judgement. However, there are also deeper structural and procedural factors which, as the next sections of this chapter argue, led to defective decision making in the international financial institutions.

Groupthink and the approach of the IMF and the World Bank to Mexico in 1994

In this section I will first examine whether *antecedent conditions* of Groupthink were present in the institutions in the period up to the 1994 crisis, then show the evidence of *symptoms of Groupthink* and finally give details of *defective decision making.*

Antecedent conditions of Groupthink

The first cluster of conditions discussed in the preceding section concerns the character of the group involved in taking decisions. In particular, cohesion, insulation and homogeneity were given as important antecedent conditions for Groupthink. All three were strongly present in the groups working on Mexico within the IMF and the World Bank. In each organization there was a high level of group cohesion in the early 1990s, facilitated greatly by specialization in Mexico of staff and by the status accorded to working within the Mexican team. I say this while recognizing that by the 1990s Mexico was not considered quite as 'exciting' or 'demanding' (to quote staff members) a case as Russia or Eastern Europe. Nevertheless, the importance of Mexico within the institutions' work (as detailed below) ensured that Mexico was still a high status task for their personnel.

'Insulation' was a problem in both these large organizations. Neither was open to external analysis or even, it would seem, to much debate with analysts outside the institutions. I accept here the relative point that the IMF is a smaller, more disciplined, more secretive and more insular organization than the World Bank, the larger staff and wider relations with state and non-state actors of which make it more porous. Surprisingly, as the Mexican crisis approached there seems not to have been much sharing of analysis or information even between the Fund and the Bank. To some extent their overall insulation is understandable, given that each organization has a large and highly qualified research staff to rely upon and given that some of the information they deal with is highly confidential. However, the cost of such insulation (as will be shown below) is that it makes organizations much more vulnerable to Groupthink.

Finally, homogeneity is clearly evident in the teams dealing with Mexico. Indeed, there is ample evidence of homogeneity among all personnel within the Fund and Bank. For example, in terms of background and training, a study of senior employees in the World Bank has found that 80 per cent of high-level staff in its Policy, Research and External Affairs Department have trained in economics and finance at institutions in the United States and Britain (Stern and Ferreira 1993). In the IMF some 90 per cent of employees with PhDs have received them from universities in the US and Canada (Clark 1996: 9). As will be shown below, homogeneity within both institutions is also reinforced by decision-making procedures.

In the period up to Mexico's crisis, the two organizations also shared structural defects that made them vulnerable to Groupthink. Two general kinds of procedural weakness highlighted above seem to apply to this case: unrigorous methodological procedures and directive leadership. In 1994 the methodological procedures used let the institutions down: there was virtually no 'looking beyond' the upbeat scenario, towards alternative futures the Mexican economy might be facing. Furthermore, officials involved at the time say that little effort was made to consider a contingency plan, in the event their positive assumptions should prove incorrect.

In examining the structure of the Fund and of the Bank, one is compelled to ask what kind of questioning and rigour was exercised by the various tiers of decision makers. For example, given the importance of Mexico to international stability, did the Executive Board of the IMF subject staff policy to close enough scrutiny? Or, indeed, did they subject it to any scrutiny at all? This is, after all, part of their responsibilities – not as representatives of member states, but as members of the organization. From interviews with some of those involved, my own impression is that Executive Board members did not robustly pursue doubts or concerns they had about Mexico in the period up to 1994.

A further element of procedural weakness lies in the degree of 'directive' leadership within teams at the organizations. To some extent this reflects necessary chains of command, responsibility and accountability. However, the hierarchical nature of both institutions means that sometimes disagreements will be resolved by appeals to a higher level of the hierarchy (as opposed to peer scrutiny). The results are highlighted by authors of the World Bank history, who note that in that organization particular ideas are maintained and perpetuated and change is top-down (Stern and Ferreira 1993). Similarly, alternative or critical views are discouraged within the Fund through its deliberate policy of keeping its staff small, with a low turnover, and although this has resulted in sound research, it has also meant that the employees are slow to 'experiment and innovate' (Kuczynski 1988: 124).

Rather alarmingly, the potential pitfalls of hierarchy and directive leadership were exacerbated in the case of Mexico by members of the group having incomplete access to information. I refer here to a practice – which long predates the 1994 crisis and which has been mentioned to me by officials in the Mexican government, the IMF and the World Bank – whereby senior Mexican officials shared highly confidential information with just one senior member of a Bank or Fund team. In the hands of one team member, this kind of information can further entrench Groupthink by preventing equal participation in discussions.

The evidence of symptoms of Groupthink

The symptoms of Groupthink were summarized above under the headings overestimation of the group by its members, closed-mindedness, and pressures for uniformity. This section will present the evidence of these symptoms in the Fund and Bank up to the crisis of 1994, looking first at the illusions that arose within the groups monitoring the Mexican economy.

It is evident that the organizations shared a clear and focused set of beliefs about the Mexican economy. There are important practical reasons for such a mindset. Operationally, both organizations need a clearly enunciated, 'consistent' framework for analysis and policy prescription. This is because each institution sends junior officials to countries across the world. For the institutions to retain their identity and mandate, they need to ensure that all staff use the same framework and share the same understanding of the organization's tasks. Yet this can all too easily lead to an illusion of invulnerability, closed-mindedness, pressures for uniformity, and a screening out of warnings and information.

What became clear after Mexico's crisis at the end of 1994 was that only one scenario had been considered in 19th Street, Washington. Staff at both institutions seemed almost blind to more negative possibilities. Indeed, after the crisis a very senior World Bank employee pointed out this blindness, commenting: 'What is to some extent intriguing ... is not that the Mexican economy faced a major currency crisis, but that so many observers were shocked by this turn of events'. In his view the 'prophetically similar crisis' suffered by Chile in the 1970s might have alerted officials (Edwards 1996: 176). Yet such a scenario was not being considered. Rather, analyses of Mexico's situation were characterized by over-optimism (an illusion of invulnerability) and by a screening out of any evidence that ran counter to the group's beliefs and story (an illusion of unanimity).

Importantly, as Mexico headed towards crisis, several analysts *outside* the IMF and the World Bank managed to read the signals. Throughout 1994 highly respected economists issued a variety of warnings. Among the more famous were Rudiger Dornbusch, who advocated an immediate devaluation (Dornbusch and Werner 1994), and Guillermo Calvo, who proposed not a devaluation but an urgent arrangement with the US Treasury (Calvo 1994). Most warnings focused on the appreciation (or 'overvaluation') of the peso and what it reflected and implied for the economy. The critics of government policy highlighted the lack of economic growth and the fragility of monetary and exchange rate policy.

However, while questions about the sustainability of Mexico's reforms were debated by economists outside the IMF and World Bank, within the organizations there was an overwhelming consensus, based around the success story. For example, the Fund's *Country Report* on Mexico of January 1994 recognizes some of the danger signs: both that the Mexican currency was appreciating and that net inflows to the public sector were increasing. Yet the interpretation was: 'It was felt that such a real appreciation [i.e. a small ongoing appreciation] would not affect export competitiveness significantly because of the positive effects of the structural reforms.' Later in the appraisal: 'During 1993 the peso continued to appreciate in real effective terms as customarily measured and eroded further the margin obtained in the 1980s. However, the strong expansion in manufacturing exports would indicate that the structural reforms in recent years and wage restraint have compensated so far' (IMF, *Country Report* of January 1994, following 1993 Article IV consultations with Mexico: 7 and 12).

The rationale for the positive interpretation was a doctrinal one. Staff in both organizations maintained the belief throughout 1993–4 that Mexico's current account deficit was not a cause for undue concern because it was essentially a *private sector phenomenon*. They argued that as long as public sector finances were (or seemed to be) more balanced, the private sector could be relied upon to adjust itself. Yet it is unclear whether there is any real evidence of an actual case where the private sector has adjusted to such deficits without a damaging spillover into public finances.

Not only were officials in both international financial institutions continuing to interpret events according to one rather narrow framework, they had also insulated themselves and did not seek out external sources of information. For example, the IMF staff relied throughout 1993–4 on the debt data published by the Mexican Central Bank (with a two to three months' time-lag). What they might have done – indeed what some other financial actors, such as Reuters, did – was track the Mexican government's debt by following the results of auctions of government securities. The crucial point here is that alternative sources of information were available, yet personnel at the Fund chose to rely on what the Mexican government was making available to them. They were even prepared to endorse this information, by using it as a basis for giving assurances about the Mexican economy to the Bank for International Settlements in mid-1994.

Looking back, what we find is that while the IMF and the World Bank issued their usual caveats and concerns in economic reports and forecasts, as did some credit rating agencies and many private investment institutions, they held fast to the view that the appreciation of the Mexican currency was a natural concomitant of capital inflows and foreign investment and reflected a high rate of absorption into the Mexican economy (see the private investors' forecasts cited in Hale 1996). Debt, or a trade deficit, in this view, was not a problem as long as it was in the private sector.

This belief in Mexico's reform process buttresses optimistic accounts of the country's prospects and covers up warnings or evidence to the contrary in a host of Fund and Bank publications. Indeed even after the August 1994 elections, both organizations were prepared to continue giving upbeat and optimistic assessments of the Mexican economy. Their reports and statements tended to report sources or signals from the markets that were *positive*, yet only very exceptionally to pick up and report any major *negative* signs or outside commentaries.

The screening out of any alternative information or warnings coincided neatly with an optimism which, in retrospect, looks ever less warranted by the facts, to which the organizations should have paid more attention at the time. This optimism rested largely on the belief that Mexico's successful programme of stabilization, privatization and deregulation, topped off by NAFTA and OECD membership, gave it a credibility and strength which would carry it through temporary difficulties. To maintain this view, even in the face of evidence to the contrary, was astonishing. Such an upbeat atmosphere within the decision-making group and among the other participants (the Mexican government and the Boards and management of both organizations) made it all too easy for standards of evidence and ongoing probity to slide.

To further exacerbate the potential for faulty decision making resulting from overestimation of the group and closed-mindedness, there were also other pressures at work in the institutions – pressures for uniformity. We have seen already that hierarchy can impose a 'top-down' form of dispute resolution within an institution. One problem with a hierarchical structure is that it creates an atmosphere in which staff tries to 'second-guess' upper management or, if relevant, the Executive Board. 'Conformity', in other words, can encourage self-censorship, marginalizing strongly critical or alternative views. Staff members in both organizations have recognized this. In the words of one Bank official: 'The ethos of the Bank is that no one challenges his supervisor, there is no room for boat rocking' (Sherk 1994: 46). This echoes a case I came across while doing research on the Mexican crisis of 1982 prior to which a young Chilean economist in the World Bank's Mexico team wrote a damning and critical report which was both pessimistic and, in retrospect, correct. Before the crisis erupted at the end of the summer of 1982, this economist was swiftly moved out of the Mexico team and into another area of the Bank.[5]

The insights into Groupthink point to an interface of psychology and group processes which explains why it was so difficult for any member to conceive of, let alone voice, doubts about the group's mindset, even in the face of evidence of fragility and risk. The inability of personnel to posit a different interpretation is borne out by what staff members were saying at the time about the agreement within the teams working on Mexico. IMF employees told me in 1994 that there was virtually no disagreement – even as Mexico was moving closer and closer to crisis.

Defects in decision making

The decision-making defects that result from Groupthink have been detailed above. Most of these can be seen in the case of Mexico in 1994. First, from an early date research teams failed to survey the potential negative scenarios Mexican policy makers were facing. Second, the desire to prove that Mexico was a success story seems to have overwhelmed the institutions' primary objectives: in the case of the IMF to ensure international financial and monetary stability, and for the World Bank to help to further Mexico's national development goals. Third, as the potential crisis developed, there seems to have been virtually no investigation of alternatives. Nor, in fourth place, was there an examination of the institutions' preferred choices. Fifth, the decisions taken appear to have been based on faulty evidence and a poor information search. Finally, there seems to have been a complete failure to develop a contingency plan. Overall, in other words, decision making was defective in precisely the ways the concept of Groupthink suggests.

Conclusions

What was required from the IMF and the World Bank in 1994 was an impartial and rigorous analysis and monitoring of the Mexican economy. Instead, staff in both organizations started from the presumption that, since the Mexican government had been undertaking – in an exemplary way – reforms endorsed by the institutions, the economy was unlikely to be in any serious difficulty. In retrospect neither organization, imbued as they were with their own particular economic orthodoxy (maintained throughout the organizations by hiring, training and promotion, and through hierarchy), was in a good position to generate an analysis which would be critical of any core element of the orthodoxy. Yet this was what was needed if either institution were to prepare for, or to signal, the coming crisis.

It has been argued in this chapter that the concept of Groupthink usefully highlights some of the conditions and processes which led to teams within the IMF and the World Bank 'getting it wrong' in the case of Mexico. Groupthink does not offer a testable analysis, or a particularly parsimonious explanation. Its application to the study of international organizations is limited. In this particular case, however, the concept assists in underlining and illuminating institutional and organizational features of the Fund and the Bank, which led them to have a significant blind spot in respect of the Mexican crisis. What this chapter shows is that the international financial organizations should not retreat behind the excuse that in 1994 their decision making suffered from poor information and bad faith on the part of the Mexican government. This may well have been the case, but the crisis also shows up defects in decision making within the institutions.

Notes

1 It has been alleged that the US Treasury had better information – or a more accurate, negative interpretation of information – which was suppressed for US political reasons: to bolster the strong peso in order to keep US exports to Mexico up and to prevent an increase in imports which would inflame the anti-NAFTA lobby. See the testimony of Senator Alfonse d'Amato in Senate Committee on Banking, Housing and Urban Affairs (1995).

2 The analysis in this section is based on information available in official publications, IMF *Country Reports* on Mexico, and interviews with some of the actors concerned. See IMF 1995a and 1995b, and World Bank 1995.

3 This analysis does not mean to suggest that these were the only institutions prone to these kinds of defects in decision making: see the various forecasts made by major financial and investment institutions in the latter half of 1994, which are analysed in Hale 1996.

4 Brazil was putting this argument to many institutions in Washington in late 1995. On India and South Korea see Hale 1996: 2 and 21.

5 This episode has been related to me by three Bank officials who were involved with Mexico at the time or shortly afterwards.

References

Aspe, P. (1993) *Economic Transformation: The Mexican Way*, Cambridge, Mass: Massachusetts Institute of Technology.

Callaway, M. and Esser, J. (1984) 'Groupthink: Effects of Cohesiveness and Problem-Solving Procedures on Group Decision Making', *Social Behaviour and Personality*, 12(2): 157–64.

Calvo, G.A. (1994) 'Comments' (on Dornbusch and Werner), *Brookings Papers on Economic Activity*, 1994(1): 298–303.

Clark, I. (1996), 'Should the IMF Become More Adaptive?', *IMF Working Paper*, Washington DC: IMF.

Dornbusch, R. and Werner, A. (1994) 'Mexico: Stabilization, Reform, and No Growth', *Brookings Papers on Economic Activity*, 1994(1): 253–315 (including comments).

Edwards, S. (1995) *Crisis and Reform in Latin America: From Despair to Hope*, New York: Open University Press.

—— (1996) 'Exchange-Rates Anchors, Credibility, and Inertia: A Tale of Two Crises, Chile and Mexico', *American Economic Review: Papers and Proceedings*, 86(1): 176–80.

Esser, J. (1998) 'Alive and Well after 25 Years: A Review of Groupthink Research', *Organizational Behavior and Human Decision Processes*, 73(2/3): 116–42.

Foot, R., MacFarlane, N. and Mastanduno, M. (2003) *US Hegemony and International Organizations*, Oxford: Oxford University Press.

George, A. (1997) 'From Groupthink to Contextual Analysis of Policy-Making Groups' in P. 't Hart, E. Stern and B. Sundelius (eds) *Beyond Groupthink: Political Group Dynamics and Foreign Policy-Making*, Michigan: University of Michigan Press, 35–54.

Hale, D. (1996) 'Lessons from the Mexican Crisis of 1995 for the Post Cold War International Order', Draft chapter for *The World Bank Report on Mexico*, Washington DC, February.

IMF (1995a) 'Evolution of the Mexican Peso Crisis', in *International Capital Markets: Developments, Prospects, and Policy Issues*, Washington DC: IMF, 53–69.

—— (1995b) *World Economic Outlook: A Survey by the Staff of the International Monetary Fund*, Washington DC: IMF.

Janis, I. (1972) *Victims of Groupthink: A Psychological Study of Foreign-Policy Decisions and Fiascoes*, Boston: Houghton Mifflin.

—— (1982) G*roupthink*, Boston: Houghton Mifflin.

Kuczynski, P.-P. (1988) *Latin American Debt*, Baltimore: Johns Hopkins Press and Twentieth Century Fund.

Leana, C.R. (1985) 'A Partial Test of Janis' Groupthink Model: Effects of Group Cohesiveness and Leader Behaviour on Defective Decision Making', *Journal of Management*, 11(1): 5–17.

Lebow, R.N. (1981) *Between Peace and War. The Nature of International Crisis*, Baltimore: Johns Hopkins University Press.

McCauley, C. (1989) 'The Nature of Social Influence in Groupthink', *Journal of Personality and Social Psychology*, 57(2): 250–60.

Ripley, B. (1993) 'Psychology, Foreign Policy and International Relations', *Political Psychology*, 14(3): 403–16.

Roberts, J.M. (1988), *Decision-Making During International Crises*, Houndmills: Macmillan.
Senate Committee on Banking, Housing and Urban Affairs (1995) *Report on the Mexican Economic Crisis*, 29 June, Washington DC: Senate Committee on Banking, Housing and Urban Affairs.
Sherk, D.R. (1994) 'Emerging Markets and the Multilateral Development Banks', *Columbia Journal of World Business*, 29(2): 44–52.
Stern, N. and Ferreira, F. (1993) 'The World Bank as "Intellectual Actor"', *Development Economics Research Programme Discussion Paper*, DEP/50, London: STICERD, London School of Economics and Political Science.
't Hart, P., Stern, E. and Sundelius, B. (eds) (1997) *Beyond Groupthink: Political Group Dynamics and Foreign Policy-Making*, Michigan: University of Michigan Press.
Turner, M.E., Pratkanis, A.R., Probasco, P. and Leve, C. (1992) 'Threat, Cohesion, and Group Effectiveness: Testing a Social Identity Maintenance Perspective on Groupthink', *Journal of Personality and Social Psychology*, 63(5): 781–96.
World Bank (1995) *Global Economic Prospects and the Developing Countries*, Washington DC: World Bank.

7 UNHCR's decision making on internally displaced persons

The impact of external and internal factors on policy strategy

Raquel Freitas

Introduction

Since the end of the Cold War, international organizations have become more salient actors in the international political system. Several changes in their international environment have enhanced their policy autonomy *vis-à-vis* the member states (Reinalda and Verbeek 1998). Such an increase in policy autonomy, however, is not an outcome that follows these changes automatically. External changes may provide a window of opportunity for international organizations to attempt to increase their autonomy, but they do not explain *whether*, or *how*, intergovernmental organizations (IGOs) make use of such a window when they have to make specific policy choices. In order to answer these questions it is necessary to incorporate the IGO's internal environment in the analysis. The purpose of this chapter is to identify those mechanisms through which changes in the international environment may result in increased IGO autonomy. Mechanism here refers to the interaction between actors and processes, both internal and external to an organization, which is reflected in its decision-making dynamics.

This chapter investigates a case in which an international organization, the United Nations High Commission for Refugees (UNHCR), is striving to define its position with regard to the provision of a controversial service: assistance for so-called internally displaced persons (IDPs). UNHCR has a past of continuous task expansion into large-scale humanitarian assistance programmes and into an increasingly operational role. Since the 1970s UNHCR has progressively included IDPs in its programmes, but mostly on an informal basis. IDPs have the same needs and difficulties as refugees, but the international community has long ignored their rights because IDPs, in contrast to refugees, do not cross international borders. In the past ten years a rudimentary regime for IDPs has been emerging, through the elaboration of *The Guiding Principles on Internal Displacement.* It defines IDPs as 'persons or groups of persons who have been forced or obliged to flee or to leave their homes or places of habitual residence, in particular as a result of or in order to avoid the effects of armed conflict, situations of generalized violence, violations of human rights or natural or human-made disasters, and who have not crossed an internationally recognized State border' (United Nations Commission on Human Rights 1998: 2). The 1990s witnessed an increase in international attention given to the plight of IDPs. This raised the problem of defining international responsibility for their assistance and protection. Contradictory pressures on UNHCR came from both outside and inside the organization. In the end, the organization chose to continue its actual assistance to IDPs *without* striving for a formal expansion of its mandate. Although UNHCR's involvement with IDPs has been commended and requested by several General Assembly Resolutions, the organization does not have mandated responsibility for this group. According to the organization's criteria, each instance should in principle be requested, or sanctioned, by the concerned state and/or by a competent organ of the United Nations. Two aspects of UNHCR's response are the objects of further inquiry here. First, why has UNHCR avoided formalizing task expansion, contrary to what could have been expected from an organization when such an opportunity occurs? Second, how has UNHCR been able to pursue its policy choice in this situation despite contradictory pressures?

In this chapter I argue that changes in the external environment of UNHCR provided a window of opportunity for the organization to expand its mandate into assisting and protecting IDPs. However, internal divisions between UNHCR's departments made such a move impossible. Political brokerage by the High Commissioner at the time, Ms Sadako Ogata, resulted in a solution that satisfied all parties: no expansion of mandate despite expansion of assistance. I will first sketch the internal and external environments of international organizations. Subsequently, I will stipulate expectations of how pressure from these environments is likely to translate into policy changes. Next, I will apply this analytical framework to UNHCR policies towards IDPs during the 1990s, when this issue – which corresponded to the ten years of High Commissioner Ogata's mandate – assumed international relevance.

Two organizational environments

The external environment

The external environment in which an international organization is embedded provides the broad context in which decisions are made, by framing the boundaries of possible choices. The international context in which international organizations have to operate has changed considerably over the last few decades. For most of the twentieth century the international system was predominantly *state-based*, based on the norm of (internal and external) sovereignty of the state. In the course of the twentieth century, however, a different norm began competing with sovereignty as a source for legitimate action. This was accelerated by the recognition of crimes against humanity, human rights, and the condemnation of apartheid policies, as well as by the institutionalization of such norms in various international organizations. This so-called *world polity system*, starting from the premise of human rights, challenges the view that the international community should not interfere in a state's internal affairs (see Cox 1997; Mills 1998; Rosenau 2000).

Both kinds of norm are present in the United Nations Charter. In principle they are not contradictory, except when a sovereign state does not ensure the protection of the human rights of its citizens. Although the protection of human rights remains formally the prerogative of the state, the international community has been progressively legitimizing an international responsibility for such protection, in particular after the lifting of the ideological and strategic concerns that dominated the Cold War superpower struggle. Thus, elements of an international polity can be said to be arising, although little agreement exists about the scope and significance of the change (see March and Olsen 1998).

The potential contradictions between different structures and normative frameworks provide a source for change that may lead to increased policy autonomy of IGOs. Indeed, through the clash of different sets of normative structures, new international issue areas arise that reflect the contradictions between state-centric structures and world polity structures. While traditionally these 'newly internationalized' issue areas were the domain of the nation-state, they are now in the process of becoming of international concern. This raises the question of whether it is legitimate for the community of states to address these issues, as they did not previously have 'decisional authority' over internal affairs of other states. States may now actually share this authority with IGOs.[1] Concomitantly, all the time, many new tasks and expanded responsibilities emerge, for which there is no specific, coordinated policy or organization (Meyer 1994: 51–3). This is the case in areas of global governance ranging from climate to technological change (see Reinicke and Deng 2000).

By expanding into these new issue areas, IGOs become indispensable providers of certain services. This type of task expansion in principle gives them added leverage in decision making (Groom 1978). Compromises are made concerning the scope of IGOs' activities that may result in more autonomy for intergovernmental decision making than was the case with traditional state-centric issue areas. Often in these situations, states lack a clear policy preference. Sometimes the issue is complex enough to impede agreement among the different countries that in principle control the IGO. Such lack of coordination produces situations of complexity and conflict, which 'open up possibilities for discretion and strategic behaviour by actors, both individuals and organisations' (Scott 1994: 75). IGOs tend to exploit these differences in the external environment to increase their autonomy (Ness and Brechin 1988) and to enforce their own preferences (Torenvlied 1996).

From the clash between two different world conceptions arise new issue areas for which no standard conduct of behaviour exists – such as the case of IDPs – and which thus open up windows of opportunity for IGOs to expand. However, whether, and how, an IGO chooses to make use of this window of opportunity is not always self-evident. A look at internal mechanisms is needed in order to understand specific choices.

Internal environment

At least two different perspectives on the evolution of an IGO can be distinguished. On the one hand, traditional organizational theory suggests that the inherent interest of an organization that has to survive in inter-organizational battles lies in an expansion of its budget, tasks and the number of personnel employed. As it expands into new activities, its originally stated goals are redefined – whether formally or implicitly. Other approaches emphasize that organizational goals are strongly shaped by certain norms that dominate the bureaucracy. The organization's interests themselves vary, are often in flux, and depend on the interaction between its staff and the environment (Barnett and Finnemore 1999: 706). This requires the relaxation of the assumption that an organization is a unitary actor. Katzenstein *et al.* (1998) make precisely this point in respect of IGOs. Just like states, they should not be seen as unitary coherent actors with clearly defined interests or preferences (also March 1988a). Within organizations, seen as political systems involving multiple actors with inconsistent preferences (March 1988b: 15), different subunits exist that develop different cultures, perspectives and interests, which can range from unit-specific objectives to personal convictions and normative dilemmas. From the perspective of traditional organizational theory, one would expect UNHCR to welcome the institutionalization of yet another set of tasks, namely a role for UNHCR regarding the problem of IDPs, all the more so because of UNHCR's past tradition of formal task expansion.

The progressive expansion of activities was, in geographical terms and in the number and type of populations of concern, included in its mandate. It also included a shift from a focus on a supervisory role to a focus on operational relief and humanitarian assistance activities. The supervisory function ensured UNHCR's considerable reputation and leverage as an impartial arbiter for and defender of refugees in the world (Anonymous 1997). At the same time the expansion into categories of concern for which there was no defined international responsibility increased its power as a humanitarian agency, as well as its funds, while initially maintaining its appearance of a depoliticized and supervisory authority (Barnett and Finnemore 1999).

However, an IGO's strength can also be its weakness. Newly assumed tasks may conflict with old ones. Moreover, task expansion increases the number of organizational units. The combined increase in tasks and in organizational units to execute them may lead to internal divisions caused by conflicting priorities within the organization and eventually to organizational dysfunction. This tension between roles has marked most of UNHCR's evolution. It has become more evident in the past 20 years, when the increase in operational as well as relief and assistance-dominated activities started to undermine the provision of the core mandate supervisory functions, such as assisting states in the appropriate application of the 1951 Convention on the Status of Refugees. This conflict came to a head in the debate concerning UNHCR's role with IDPs.

UNHCR's organizational structure has evolved alongside its expansion of activities, and has had an important impact on the general policy lines of the organization. Within the UNHCR a divide exists between the *regional* bureaus, which are predominantly operational and more closely linked to the field offices, and the *legal* ones, such as the Division of International Protection (DIP). DIP has developed a legalistic approach and 'tends to view the UNHCR and itself as the refugee's lawyer and as the protector of refugee rights under international law' (Barnett and Finnemore 1999: 725), while the regional bureaus are more liable to give in to state or operational constraints in the field. This demonstrates a cultural conflict between more narrow organizational goals, linked to the supervisory functions of the organization, and broader organizational goals that have progressively been incorporated into UNHCR's role. This became particularly apparent in the ten years of leadership (1990–2000) of High Commissioner Ms Sadako Ogata, who had a declared disdain for lawyers (Goodwin-Gill, quoted in Chimni 1998: 353). The more UNHCR embarked on operational involvement, the more it recruited non-lawyers to its ranks and the further internal divisions increased (Interview with UNHCR official, 3 October 2002). The differences in perception among UNHCR staff ensuing from different experiences and backgrounds thus fed the potential for bureaucratic battles within the organization (Interview with UNHCR official, 11 December 2000).

In fact, over the years the authority and influence of DIP eroded to a point where advice was generally sought only after decisions had been made by policy and programme staff, with the aim of legitimizing these decisions (Anonymous 1997). This became a serious concern for a group of non-governmental organizations (NGOs), which, in a letter to UNHCR's Executive Committee, underlined the importance of restoring the primacy of DIP: 'The Division of International Protection should once again be mandated to play the leading role in the decision making on UNHCR's priorities. Moreover, re-establishment of the authority of the Division should of course also be felt and reintegrated in other parts of the organization' (Working Group on International Refugee Policy 1999: 218).

To summarize, the traditional organizational perspective would expect the UNHCR to take the window of opportunity and to welcome the suggestion made by actors in its external environment, such as states and NGOs, to expand its formal mandate into the area of IDPs. A perspective that stresses internal divisions based on different organizational cultures regarding task definition, however, would not automatically predict the same outcome. The UNHCR's policy is more likely to be the outcome of the tension between these conflicting task definitions. How to account for this outcome?

Two-level game?

An IGO, such as the UNHCR, has to strike a balance between its external and its internal environment. Responding inadequately to either may jeopardize its functioning. Organizational leadership could be the bridge between these two sources of pressure (see Haas 1964; Reinalda 1998) and could create the conditions for the management of different, often contradictory or even unclear, interests within and outside the organization.

Externally, the organization is influenced by the policies and strategies of other international organizations in the humanitarian system, both within and outside the UN, as well as NGOs. All of these form a complex network that works closely together on the coordination of humanitarian programmes, but they are also competing fiercely for territory and funds. States are a major source of external and internal pressure, in particular the members of the Executive Committee and the Standing Committee which together form the governing body of the UNHCR. Cox and Jacobson (1973: 15–18) consider states as at the same time external environment forces and, through the process of representation in the governing body, participant subsystems of IGOs. States, then, constitute both the external environment in which the organization moves and an internal source of pressure, which within the UNHCR is exercised through the annual meeting of the Executive Committee and the periodical meetings of the Standing Committee, where states have the opportunity to express their preferences. Such preferences can also be indicated in other more informal ways, such as briefings on specific programmes, informal donor briefings, bilateral meetings between staff and the representatives of the different states with a stake in UNHCR's activities, and lastly but most importantly, through the funding of programmes. Organizational subunits form the other major group of internal actors.

In order to satisfy both internal and external actors that are a source of pressure in decision making, UNHCR's leadership is expected to devise policies that include a wide range of policy choices acceptable to all. Putnam (1988: 437) has designated this the 'win-set' – those options that satisfy all relevant actors with an interest. The resulting policy ambiguity is an important tool for actors mediating between the internal and external environment to retain leverage over decision making and mobilize support for policies. Representatives of IGOs often have the advantage, in particular at times when states do not have clear preferences or cannot find agreement among themselves. Indeed, one way to achieve this is to make use of vague policy proclamations and emphasize creative autonomy. '[A]dministrative agencies seem likely to adapt to a history of ambiguous, contradictory, and grandiose policies' (Baier *et al.* 1988: 160). Ambiguity can thus be exploited for unambiguous ends (March 1988b: 15).

Analysis

In this section I will analyse UNHCR's policies towards IDPs by combining three perspectives. The perspective of the external environment suggests that UNHCR will make use of the opportunity to formally expand its mandate into the area of IDPs. That of the internal environment proposes that such a decision would depend on the conflict between two opposing organizational cultures regarding UNHCR's role. The perspective of the two-level game propounds that UNHCR's leadership will strike a balance between pressures from both environments, but, exploiting the expected differences between external actors, will succeed in promoting an outcome that is closer to the preferences of internal actors.

External environment explanation

UNHCR had the opportunity to formalize a full mandate for IDPs and was even put under pressure by some states to accept such a mandate. In 1993, the Netherlands proposed that the organization be assigned general competence for IDPs. The Representative of the Secretary-General on IDPs, Francis Deng, supported this in that year's report. But neither UNHCR nor the Executive Committee endorsed the idea (Cohen 1998: 6). In 1997, at the time of the UN reform when UNHCR was approached on the issue, the reaction was to a large extent the same, mainly due to disagreement by other humanitarian agencies (Loescher 2001: 292). In January 2000, the United States Ambassador to the United Nations, Richard Holbrooke, strongly urged the international community to come up with a solution to the problem of IDPs. He clearly exhorted UNHCR to take on responsibility for these populations, based on its expertise and on the practical irrelevance of a distinction between refugees and internally displaced persons, whom he designated 'internal refugees' (Statement to the Security Council on 13 January 2000, and to ECOSOC on 20 July 2000, US/UN Press Release #95, 2000). Several NGOs, such as Human Rights Watch, Médicins Sans Frontières and the International Rescue Committee, also supported this proposal, although no overall agreed position existed among NGOs or within the humanitarian community in general. Indeed, many of the humanitarian agencies were against such a broad expansion of the role of the UNHCR (McElhinny 2000).

However, even if for different reasons, most states have so far been very cautious in the area of IDPs. Until recently government-defined positions regarding international responsibility for protection and assistance of IDPs have been very rare. Above all, clear coalitions among countries to defend a specific policy line are almost non-existent, in the absence of consensus on the best solution for the IDPs' problematic situation. Moreover, the tension between the norm of sovereignty and the right to humanitarian intervention still prevails. This is shown, for example, in the difficulty certain G77 states have in accepting the *Guiding Principles on Internal Displacement* by the UN Secretary-General's Representative for IDPs, Francis Deng.

In fact, most actors could not agree on the best policy option. Some of the states reacted negatively to the international community's intrusion into the realm of sovereignty. Given such a policy vacuum it would have been possible for UNHCR to step in and take over the international responsibility for IDPs. Indeed, the absence of clear state policies and of agreement between these actors on the best option for allocating international responsibility for IDPs, or even on whether to address the issue, gave UNHCR ample policy autonomy. Yet it exploited this freedom of manoeuvre not by expanding its formal mandate, but by maintaining the ability to decide on a case-by-case basis whether to intervene in the area of IDPs.

Internal environment explanation

As was shown, the historical evolution of UNHCR led to a goal redefinition with regard to expansion. In addition, two interrelated kinds of internal division have contributed to this redefinition, as was particularly evident in the case of UNHCR's role with IDPs. First, divisions that derived from the very structure of the organization and, second, those that were rooted in the contradictions inherent in a role with IDPs. In some cases such a role would mean a clash with UNHCR's protection function, since protection remains the responsibility of the country of origin. Carrying out protection activities might endanger the ability to provide assistance, if those activities are performed without the agreement of the state. Further, given the serious shortage of funds in recent years, assuming responsibility for IDPs would have involved much greater costs and thus could have caused a reduction in the programmes for refugees.

Such contradictions led to the coexistence of *three types of stated position* within UNHCR regarding the best policy for IDPs. First, that of those normally considered the '*pragmatists*' (Interview with UNHCR official, 3 October 2002), who support a role with IDPs primarily on the grounds that it is very often operationally problematic and morally untenable to distinguish between the two populations (UNHCR 2000a: 215). Second, that of those who think UNHCR has been drifting away from its core mandate and should return to it (the '*traditionalists*' and more legal-oriented staff members). Finally, that of those who argue that UNHCR should become involved on a case-by-case basis: '*pragmatism out of necessity*', in the words of Steven Corliss, Special Assistant to the High Commissioner (Interview, 30 November 2000). This last seems to be the dominant position in the agency. These divergences are even more visible in decisions on involvement when the link with refugee operations is not clear, as was the case in UNHCR's intervention in Colombia, where regional bureaus stimulated much of the work of persuasion and coalition building to support involvement (Interview with UNHCR official, 30 November 2000).

Within the state participant subsystem not even the United States government had a policy on IDPs, despite the personal efforts of Richard Holbrooke in 2000 to push the establishment of concrete measures to address the problem forward (Interview with US government official, 28 November 2000). At that time some representatives ventured to state their own positions on the issue even if they did not have specific instructions, although the issue featured less prominently in subsequent meetings of the Executive Committee and of the Standing Committee except when it was closely related to a discussion about other categories. This is due to the fact that many state representatives' instructions are the result of compromises between different ministries or agencies, which frequently have not yet fine-tuned their positions (where they have them at all), leaving the representative without a clear official position. This is the case, for example, with the European Union (Rudge 2002), Switzerland (Interview with Swiss government official, 15 December 2000), Japan (Interview with Japanese government official, Hajime Kishimori, 5 December 2000) and the US (Kunder 1999; McElhinny 2000; US General Accounting Office 2001). The result has been that, within UNHCR, the patterns of state recommendations regarding UNHCR's possible involvement with IDPs have become dependent on the moral or practical considerations of the state representatives on the issue, combined with a few policy guidelines.

The internal environment of UNHCR and its subunits was thus highly divided on the issue. No compromise between the organizational roles put forward by the internal bureaucratic rivals seemed in the offing. At the same time member states often had no clear policy guidelines and thus could not impose a certain policy line on the organization. This situation offered the conditions under which organizational leadership could have a decisive impact.

Leadership

What IDP policy did the UNHCR leadership eventually adopt, in the wake of external and internal pressure? It opted for a solution that served the pragmatic need to halt the institutionalization of further expansion and to keep decisions on involvement in IDP operations away from mandate incorporation, while at the same time not alienating the organization's role with IDPs. This so-called *ad hoc* approach remained the most desirable. In this way the funds for 'high-profile' emergencies continued to be an important source of organizational vitality. Moreover, it strengthened UNHCR's position in its turf wars with other organizations. Most importantly, it enabled UNHCR to avoid becoming involved in situations that proved too complex or unmanageable, or lacked adequate funding.[2]

UNHCR has thus been sending contradictory signals by systematically refusing to take on the responsibility for IDPs, even if it does seem willing to maintain its role and to provide leadership and coordination in the UN system. When pressed by states or by members of the humanitarian community to take on an expanded mandate, UNHCR responded by pointing to the impossibility of a single humanitarian organization dealing with so complex an issue. It usually gave as its main concerns the resource implications and the resistance of sister agencies (McElhinny 2000), while affirming its commitment to the cause. Subsequently UNHCR would issue policy papers, giving the conditions and criteria for its involvement.[3] These position papers were effective in that they enabled the organization to make decisions on the definition of its own mandate, allowing it to keep its responsibilities largely dependent on its own judgement. The consistent caution with which UNHCR has reacted seems to substantiate the interpretation that the papers serve to affirm UNHCR's wish to retain autonomy in deciding when and where it will become involved, without formalizing a responsibility or completely withdrawing from the issue area. All policy papers basically outline UNHCR's own stipulations for involvement, which include technical and operational criteria as well as requirements for donor countries, making involvement dependent especially on the availability of resources. The papers also include the possibility of in each situation defining who are to be considered 'IDPs of concern', meaning not all IDPs in a given country will benefit from UNHCR's activities.

In the words of Garling, these criteria 'allow the UNHCR flexibility without imposing formal mandatory obligations [and] have allowed UNHCR considerable discretion in deciding when and how to intervene on behalf of internally displaced groups'. The criteria could further serve to 'protect UNHCR from entering situations where there was no real political will to resolve an internal displacement crisis, and which might thus render its solutions expertise irrelevant and its available resources inadequate' (Garling 2000: 6).

Having simply stated 'an interest in the protection and welfare [of IDPs]' (UNHCR 2000b: 11), and not accepted a mandate, UNHCR has been accused of taking an *ad hoc* approach and of lack of predictability as to when it will become involved in an IDP situation. As noted above, the development of a regime at inter-institutional level pressured UNHCR into increased accountability regarding its decisions. Indeed, the 2000 policy paper was delivered as a response to such pressures, as well as to Holbrooke's call for a broad mandate for UNHCR (Interview with Special Coordinator of the Senior Network on Internal Displacement, 30 November 2000). Although it argued for an increased role for the Division of International Protection in decision making, the 2000 position paper's internal origins are unclear. In the words of Goodwin-Gill 'though couched in quasi-legal language and purporting to make a "case" for additional activity, it does not present much of a "Department of International Protection" perspective' (Goodwin-Gill 2000a: 7). This last policy paper differs from previous ones in that its final version was actually written by the High Commissioner (Interview with UNHCR official, 11 December 2000). Unlike the other two it was not issued by DIP for internal guidance only, but was presented in the form of an external paper, widely distributed publicly (see UNHCR 2000b). This reflects the leadership's way of handling UNHCR's internal divisions. It can thus be interpreted as a deliberately political and symbolic output that does not add much to clarify UNHCR's commitment to IDPs.

Ms Ogata's mandate was marked by an inconsistency and obscurity of policy making towards IDPs, which reflects the deep internal problems and the general contradictions that a role with IDPs entails. As pointed out by Cox, '(t)he executive leadership of an international organization is pre-eminently a political task' (Cox 1996: 322). Ms Ogata had considerable political support from states, in particular because she was seen to give in to pre-eminent states' priorities (Interview with UNHCR official, 11 December 2000) while at the same time actively promoting the cause of refugees.

UNHCR's leadership has also skilfully exploited the lack of a UN system of coordination for involvement in IDP situations to push for its development, which has reduced the problem of UNHCR's overall role with IDPs. As the dominant agency in the humanitarian community, UNHCR has seconded many members of its staff to leadership positions in its efforts to create a coordination system.[4] This will enable it to influence the shaping of such system, thus retaining the necessary flexibility and allowing it to lead when it suits UNHCR's priorities.

Conclusion

Changes in the international environment explain increasing policy autonomy of IGOs, but they do not fully account for specific policy choices. In a changing and increasingly complex world, managing an IGO becomes an intricate task that requires consideration of a number of different constraints, related not only to its external but also to its internal environment. Hence the importance of addressing internal decision-making mechanisms when explaining international policy choices by IGOs, as well as of analysing the role of the leadership in bringing together the different considerations and balancing external and internal inputs.

The case of UNHCR's role with IDPs shows how the phenomenon of change led to the development of a new international issue area, which in turn produced a window of opportunity for UNHCR task expansion. The leadership of the organization took advantage of this window of opportunity to increase its policy autonomy. However, it did not do so through the traditional option of institutionalizing task expansion, which in this case would have committed the organization to a responsibility that would become detrimental to it and create negative reactions among several of the actors with a stake in its activities. Instead, it opted to ensure policy flexibility and retain decision-making capability on a case-by-case basis, thus satisfying the different actors as the situations occurred.

Notes

1 In Schmitter's model, regional integration is defined as the study 'of how national units come to share part or all of their decision-making authority with an emerging international organization' (Schmitter 1971: 232).
2 However, in concrete emergencies the organization's track record has predominantly been one of going beyond its recognized legal role, stepping into political minefields and thus abandoning any claim to autonomy (Goodwin-Gill 2000b: 29).
3 UNHCR IOM/FOM/33/93 of 28 April 1993; UNHCR IOM/87/97-FOM/91/97, of 2 December 1997; UNHCR 2000b.
4 For example, the first Special Coordinator of the Senior Inter-Agency Network on IDPs had been on the UNHCR staff, and the director of the IDP Unit at the Office for the Coordination of Humanitarian Affairs is also a former UNHCR staff member.

References

Anonymous (1997) 'The UNHCR Note on International Protection You Won't See', *International Journal of Refugee Law*, 9(2): 267–73.

Baier, V.E., March, J.G. and Saetren, H. (1988) 'Implementation and Ambiguity' in J.G. March (ed.) *Decisions and Organizations*, Oxford: Basil Blackwell, 150–66.

Barnett, M.N. and Finnemore, M. (1999) 'The Politics, Power, and Pathologies of International Organizations', *International Organization*, 53(4): 699–732.

Chimni, B.S. (1998) 'The Geopolitics of Refugee Studies: A View From the South', *Journal of Refugee Studies*, 11(4): 350–74.

Cohen, R. (1998) 'Recent Trends in Protection and Assistance for IDPs', in J.

Hampton (ed.) *Internally Displaced People: A Global Survey*, Oxford: Norwegian Refugee Council, 3–9.

Cox, R.W. (1996) 'The Executive Head: An Essay on Leadership in International Organization (1969)', in R.W. Cox and T.J. Sinclair (eds) *Approaches to World Order*, Cambridge: Cambridge University Press, 317–48.

—— (ed.) (1997) *The New Realism Perspectives on Multilateralism and World Order*, New York: Macmillan and United Nations University Press.

Cox, R.W. and Jacobson, H.K. (eds) (1973) *The Anatomy of Influence. Decision Making in International Organization*, New Haven: Yale University Press.

Garling, M. (2000) *UNHCR and Internal Displacement*, Unpublished paper, Geneva.

Goodwin-Gill, G.S. (2000a) *The International Protection of Refugees: What Future?*, Notes for a Presentation at the Institut Universitaire De Hautes Études Internationales.

—— (2000b) 'UNHCR and Internal Displacement: Stepping into a Legal and Political Minefield', *World Refugee Survey 2000*, Washington DC: United States Committee for Refugees, 26–31.

Groom, A.J.R. (1978) 'International Organisation in World Society', in P. Taylor and A.J.R. Groom (eds) *International Organisation: A Conceptual Approach*, London: Pinter, 152–62.

Haas, E. (1964) *Beyond the Nation-State. Functionalism and International Organization* Stanford: Stanford University Press.

Katzenstein, P.J., Keohane, R.O. and Krasner, S.D. (1998) 'International Organization and the Study of World Politics', *International Organization*, 52(4): 645–85.

Kunder, J. (1999) *The US Government and Internally Displaced Persons. Present but Not Accounted For*, Brookings Institution and United States Committee for Refugees.

Loescher, G. (2001) *The UNHCR and World Politics. A Perilous Path*, Oxford: Oxford University Press.

March, J.G. (1988a) *Decisions and Organizations*, Oxford: Basil Blackwell.

—— (1988b) 'Introduction: A Chronicle of Speculations About Decision-Making in Organizations' in J.G. March (ed.) *Decisions and Organizations*, Oxford: Basil Blackwell: 1–21.

March, J.G. and Olsen, J.P. (1998) 'The Institutional Dynamics of International Political Orders', *International Organization*, 52(4): 943–69.

McElhinny, J. (2000) *Fixing Responsibility for the Internally Displaced*, International Migration Policy Program, at www.ceip.org/files/events/fixingresponsibility.asp, accessed on 23 February 2001.

Meyer, J.W. (1994) 'Rationalized Environments' in W.R. Scott and J.W. Meyer (eds) *Institutional Environments and Organizations*, Thousand Oaks: Sage Publications, 28–54.

Mills, K. (1998) *Human Rights in the Emerging Global Order*, London: MacMillan.

Ness, G.D. and Brechin, S.R. (1988) 'Bridging the Gap: International Organizations as Organizations', *International Organization*, 42(2): 245–76.

Putnam, R. (1988) 'Diplomacy and Domestic Politics: The Logic of Two-Level Games', *International Organization*, 42(3): 427–60.

Reinalda, B. (1998) 'Organization Theory and the Autonomy of the International

Labour Organization' in B. Reinalda and B. Verbeek (eds) *Autonomous Policy Making by International Organizations*, London: Routledge, 42–61.

Reinalda, B. and B. Verbeek (eds) (1998) *Autonomous Policy Making by International Organizations*, London: Routledge.

Reinicke, W.H. and Deng, F. (2000) *Critical Choices: The United Nations, Networks, and the Future of Global Governance*, Ottawa: International Development Research Centre.

Rosenau, J.N. (2000) *Thinking Theory Thoroughly. Coherent Approaches to an Incoherent World*, Boulder: Westview Press.

Rudge, P. (2002) *The Need for a More Focused Response: European Donor Policies Toward Internally Displaced Persons (IDPs)*, Washington DC: Brookings Institution, Norwegian Refugee Council, United States Committee for Refugees.

Schmitter, P.C. (1971) 'A Revised Theory of Regional Integration', in L.N. Lindberg and S.A. Scheingold (eds) *Regional Integration: Theory and Research*, Harvard: Harvard University Press, 232–64.

Scott, W.R. (1994) 'Institutions and Organizations: Toward a Theoretical Synthesis', in W.R. Scott and J.W. Meyer (eds) *Institutional Environments and Organizations*, Thousand Oaks: Sage Publications, 55–80.

Torenvlied, R. (1996) 'Political Control of Implementation Agencies. Effects of Political Consensus on Agency Compliance', *Rationality and Society*, 8(1): 25–56.

United Nations Commission on Human Rights (1998) *The Guiding Principles on Internal Displacement*. Addendum to the Report of the Representative of the Secretary-General, Mr. Francis M. Deng, UN Doc. E/CN.4/1998/53/Add. 2, 11 February.

United Nations High Commissioner for Refugees (2000a) *The State of the World's Refugees: Fifty Years of Humanitarian Action*, Oxford: Oxford University Press.

—— (2000b) *Internally Displaced Persons: The Role of the UNHCR*, Geneva: UNHCR, 6 March.

US General Accounting Office (2001) *Internally Displaced Persons Lack Effective Protection. Report to the Chairman and the Ranking Minority Member, Committee on Foreign Relations, U.S. Senate*, Washington DC: United States General Accounting Office.

US/UN Press Release #95 (2000) *Statement by Ambassador Richard C. Holbrooke, United States Permanent Representative to the United Nations at the Humanitarian Affairs Segment, ECOSOC, 20 July*, New York.

Working Group on International Refugee Policy (1999) 'Report of the International Conference on the Protection Mandate of UNHCR', *Journal of Refugee Studies*, 12(2): 203–20.

Part V

Conflicts of loyalty

8 Are world leaders puppets or puppeteers?

The sherpas and decision making within the G7/G8 system

Nicholas Bayne

Introduction

The G7 – now G8 – summits were launched in 1975, with three objectives: (1) developing collective management of the world economy, to replace American hegemony; (2) reconciling the domestic and external pressures generated by interdependence; and (3) mobilizing political leadership to resolve problems beyond the reach of bureaucracies. Though 'globalization' has now replaced 'interdependence' and a political agenda has been added, these objectives have remained remarkably constant.[1] But during the summits of the 1990s and early 2000s (see Table 8.1) the decision-making processes of the G8 have changed radically.[2] The heads of government have detached their flanking ministers and begun meeting by themselves. The supporting apparatus has become more complex and developed a life of its own. More outside contributors have become involved in the preparation of the summits and their follow-up.[3]

This chapter focuses on the personal representatives of the heads of

Table 8.1 The G7 and G8 summits of the 1990s and 2000s

G7/G8	*Year*	*Site*
G7	1990	Houston
	1991	London III
	1992	Munich
	1993	Tokyo III
	1994	Naples
	1995	Halifax
	1996	Lyon
	1997	Denver
G8	1998	Birmingham
	1999	Cologne
	2000	Okinawa
	2001	Genoa
	2002	Kananaskis
	2003	Evian

government, known as the 'sherpas', who operate at the heart of the summit process. It first asks: what is the precise function of the sherpas and what are the sources of their influence? It concludes that their influence does not derive from their agenda-setting power, nor from their capacity as an epistemic community, but rather from their ability to negotiate value-creating deals through their pivotal position between the political leaders and their bureaucracies. The second part of the chapter asks: is the primacy of the sherpas being challenged? The potential challenges come from the heads of government themselves; from the growing G7/G8 apparatus; and from actors outside government or beyond the G8 circle. This section concludes that the sherpas are losing their monopoly of power. But they still exercise more influence on the summit outcome than any other single group of actors.

The sherpa process

This section explains how the sherpas became part of the summit process and goes through the different stages of their activity. It seeks to define exactly what the sherpas contribute to the process and the sources of their influence.

Origins

The G7 summit was conceived as a personal encounter of the leaders of the world's most powerful economies. The founders believed that this would enable them to better understand both the domestic problems of their peers and the international responsibilities they all shared. It would enable them to solve problems that had baffled their bureaucrats, who ought to be kept out of the process entirely. But even before the leaders met, it became clear that this vision was unrealistic. The subject matter of international economics was too complex for the heads to reach decisions without some preparation. So they reconciled themselves to playing roles written for them by the sherpas, their personal representatives charged with preparing the summits.

The sherpas are all government officials, chosen either for their closeness to the head of government or for their seniority in their parent department, usually the foreign or finance ministry.[4] The former criterion always prevails in France, Britain and Italy, the latter in Japan. Being a sherpa is not a full-time activity. Sherpas combine their role in summit preparation with a position either on the personal staff of the Head of Government or near the top of their parent bureaucracy.

The cycle of summit preparations by the sherpas

Summit preparations are concentrated in several meetings each spring, to select the agenda and start drafting the necessary documents. The task for the first sherpa meeting of the year is to set the summit agenda.

Agenda setting

The summit agenda is always under pressure and the sherpas are squeezed from two directions. On the one hand, there is pressure from the heads of government for new topics, to make the next summit look innovative. On the other hand, many of the difficult issues that come up often need repeated summit treatment, such as international trade or debt relief. Throughout the 1990s and early 2000s, the summits kept on adding new items – employment, information technology, infectious diseases, Africa – without deleting old ones. Thus the innovative ideas of earlier years become recurrent themes later. The sherpas have to balance the heads' demand for innovation against the ongoing summit programme, consisting of items started but not completed in earlier years. Agenda setting for the sherpas largely consists of deciding what to leave out.

Negotiating G8 agreements

Once the agenda is set, the sherpas begin work on the package of agreements that could emerge from the summit. These fall into three groups: endorsement of work in progress; stimulating agreement at lower levels; and promoting agreement at the summit itself.

Summit endorsement

Over the years, endorsement has made up the largest part of the summit agenda and documentation. It consists of the heads of government putting their authority behind work that is going on elsewhere. This may be activity generated by earlier summits, so that the heads give their blessing to work in progress. G8 governments also find it helpful to have the endorsement of their peers at summit level for policies they have decided to adopt already, since this can be used in overcoming domestic opposition.

This aspect of the summit is most subject to inflation. There is a strong incentive for G8 governments to expand the policies which carry summit endorsement. But the wider this endorsement is given, the more diluted its value becomes. The sherpas try to limit the list of issues offered for endorsement. This was successfully done at Kananaskis in 2002, when the Canadian hosts focused the discussion on a few subjects only. But this self-restraint is unusual. Once the heads have lent their authority to a particular subject they become reluctant to abandon it, for fear others should conclude that they have ceased to care about it.

Stimulating agreement at lower levels

A more demanding technique is using the prospect of summit discussion to bring about agreement at lower levels. The sherpas use the imminence of discussion among the heads of government to stimulate other parts of government into making the moves necessary to produce agreement. This may be used to resolve differences between G8 members, or to launch initiatives in wider international contexts.

A good example is seen in the international financial architecture agreed after the Asian crisis. The essential work on this was done by the G7 finance ministers and their deputies. On some issues there were deep divisions between them, but the approach of the summits in Birmingham in 1998 and Cologne in 1999 gave them an incentive to resolve these differences. The sherpas prepared for a discussion among the heads of government at both summits. But since the contentious issues had been resolved by the time they met, the heads simply endorsed what their finance ministers had agreed, without adding anything themselves.

The same process operated, more controversially, in international trade. In the Uruguay Round the summit three times failed to resolve differences among the G7. In 1993, however, the sherpas arranged that G7 trade ministers should meet as the 'Quad' (the US, EU, Canada and Japan) just before the Tokyo III summit. The imminence of the summit encouraged the ministers to reach agreements that opened the way for the Uruguay Round's final completion in December 1993. There was similar G7 discord leading up to the disastrous meeting of the World Trade Organization (WTO) in Seattle in 1999. But in 2001 the imminence of the Genoa summit encouraged the European and American trade negotiators to settle their differences, which facilitated agreement at the WTO meeting in Doha later that year.

Promoting agreement at the summit itself

The two techniques described so far cover most of the summit content. Often the sherpas' work will produce the most important evidence of G7/G8 cooperation, without the heads of government having to intervene personally at all. But the sherpas know the heads are not happy when everything at the summit has been 'pre-cooked'. The sherpas therefore exploit the heads' wish for some achievements of their own and provide scope for them to go beyond what has been prepared for them. Otherwise, the heads will be tempted to take their own unprepared initiatives, as will be described later.

Sometimes the sherpas provide for the heads to use their own authority to give impetus to a wide-ranging or innovative programme. The work on mobilizing information technology (IT) for development at Okinawa 2000 and the launch of the Global Funds for AIDS, malaria and tuberculosis at Genoa 2001 are examples of this. At other times the sherpas set up agreements that can only be confirmed by the intervention of the heads themselves. This applied to the peace arrangements for Kosovo in 1999. Detailed preparations had been made, but everything hinged on the position of Yeltsin, which only became clear when he reached the Cologne summit in person.

Equally the sherpas enable the heads of government to reach agreements which are not attainable at lower levels. Debt relief for impoverished countries provides successive examples of this technique throughout the 1990s and again in the 2000s. At London III 1991, Naples 1994, Lyon 1996 and Cologne 1999, the heads succeeded in advancing agreement on this subject further than their finance ministers had taken it. Shortly before Kananaskis 2002, the G7 finance ministers had failed to agree on a figure for replenishing the World Bank's Trust Fund to finance debt relief, because of hesitation by the Americans. At the summit, however, Bush agreed with his colleagues on a figure of $1 billion.

Because the sherpas cover the whole range of summit issues, they can sometimes identify links between subjects that enable deals to be struck that were not available below summit level. This happens rarely, but Kananaskis provides a good example. The United States was seeking matching finance from its partners of $10 billion over ten years, to clean up nuclear and chemical weapons in the former USSR. Bush's readiness to accept a figure for debt relief replenishment was a key factor in getting the Europeans, Japan and Canada to make firm commitments on weapons of mass destruction.

Of course, this strategy does not always work. This is shown by the summits' treatment of environmental issues. Early summits were able to stimulate new thinking before the UN Conference on Environment and Development in Rio de Janeiro in 1992. However, as discussion moved from broad ideas to specific commitments, it became harder to overcome differences between the United States and Europe. At Denver 1997 and Okinawa 2000, in advance of climate change meetings in Kyoto and The Hague, raising the issue to head of government level did not resolve the disagreements. Genoa 2001 took place under the shadow of Bush's rejection of the Kyoto Protocol, though this still helped the other G8 members to present a common front.

Domestic motivation

When the sherpas prompt the heads of government to go a bit further at the summit than their officials or other ministers can, this usually reflects a judgement on the balance between domestic and international advantage of reaching agreement. The Kosovo settlement was unpopular in Russia, but Yeltsin did not want to alienate the support of the G7. The Cologne agreement on debt relief was prompted by strong public interest in debt relief. But domestic considerations at this level can work in the wrong direction as well. On environmental issues the strongest domestic pressures in Europe come mainly from consumer groups and public opinion, while in North America they come from producers and business interests.

So agreement may actually be harder to reach at the summit than lower down.

Sources of influence: the sherpas as the fulcrum of the summit process

This section examines the various sources that could explain the influence exercised by the sherpas over the summit process.

At first sight the sherpas may appear to have agenda-setting power. But this is deceptive. The strongest influence on the summit agenda is exercised by the decisions of previous summits. Beyond that, the power to introduce new topics lies more with the heads of government themselves than with the sherpas. Although it looks as if the sherpas' main task is to prepare the agenda for the summit attended by the heads, in fact most of their activity consists of pre-negotiation of agreements, which the heads should either endorse or complete.

It could also be argued that the sherpas make up an epistemic community. But this too is a misinterpretation of their function. Epistemic communities, as defined by Peter Haas, have 'recognised expertise and competence in a particular domain and an authoritative claim to policy-relevant knowledge within that domain or issue-area' (Haas 1992: 3). The subject matter of the summits is so diverse and open-ended that no group of individuals could claim knowledge of it all. The sherpas make use of epistemic communities, both nationally and internationally.[5] Epistemic communities also contribute to the summit process independently. But the sherpas themselves do not constitute an epistemic community.

One key to the sherpas' influence is that they reproduce the dynamics of summit meetings at their own level. Sherpa meetings are small and discussion is frank, with plenty of personal interaction. The sherpas have the advantage over the heads of government in that they meet several times, usually over several days, rather than have a single meeting under pressure of time. They get to know each other well, they understand each others' domestic background and they develop a sense of solidarity and shared responsibility. The sherpas become adept both at seeing what arguments would prove convincing, against their colleagues' domestic backgrounds, and at picking up ideas from the others which they can use to good effect back home.

The close interaction among the sherpas affects their choice of negotiating strategies. John Odell has divided negotiating strategies into three types: *value claiming*, where one party advances its objectives at the expense of others; *value creating*, which looks for benefits shared among all parties; and *mixed strategies*, combining the two (see Odell 2000: 27–38). The sherpas try to devise value-creating agreements or packages which provide something for everyone. This approach, for example, enabled the G7 members to reach an agreed strategy on a new trade round in the WTO at the Genoa summit of 2001. It also enabled them to identify the link between debt relief and cleaning up nuclear and chemical weapons which led to agreements on both at Kananaskis 2002. Value-claiming strategies seldom provide a basis for summit accord. The tendency of both the United States and the European Union to pursue value claiming in global environmental issues like climate change has frustrated the efforts of the sherpas to construct agreements in this field.

The sherpas exert a dominant influence over the summit outcome because they serve as the fulcrum in the summit process, between the political reflexes of their patrons and the bureaucratic pressures of the national government machine. The sherpas, through their links with their patron heads of government, can assess the political pressures at work on them and judge how these can be used to promote international agreement at the heads' own level. Their influence thus feeds upwards. But at the same time, the sherpas use the authority they derive from their patrons to stimulate their national bureaucracies to come to agreements they would not achieve on their own. In this way their influence feeds downwards.

The sherpas use their regular contacts with their fellow sherpas as the basis for two different types of 'two-level game', of the kind identified by Robert Putnam. In Putnam's model, Level I is the game on the international board, Level II the game on the domestic board (see Putnam 1988: 427–60). Sherpas play one Level II game with their patron heads of government and a second with their national administrations. With the heads they are usually trying to harness their innovative instincts, so as to promote workable agreements. With the government machine they seek to overcome bureaucratic inertia. At both levels they use their close links with their fellow sherpas to increase the possibilities of 'reverberation', in Putnam's usage, whereby international pressures help to produce policy decisions domestically. This ability to pursue two-level negotiating strategies, rather than agenda-setting power or the attributes of an epistemic community, is the foundation for the sherpas' influence.

Challenges to the sherpas

The sherpas' pivotal position, analysed above, has come under increasing challenge in the late 1990s and early 2000s, as a result of changes elsewhere in the decision-making process. The heads of government may seek to pursue their innovative ideas themselves, bypassing the sherpas. The bureaucracy may use the inexorable growth of the subjects addressed at the summits to overwhelm the sherpas. Other players outside the government circle or the G8 membership may try to influence proceedings. Each of these challenges are examined in this section of the chapter.

Challenges from the heads themselves

The heads of government accepted the need for substantive summit preparation at an early stage. But the prospect of informal and spontaneous contacts, during which they could develop their own ideas, has never ceased to exercise a powerful attraction on them. In the 1990s they moved to re-create the summit in this image.

Summit format

The heads increasingly complained that the summit procedures were too bureaucratic, giving them no scope to have their own input. After several abortive attempts at reform, major changes were introduced at the Birmingham summit of 1998 on Blair's initiative. Up until then, the heads of government had been flanked at the summits by their foreign and finance ministers. But only the heads came to Birmingham, with foreign and finance ministers meeting a few days earlier. Blair proposed an economic agenda of only three closely defined items, which allowed the documents issued to be pruned severely. 'Heads-only summits' with a limited agenda have now become firmly established, giving the heads greater freedom to develop their own ideas.

Innovation

While the sherpas try to impose order on the agenda, the heads are instinctively innovative. Each G8 country hosts the summit in turn. Every year, the host head of government tries to make 'his' summit stand out from the others and will propose as innovative an agenda as the others can accept. This is the point at which the host has most influence over the proceedings and few can resist a personal initiative.

Innovation by any of the other heads of government can happen at the summit as well. Hitherto this has more often been procedural rather than substantive. Ideas for brand new policies rarely succeed unless they have been filtered through the preparatory process.[6] But new procedural proposals launched at the summit itself are more common and likely to produce agreement. Clinton made his mark at Tokyo III 1993, his first summit, by suggesting a special meeting of G7 employment ministers – and Chirac did the same at his first summit, Halifax 1995. Some summit heads also have had personal crusades, particularly Kohl, who insisted on getting environmental issues onto the agenda.

Political reflexes

At the summit, the heads' political instincts can lead them to reject what the sherpas have prepared and to go their own way. The heads will often react to sudden crises which happen just before a summit. For example, because terrorists attacked US servicemen in Saudi Arabia just before Lyon 1996, Clinton persuaded his colleagues to convert material prepared on international crime into an action programme against terrorism. On other occasions the heads' political sense tells them that the conclusions prepared for the summit are not adequate. At Genoa 2001, after the G8 heads had met African leaders over dinner, they decided the conclusions prepared on Africa were insufficient. They produced a brief 'Genoa Africa Plan' on the spot and created a G8 Africa Group, which drew up an Africa Action Plan for adoption at Kananaskis 2002.

These interventions by the heads, against the grain of the preparations, are different from deals struck on the basis of the preparatory work, discussed earlier in this chapter. The heads also make personal use of the summit, independently of the sherpas, to respond to domestic pressures or to advance their domestic agenda. Thus Kohl's concern with the environment reflected strong public interest in this subject in Germany. Clinton hoped that having Africa on the agenda for Denver 1997 would help him in his plans to upgrade US policy towards that continent.[7] Blair in 1998, as a newly elected left-of-centre leader, used the summit to advance his own domestic objectives in employment.

The growing freedom of the heads of government to launch their own initiatives, often for domestic political reasons, to some extent puts the position of the sherpas at risk. As this analysis shows, the heads seldom go beyond procedural innovations and they still rely on the sherpas for most policy changes. However, the treatment of Africa marks a new departure. Not only did the heads launch the Genoa Africa Plan on their own initiative, but they also created a special group, separate from the sherpas, to implement it.[8] If this should become standard practice, the sherpas' pivotal role would be threatened.

Challenges from the G7/G8 apparatus

The G7/G8 apparatus has expanded greatly since the summits began. At the outset foreign and finance ministers attended the summit, flanking their heads of government. But during the 1980s each group gradually asserted its independence. Since Birmingham, both groups meet just before the summit, but no longer attend it; they also have their own cycle of meetings throughout the year.

Meanwhile, in the 1990s other ministers became associated with the summit, largely thanks to personal initiatives by the heads of government themselves. Regular or periodic meetings of environment ministers (promoted by Kohl), employment ministers (backed by Clinton, Chirac and Blair), energy ministers (started by Yeltsin), education ministers (thanks to Schröder) and interior and justice ministers are held both to prepare for summits and to carry out instructions from the heads. Each has its own apparatus of supporting officials.[9]

Once the summit became a meeting of heads of government only, these separate ministerial groups no longer felt bound to preserve the strict G7 or G8 format. G8 foreign ministers have invited selected other countries to join them for meetings focusing on specific problems – for example, on Balkan stability in June 1999. The G7 finance ministers have created a new permanent grouping, the G20, linked to monetary reform in the International Monetary Fund (IMF), which includes major developing countries such as Brazil, China, India and South Africa.[10]

The growth of this ministerial apparatus is due to a combination of two factors. The first is the growing complexity of the issues reaching the summit. Often they cannot be resolved at a single meeting and require iterative treatment. The second is the wish of the heads of government for more freedom of action. The initiative for ministerial groups has come from the heads themselves, not from the sherpas. Issues that are treated by these other G7/G8 groups pass out of the direct oversight of the sherpas. In some respects it is a relief for the sherpas to see some issues removed from their responsibility. Even now, the array of G8 ministerial meetings is so bewildering that the sherpas' time is increasingly spent sifting their results, rather than responding to the heads' own wishes. Yet the sherpas still control what items go to the summit itself and in what form.

Challenges from outside forces

In addition to personal initiatives by the heads of government and the growth of the G8 governmental apparatus, the pivotal position of the sherpas may be challenged by the increased involvement of non-G8 governments and of non-state actors, especially business and non-governmental organizations (NGOs). These new actors influence both summit preparation and follow-up.

Summit preparation

Throughout the 1970s and 1980s, the G7 governments kept summit preparation firmly in their own hands. Other governments had little chance of influencing the process directly, apart from other member states of the European Community. The non-G7 members of the Organization for Economic Cooperation and Development (OECD) would use its annual ministerial meeting to make their views known. As for non-government influences, these barely went beyond visits to the G7 host by business and trade union delegations under OECD auspices.

During the 1990s the hermetic character of summit preparations began to loosen up and this has accelerated since 2000. The involvement of supporting ministers in the preparatory process enabled both the staff of international institutions and other governments to become involved. A more radical move was made in 2000, when most G8 heads met a group of leaders from developing countries before the Okinawa summit.[11] Before Genoa 2001 all the G8 heads met a group of African leaders, who – as noted earlier – urged the G8 to underwrite their efforts to revive their troubled continent. This led to an even greater integration of the African presidents at Kananaskis 2002, where they were present as the Steering Committee of the New Partnership for Africa's Development (NEPAD) and were full participants in the discussions on Africa.

Non-state actors have also made advances. In 2000, the Japanese prepared for the treatment of information technology at the summit by inviting major multinational companies to a special conference before Okinawa. Most of its findings were incorporated in the document agreed at the summit. The involvement of NGOs took off at Birmingham 1998, where the Jubilee 2000 Campaign organized a march of 50,000 people calling for debt cancellation. In 2000 the Japanese provided an NGO centre at Okinawa and involved NGO groups in consultations with their sherpa team.[12] The Italians made similar preparations for Genoa 2001, but these plans were abolished due to violent rioting. Because of this, and also because of security concerns after the terrorist attacks of 11 September 2001, Canada hosted the 2002 summit in a remote mountain resort and kept all demonstrators at a safe distance. But this isolation is not likely to endure.

Summit follow-up

In contrast to the preparations, summit follow-up has relied on other actors from the outset. The summits of the 1970s and 1980s largely delegated the responsibility for implementing their decisions to bodies like the OECD, the IMF and World Bank and the General Agreement on Tariffs and Trade (GATT). The summits handed down their decisions as *faits accomplis*, without systematic advance contacts with the wider institutions. The G7 leaders expected their conclusions to be adopted more widely without further debate.

This approach could no longer work in the 1990s. More countries became active in the global economic institutions and they would not accept being dictated to by the G7. The G7 members conducted a review of international institutions, from Naples 1994 to Denver 1997, and realized that they would have to use more tact and persuasion to get their ideas for reform accepted by the wider international community. Meanwhile, the summits have moved further into policy areas where the institutions are inadequate, such as crime and money-laundering. This has encouraged the creation of separate G7 and G8 groups, such as of the interior and justice ministers.[13]

During the 2000s private business and NGOs have become involved in summit follow-up and they have created several epistemic communities in the process.[14] The priority given to IT at Okinawa led to the creation of the 'Dot-Force' to overcome the digital divide. This had strong participation from business and from NGOs, who were also involved in two other programmes launched at Okinawa: the campaign against infectious diseases in poor countries and the task force on renewable energy. The reports on these subjects presented at Genoa 2001 showed an impressive synergy of public and private actors. The constructive contribution of the NGO members contrasted with the riots on the streets.

The involvement of outside forces – non-G8 governments, international organizations and non-state actors like business and NGOs – is essential to give greater legitimacy to the summit process. This process has gathered strength since the Birmingham summit changed the format of the event and gave the heads of government more scope to reach out beyond the traditional circles of the G8 apparatus. The expansion of G7/G8 meetings at lower levels has also contributed to this trend.

This outreach has brought new responsibilities to the sherpas. Nationally, they now spend more time in contacts with bodies outside government which express an interest in the summit and its agenda. The task of the host country sherpa involves regular contacts with the international NGO community, with non-G8 governments and with international organizations. The participation of business and NGOs has the merit of tapping into additional sources of expertise and financial support. But these new players are not easily integrated into the existing framework of international institutions normally charged with summit follow-up. Originally the sherpas took little interest in summit follow-up, since this was entrusted to established organizations. Now they continue their work after the year's summit is over, to maintain an oversight over the implementation of G8 decisions.

Conclusions: who pulls the strings?

The early development of the summits made the sherpas pivotal in the G7 process. They are a small, close-knit group of officials who simulate the dynamics of the summit meetings at their own level. Their authority, as personal representatives of the heads of government, enables them to stir up sluggish bureaucratic procedures and to stimulate agreement at lower levels without the heads having to intervene directly. But they are also indispensable to the heads, in bringing issues to a point where a brief meeting between them can conclude agreements that could not be reached elsewhere. They owe their influence to their position as the fulcrum between political leadership and bureaucratic processes.

The power of the sherpas has been challenged in the 1990s and 2000s, from three directions. In each case this reflects the problems created for the sherpas by the advance of globalization. The summit agenda has become more complex and politically more sensitive, as international pressures penetrate deeper into domestic policy making. As more countries become active in the international system, the summit has needed wider outreach to give it legitimacy.

The sherpas have responded to the three challenges as follows:

From the heads of government themselves. In a sense, the sherpas did their work too well, leaving the heads too little personal initiative. The heads have shortened their agenda and cut loose from their supporting ministers. This gives them greater freedom for their own innovative moves, often driven by domestic political motives. But the heads on their own seldom advance beyond procedural initiatives. They still need the sherpas to prepare them for most policy decisions.

From the G8 apparatus. The growth of G7/G8 ministerial meetings, each with their supporting official groups, results in issues escaping from the sherpas' strict control. In fact the complexity of the G8's subject matter is more than the sherpas could encompass on their own and it is a relief to have some of it taken off their hands. The sherpas still maintain their grip on the issues that go to the heads of government and the way they are presented.

From outside forces. Greater summit outreach increases accountability, at some cost to efficiency. It is hard work to reconcile the different aims and working methods of governments, international organizations, business and NGOs. Involving a wider range of actors adds to the burdens on the sherpas. Their responsibilities do not end with the summit itself, but they have to extend their oversight to the implementation of decisions.

The role of the sherpas has become more demanding, while there has been some erosion of their power. They no longer enjoy the same monopoly position they had in the 1970s and 1980s. But they are still the most influential figures in determining which issues go to the summit and which agreements are concluded there.

Notes

1 These objectives are analysed in Putnam and Bayne 1987: 13–35, and Bayne 2000: 3–15 and 191–217.

2 Nearly all the examples of decision making from the summits of the 1990s in this chapter are taken from Bayne 2000: chapters 5, 8 and 10. For the 2000 Okinawa summit, see Bayne 2001; for the 2001 Genoa summit, see Bayne 2002; for the 2002 Kananaskis summit, see Bayne 2003.

3 Although the G7/G8 summit has its own decision-making process, it is not strictly an international organization according to the criteria set out in Jacobson 1984: 77–98.

4 A complete list of the summit participants, including the sherpas, from the beginning up to 2000 is in Sherifis and Astraldi 2001: 217–53.

5 For example, the UK sherpa drew on an epistemic community on renewable energy before the Okinawa 2000 summit and this was carried through into the summit decisions. See Budd 2003.

6 The classic example of a new policy introduced at the summit without preparation is the agreement on hijacking from Bonn I 1978 – see Putnam and Bayne 1987: 87.

7 Bush was likewise content to give high priority to Africa at Kananaskis, in advance of his own visit to Africa planned for 2003.

8 It is worth considering whether the G8 Africa Group should be regarded as an epistemic community. Some of its leading members, like Bob Fowler (Canada) and Michel Camdessus (France), have knowledge of Africa. But this is not their only or even their principal expertise.

9 For an analysis of this development, see Hajnal 1999: 35–44.

10 See Kirton 2001 for an account of the G20 and its role. The G20 chair passed in 2002 from Canada to India, a non-G8 country.

11 This meeting was arranged without difficulty. But in 1989 the G7 heads had rejected Mitterrand's proposal that they should meet non-G7 leaders. See Attali 1995.

12 On the summit and the NGOs of civil society, see Hajnal 2002.

13 One early example is the Financial Action Task Force against money-laundering, founded at the Paris 1989 summit – see Bayne 2000: 66.

14 Both the Dot-Force and the task force on renewable energy, created at Okinawa 2001, should be regarded as epistemic communities. The latter has links with other environmental groups, analysed in Gough and Shackley 2001.

References

Attali, J. (1995) *Verbatim III*, Paris: Fayard.

Bayne, N. (2000) *Hanging in There: The G7 And G8 Summit in Maturity and Renewal*, Aldershot: Ashgate.

—— (2001) 'Managing Globalisation and the New Economy: The Contribution of the G8 Summit', in J.J. Kirton and G.M. von Furstenberg (eds) *New Directions in Global Economic Governance*, Aldershot: Ashgate: 23–38.

—— (2002) 'Impressions of the Genoa Summit', in M. Fratiani, P. Savona and J.J. Kirton (eds) *Governing Global Finance*, Aldershot: Ashgate: 199–210.

—— (2003) 'Impressions of the Kananaskis Summit', in M. Fratianni, P. Savona and J.J. Kirton (eds) *Sustaining Global Growth and Development*, Aldershot: Ashgate, 205–13.

Budd, C. (2003) 'G8 Summits and their Preparation', in N. Bayne and S. Woolcock (eds) *The New Economic Diplomacy*, Aldershot: Ashgate: 139–46.

Gough, C. and Shackley, S. (2001) 'The Respectable Politics of Climate Change: The Epistemic Communities and NGOs, *International Affairs*, 77(2): 329–45.

Haas, P. (1992) 'Introduction: Epistemic Communities and International Policy Coordination, *International Organization*, 46(1): 1–35.

Hajnal, P. (1999) *The G7/G8 system*, Aldershot: Ashgate.

—— (2002) 'Partners or Adversaries? The G7/G8 Encounters Civil Society', in J.J. Kirton and J. Takase (eds) *New Directions in Global Political Governance*, Aldershot: Ashgate, 173–84.

Jacobson, H.K. (1984) *Networks of Interdependence. International Organizations and the Global Political System*, 2nd edn, New York: Alfred A. Knopf.

Kirton, J.J. (2001) 'The G20: Representativeness, Effectiveness and Leadership in Global Governance', in J.J. Kirton, J.P. Daniels and A. Freytag (eds) *Guiding Global Order: G8 Governance in the Twenty-First Century*, Aldershot: Ashgate, 143–72.

Odell, J.S. (2000) *Negotiating the World Economy*, Ithaca and London: Cornell University Press.

Putnam, R.D. (1988) 'Diplomacy and Domestic Politics: The Logic of Two-Level Games, *International Organization*, 42(4): 427–60.

Putnam, R.D. and Bayne, N. (1987) *Hanging Together: Cooperation and Conflict in the Seven-Power Summits*, London: Sage.

Sherifis, R.F. and Astraldi, V. (2001) *The G7/G8 from Rambouillet to Genoa*, Milan: FrancoAngeli.

9 An institutionalist perspective on EU committee decision making

Jarle Trondal

Introduction[1]

There is a shortage of empirical studies on how international organizations work. This poses a challenge to the research community, because national parliaments, governments and central administrations are challenged by international organizations in day-to-day decision making. Some international organizations transform nation-state dynamics more than others, because they pose challenges to the Westphalian ideal of territorial state sovereignty (Biersteker 1999). The supranational and transgovernmental polity of the European Union (EU) is one tangible example. This chapter highlights the internal decision-making dynamics of the EU by analysing the identity and role orientation of EU decision makers. In particular, I analyse a specific segment of the Brussels bureaucracy, where different decision-making dynamics collide – the EU committees. These committees are composed of national and EU civil servants and they are thus adequate laboratories for studying what happens when different decision-making dynamics meet. The Commission expert committees (ECs) prepare decisions for the Commissioners, the Council working parties (CWPs) have a similar function for the Council of Ministers, while the so-called comitology committees (CCs) assist the Council in controlling delegated powers in the European Commission.

Decision making in international organizations is about creating optimal and efficient institutions and aggregating interests towards equilibrium, creating preferences, meaning, identities and roles, and transforming these into integrated regulative, cognitive, normative and symbolic arrangements (March and Olsen 1994: 265; Barnett and Finnemore 1999). Hence, decision making within international organizations also pertains to the less acknowledged aspects of actor socialization and re-socialization, identity change and role play. The identities and roles activated by individual decision makers are moulded institutionally, through processes of matching perceptions of appropriateness to particular situations and through the systematic and routine allocation of attention. Departing from, first, a 'sociological' and then a 'cognitive' perspective on decision making, this chapter argues for middle-range institutionalist theorizing on European integration and on EU committee decision making. My endeavour is to reveal institutional conditions whereby national decision makers evoke *particular* roles and identities when participating in EU committees.

Studies of European integration and domestic change have increasingly transcended the *sui generis* distinction between intergovernmentalism and neo-functionalism that dominated earlier theorizing on European integration, by applying institutionalist approaches from political science and organizational studies (e.g. Schneider and Aspinwall 2001). I argue that this conceptual divide between intergovernmentalism and neo-functionalism may be overcome and *bridged* by introducing a generic institutionalist approach. This bridge-building exercise is done by specifying the institutional conditions under which different decision-making dynamics prevail within EU committees, be they intergovernmental, functional or supranational dynamics. Committees are 'generic features of modern political life', important venues for regulative decision making in the EU and important arenas where national and supranational decision makers meet, interact, persuade, argue, bargain, adapt, learn and re-socialize (Christiansen and Kirchner 2000: 12). EU committees primarily exemplify three decision-making dynamics: (1) defence of nation-state preferences (intergovernmentalism), (2) provision of neutral expertise (functionalism), and (3) defence of the 'common European good' (supranationalism). Based on this, I pose the following question: to what extent do national civil servants adopt intergovernmental, supranational or functional loyalties, roles, identities and allegiances when attending EU committees? Assuming that the functional and supranational identities transcend the existing nation-state order, I treat the intergovernmental dynamic as my null hypothesis and explicate institutional conditions that trigger supranational and functional dynamics. This question pertains to the problematic nature of the transformative power of international organizations in general and of the EU in particular (Barnett and Finnemore 1999). EU institutions and EU committees are important laboratories for the study of transformational change, because they are strongly institutionalized and bring together national and community officials in day-to-day decision making. Based on the *most likely* research design, I expect national civil servants to more strongly adopt supranational and functional roles, identities, loyalties and allegiances in EU committees than in other international organizations, such as the North Atlantic Treaty Organization (NATO), the United Nations (UN) and the World Trade Organization (WTO).

I employ generic institutionalist arguments on institutional 'mattering'. In addition, I specify the conditional validity of particular institutional mechanisms (Börzel and Risse 2000). Departing from sociological and cognitive institutional perspectives, I suggest a multi-level institutionalist approach focusing on the impact of national *and* EU institutions. I thus accept the multi-level governance concept, but do not use it as an explanatory device. To explain the roles, identities, loyalties and allegiances of civil servants I focus on their *multiple institutional embeddedness*. Multiply-embedded civil servants face competing expectations and perceptions concerning what roles to play and what allegiances to emphasize in different situations (Trondal 2000; Egeberg 2001). Assuming that a mix of different institutions moulds civil servants' roles, identities, loyalties and allegiances, I suggest seven *ceteris paribus* clauses that explicate the causal arrows and the expected empirical implications. The highlighted hypotheses are suggestive, although not exhaustive. They are outlined theoretically and illuminated empirically throughout this chapter.

The chapter proceeds in four steps. The first section outlines a middle-range institutionalist approach and *seven operational hypotheses* on how domestic and EU institutions 'matter'. The next section introduces the data and methodology. I then move on to an empirical illustration of the seven hypotheses. The final section gives comparative assessments of decision making in EU committees and in other international organizations.

A middle-range institutionalist approach

The roles, identities and allegiances adopted by individuals are causally salient, because they provide cognitive, normative and ethical precedents and generalized prescriptions for how to act in different situations. Roles and identities taken by incumbents in public administration are chiefly the product of primary and secondary institutional socialization (Egeberg 2001). This chapter focuses on the roles and identities as institutionally constructed at the crossroads of national civil services and the EU. To account for national and European institutional 'mattering' I employ 'sociological' and 'cognitive' institutionalist approaches. Whereas the sociological perspective underscores roles and identities as products of the logic of appropriateness, the cognitive perspective explains role and identity construction through the confined rational choices made by humans (March and Olsen 1995). I rule out 'pure' rational-choice institutionalist accounts, which basically reduce roles and identities to a question of optimization of expected utility.

The cognitive argument stresses that organizations serve as buffers against information and thereby simplify the stimuli incumbents are exposed to. The confined and local rationality of individuals is subsequently aggregated systematically into organizational rationality by this buffer function. Consequently, the systematic selection of information and relevant premises for decision making and role enactment mould how organizational members think, feel and act. The 'sociological' argument stresses that institutions and individual roles are historical products and that institutional change is accompanied only by incremental changes in collective and individual roles and identities. Whereas a cognitive perspective focuses on the allocation of scarce attention among constricted rational actors, the sociological perspective focuses on how actors match identities and roles to particular situations, and on the fact that this matching process takes time, is inefficient and is path-dependent (March and Olsen 1995). 'The central logic is that of matching one's repertoire of identities and roles to specific (institutional) situations' (Trondal 2001: 15). Hence, a *cognitive* perspective emphasizes institutions and individual roles and identities as historically efficient (roles and identities adapt efficiently to institutional contingencies), while the *sociological* approach highlights historical inefficiency (roles and identities adapt slowly and imperfectly to institutional contingencies). Whereas the *cognitive* perspective departs from a restricted rational perspective on human computational capacities, the *sociological* approach views actors as socialized humans who have normatively internalized 'patterns of behavior and role expectations which characterize the groups in which they interact' (Alderson 2001: 416). Normatively internalized behaviour and roles are taken for granted and thus go beyond mere behavioural compliance. Accordingly, the length and intensity of interaction within groups and the length and intensity of exposure to stimuli affect the processes of socialization of in-group behaviour and roles. 'Identities can be seen as arising from a process of socialization into socially defined relationships and roles' (March 1994: 62). Accordingly, '[t]he longer one is exposed to particular stimuli, the more one is likely to absorb these influences' (Hooghe 2001: 15). This is particularly relevant in explaining supranational roles (see below). Common to these two perspectives is the focus on institutional contingency regarding human roles, identities and behaviour.

Organizational borders are causally relevant because they create relevance criteria for particular roles and identities (Barnett and Finnemore 1999). From this premise it follows that civil servants, having several organizational affiliations, are exposed to multiple buffers against attention, logics of appropriateness, classification schemes, temporal rhythms, physical structures and artefacts, symbolic arrangements, etc. Organizations may provide more or less consistent or conflicting challenges to the organizational members and more or less ambiguous cues for action. Organizational dynamics are triggered when organizational borders and divisions are activated. For example, what happens 'when the state is embedded in more than one institution and each institution demands a different role and set of behavioral actions' (Barnett 1993: 273)?

The concept of multiple roles and identities goes beyond an either/or style of representation, as seen in the 'free agency versus mandate' emphasized by intergovernmentalists and neo-functionalists (Eulau 1959: 746). It is commonly assumed that civil servants adopt multiple roles and allegiances.[2] However, multiple roles and identities can be related in different ways: they may be hierarchically-embedded, crosscutting and/or meshed and blended (Wendt 1994: 385). I argue that roles often crosscut in different dimensions or divisions (see Radaelli 1999: 34). For example, civil servants in national sector ministries are accustomed to the role of independent neutral expert. Diplomats from the foreign ministry, however, are used to combining the sector expert role with the role of national representative. These roles are relevant in a sectoral/territorial split, but irrelevant in another division: the national/supranational. Accordingly, civil servants adopting a supranational role and identity may at the same time make a territorial allegiance, because these roles and identities crosscut each other. Moreover, different roles and identities may be more or less important to individuals in particular situations. A role that is perceived as marginal to a civil servant is less likely to outweigh a role deemed salient. Hence, civil servants tend to live with role and identity conflicts both because they attach different weights to them, and because some of them crosscut each other. Finally, roles and identities may be adopted sequentially in different institutional contexts, and thus, role conflicts may be coped with by sequential attention.

In the following subsections I will develop seven hypotheses on role and identity enactment conditioned by national and EU institutions.

Hypotheses on national institutional 'mattering'

National civil servants are primarily affiliated to their own government institution, portfolio and role. These affiliations tend to mould decision-making behaviour and role and identity perceptions because '[t]he routines of attention allocation tend to give priority to those things that are immediate, specific, operational and doable' (March and Olsen 1979: 50). For example, I expect national institutions to influence their civil servants' roles and identities more strongly than EU institutions. The following hypotheses are based on the sociological and cognitive perspectives on organizations and draw on fairly general principles in organizational life.

H1: Bureaucrats from federal polities *are more likely to adopt a supranational role than those from unitary polities*

Federal systems have vested autonomous power at the level of the sub-territories – as in the German *Länder*. Hence, federal systems to a large extent have decentralized the power-base. Moreover, the sub-territories of federations are normally represented at federal level – as in the German *Bundesrat* (Egeberg 2001). Accordingly, civil servants at federal level are accustomed to complex systems of multi-level decision making on the domestic stage (Hooghe 2001: 102). They are thus likely to adapt more easily to the multi-level structure of the EU in general, and within the EU committees in particular. They are inclined to be more supportive of sharing sovereignty across territorial levels and of strengthening supranational powers. Civil servants from unitary states, by contrast, are less familiar with the give-and-take bargaining across governmental tiers on a domestic level. They are therefore likely to be less adaptive to the supranational experience within EU committees than federal civil servants (Beyers and Trondal 2003). The supranational experience is less likely to collide with pre-existing cognitive maps and logics of appropriateness among federal officials than among civil servants from unitary states.

H2: Bureaucrats used to specialized vertical organizational structures *are more likely to adopt sectoral and supranational roles than those used to vertically non-specialized organizational structures*

Generally, integrated and coherent polities are more robust towards external demands and penetration than fragmented and disintegrated polities. H2 postulates that vertically specialized structures are conducive to sectoral and supranational roles and identities among civil servants (Egeberg 2001). Sectoral and functional roles may reflect the vertical organization routing the political signals and demands downward in the hierarchy. Civil servants may therefore act as independent and neutral sectoral experts within EU committees, because they have the leeway to do so. Moreover, the lack of hierarchical control and direction within vertically specialized structures enhances the ability to act independently and adopt *new* supranational allegiances (Beyers and Trondal 2003). Civil servants from lower echelons in the national hierarchy are accustomed to professional autonomy and the appropriateness of role flexibility and freedom of manoeuvre, and are thus inclined to make new supranational allegiances when faced with supranational EU committees.

H3: Bureaucrats from sectoral ministries *are more likely to adopt sectoral and supranational roles than diplomats from the foreign ministry and the permanent representation in Brussels*

Sectoral organizational structures are conducive to the emergence of sectoral roles and identities because civil servants are exposed to sectoralized information, considerations, criteria for success, cues for action, etc. Moreover, the enactment of supranational roles and identities among EU committee participants may be accompanied by a lack of coordination from the foreign ministry. 'Not being reminded of their "national missions" on a daily basis in Brussels, the actors can easily lose sight of the nation-state as their primary locus of loyalty' (Trondal 2002: 473).

H4: The greater the degree of institutional misfit *between national institutions and EU committees, the more likely it is that officials will adopt a supranational role*

H4 argues that institutional misfit across levels of governance causes a perceived adaptational pressure among civil servants for role and identity shift (Cowles *et al.* 2001). Arguably, '[t]he impact of institutional compatibility reflects the compatibility of cognitive shortcuts and scripts' (Trondal 2000: 316) and similar logics of appropriateness (March and Olsen 1995). Institutional incompatibility, or misfit, is likely to challenge existing roles and identities among civil servants, because they are exposed to new sets of information and new situations that render existing roles and identities less relevant. Accordingly, institutional misfit is conducive to supranationalism among national civil servants attending EU committees.

Hypotheses on EU institutional 'mattering'

I want to suggest three propositions on how EU institutions affect civil servants' role and identity perceptions.

H5: Officials attending the ECs *are likely to adopt sectoral roles and allegiances more strongly than civil servants participating in the* CWPs *and the* CCs

In parallel with national sector ministries, the ECs are primarily organized according to a sector principle, as opposed to the CWPs and the CCs, which are principally organized on a territorial principle, mirroring the domestic foreign ministry (see H3). Accordingly, I assume that government officials attending the ECs adopt a sectoral role and identity. In contrast, participation in the CWPs and CCs primarily leads to the emergence of the perception of a national role. On the other hand, all government institutions, including EU committees, are organized according to several principles, and thus pose additional challenges to civil servants to take on several partially conflicting roles. However, I expect EC participants *mainly* to adopt an expert role, and CWP and CC participants *mainly* to emphasize a national role (Egeberg and Trondal 1999).

H6: The longer *national officials have participated in EU committees, the more likely it is that they adopt a supranational role*

According to the sociological institutionalist perspective institutional 'mattering' is subject to time lags. National civil servants first attending EU committees are not likely to become instantly re-socialized. They will probably take on roles and identities that have recently been adopted

(March 1994: 70). As civil servants interact with those from other nationalities and with Commission officials over time, it is likely that they become slowly re-socialized into supranational agents. Accordingly, the longer civil servants have participated in EU committees, the more feasible it is that they have internalized a supranational role.

H7: The more intense the degree of participation *and interaction in EU committees, the more likely it is that officials will take on a supranational role*

Whereas H6 emphasizes the causal effect of time, H7 highlights the causal weight of intensity of interaction to the understanding of supranationalism. Intensive interaction in this context refers to the number of EU committees attended, the number of formal and informal sessions joined, the degree of active involvement during discussions, joining working lunches, etc. Contact theory and small-group theory emphasize the causal importance of face-to-face interaction and contact repetition to understand role and identity change ('t Hart *et al.* 1997; Pettigrew 1998). According to Checkel (1999: 549), '[s]ocial learning is more likely where a group meets repeatedly, and there is a high density of interaction among participants'. Similarly, March (1999: 29) argues that, '[t]he interactive character of decision making extends over time so that the development of beliefs, rules, and expectations in one organization is intertwined with their development in others'.

Summing up the empirical expectations from H1 to H7, I argue that national officials are primarily moulded by national institutions such as the state system (federal or unitary), the horizontal and vertical organization of the national administration, and the degree of institutional fit across levels of governance. National civil servants are thus likely to be more intergovernmentally than supranationally oriented when attending EU committees.

Data and method

The following empirical discussion should not be considered as a finite test of the suggested propositions, but as an empirical illustration. The empirical analysis is therefore not arranged by hypothesis, but according to my twofold template: domestic versus EU institutional 'mattering'. However, I will clearly indicate which hypothesis is being examined. The data surveyed are partly based on a growing body of research on EU committees and partly on my own empirical research on EU committees. Most studies of EU committees are of a legalistic, descriptive and historical nature, mainly focusing on the comitology committees. I draw primarily on studies of EU committees that are based on interviews and surveys of the participants – covering most EU member states, as well as countries on the periphery of the Union (such as Norway). I also cover several subject areas – social policy, environmental policy, transport policy, etc. – as well as the ECs, CWPs and CCs.

Empirical illustrations

Domestic institutional 'mattering'

Beyers and Trondal (2003) compare Belgian and Swedish civil servants attending the CWPs and demonstrate how diverse national institutional arrangements result in different degrees of supranationalist orientation among these officials. It appears that Belgian officials are more supranationally oriented than Swedish officials, because of (1) the vertical and horizontal (sector) specialization of the Belgian government apparatus, (2) the federal state structure, (3) the large number of competing veto-points in the Belgian polity, (4) the great number of actors involved in national coordination who challenge the role of the foreign ministry, and (5) the lack of trust in national government compared to a high degree of trust in the EU. These observations support H1 (federalism versus unitary state), H2 and H3 (vertical and horizontal specialization of the administrative apparatus).

An early study by Scheinman and Feld (1972: 133) substantiated the causal weight of their domestic institutions in the moulding of the identities of national EU committee participants. Only recently, however, have academics begun investigating the many facets of EU committee decision making. A comparative study of civil servants from the transport ministries of five small EU member states highlights the importance of national institutions, as the primary locus of identification and role orientation (Egeberg 1999). Trondal (2002) also demonstrates that the vertical organization of the national bureaucracy matters (H2). Officials employed at agency level, below ministry level, adopt stronger sectoral allegiances than officials at ministry level. These studies also demonstrate that officials attending the CWPs take on a stronger national role than those attending the ECs. This observation partly reflects the fact that the CWP participants are more closely coordinated by their foreign ministry, which provides them with written mandates and instructions, than the EC participants (H3) (Beyers and Trondal 2003). Furthermore, Trondal (2003) demonstrates through regression analysis that anticipated career prospects do not explain civil servants' supranational orientations.

Studies also support the hypothesis on institutional fit and misfit (H4). Illustrating institutional misfit, Egeberg (1999) demonstrates that civil servants from sector ministries, particularly those attending the CWPs and CCs, are being challenged to take up new territorial roles. This observation is also supported by Jacobsson (1999), who shows that Swedish civil servants from sector ministries became increasingly aware of their national role after entering the Council system. The Swedish EU membership spurred a demand for coordinated Swedish positions among sector experts, and thereby challenged their pre-existing (sectoral) role orientations. Substantiating institutional fit, Trondal (2001) reveals that officials from the foreign ministries and from the permanent representations attending the CWPs and the COREPER (Committee of Permanent Representatives) primarily adopt a national role orientation. Due to institutional fit between the foreign ministry/permanent representation and the Council structure, the officials are *not* being challenged to change roles, but sustain and strengthen existing ones.

EU institutional 'mattering'

H5 goes beyond the EU membership/non-membership distinction by underlining the many facets of EU committee decision making. Trondal and Veggeland (2003) maintain that Norwegian and Swedish officials attending the ECs adopt fairly *similar* roles – national, functional and supranational (in order of importance). The ECs, however, have a stronger functional dynamic than both the CWPs and the CCs. Egeberg (1999) shows that CWPs are mainly intergovernmental institutions, leading officials to take on national roles and identities more than functional and supranational ones. Similar observations are made for the CCs. The ECs are revealed as having stronger functional dynamics – associated with independent expert roles among the participants (Egeberg 1999). Moreover, the fact that EU committees are organized according to several principles coincides with elements of intergovernmentalism *and* functionalism within all three classes of committee. However, supranational dynamics are stronger in the CWPs than in the other committees. Given the fact that the CWPs are also strongly intergovernmental, they seem to embody the coexistence of multiple conflicting dynamics. This may partly reflect the fact that these roles are crosscutting and of different relevance in different situations.

Over-simplistic pictures of EU committee decision making, provided for example by approaches like Wessels's fusion thesis (1998), are hereby rejected empirically. Furthermore, whereas Joerges and Neyer (1997) locate deliberative rationalism within the CCs, I underscore the many facets of EU committee decision making (H5). The CCs and the CWPs are primarily intergovernmental institutions, promoting territorial roles and allegiances among the participants. The emphasis on expert knowledge and the promotion of the 'common European good' is stronger among officials taking part in the ECs than among CC participants (Christiansen and Kirchner 2000: 8).

EU committees are sites of re-socialization towards supranational decision making. Processes of re-socialization are particularly seen among permanent representatives on temporary relocation to Brussels, and markedly so among those who interact within COREPER I and II (Lewis 1998). Intensive face-to-face interaction results in a club-like atmosphere, an *esprit de corps*, and a consensus reflex among the participants (H7) (Lewis 1998). Moreover, they develop allegiances to the EU committees more extensively than to the EU as a whole (Lewis 1998; Verdun 2000: 140). We thus witness the emergence of several small supranational 'clubs' within and around the EU committees – particularly in COREPER and the 250 CWPs (Fouilleux *et al.* forthcoming).

'The members of COREPER [and the CWPs] ... have dual tugs of loyalty' that are quite unusual in international organizations (Hayes-Renshaw and Wallace 1997: 81). As indicated, national officials have two functions: they are representatives of their member state as well as ambassadors of the EU to their own country (Lewis 1998: 483). This results in a continuous tension felt by many national 'Eurocrats' and reflects their dual institutional embeddedness in the national *and* the EU scene. According to Lewis (1998: 484), COREPER is an arena where member states develop and internalize new ways of articulating, defending and representing their self-interests. Despite the Council being primarily an intergovernmental institution, some segments of the Council structure are more supranationally oriented than others (the 'clubs'). This is particularly the case among permanent representatives, especially those of the country which holds the Presidency and those who interact frequently with people of nationalities other than their own (Hayes-Renshaw and Wallace 1997: 236; Lewis 1998). We can thus talk about a cognitive shift among some national civil servants, where 'the cognitive boundaries between the two levels have become blurred' (Lewis 1998: 500). A similar supranational shift is observed among civil servants attending the CWPs and the ECs, although more clearly in the former than in the latter (Egeberg 1999).

Studies also indicate stronger cognitive than affective changes towards supranationalism among European elites (Kerr 1973). Actors, for example, acquire greater knowledge about EU institutions and decision-making processes without developing a greater sense of loyalty to them. Changes in cognitive orientation, however, may be a prerequisite for future changes in affective orientation (Egeberg 1999: 466). These changes are mostly due to the intensity of interaction in the EU institutions (H7). Less support is found for the assumed effect of length of participation at EU level (H6).

According to Mitrany, functional loyalties would arise from experience of international cooperation generally. Research indicates that this is not a universal truth, but an insight that is valid for international and supranational organizations which are organized sectorally (for example the ECs). Ernest Haas also assumed that elite interaction within the Community institutions would be followed by elite learning and re-socialization into a community spirit at the expense of national loyalties. This study indicates that the emergence of supranational allegiances does not come at the expense of national allegiances.

Some researchers have asked if supranationalism is the result of *pre*-socialization at national level, and thus evidence of national institutional 'pre-packaging' rather than of *re*-socialization at EU level. Examples of self-selected supranationalists are observed mostly in the COREPER (Lewis 1998). In the ECs, CWPs and CCs there are fewer indications of self-selection that could indicate pre-socialization at national level. This does not mean, however, that supranationalism may not have national origins (see above).

Conclusion and comparative assessments

This chapter has challenged the current intergovernmental/neo-functionalist divide in European integration research by introducing a middle-range institutionalist account of EU committee decision making. Building bridges across this divide also implies going beyond a 'pure' rationalist and realist approach. I conceive of decision making both as processes of aggregating preferences and as those instances where preferences, roles and identities are created and discovered. National government officials who interact in EU committees are multiply embedded with multiple roles and identities. Because several roles and identities crosscut each other, they are activated under different institutional conditions. Functional roles and identities are adopted in vertically specialized organizations (H2), in ministries organized by function or sector (H3), and in the ECs (H5). Supranational roles and allegiances are taken on primarily in federal polities (H1), in vertically specialized governments (H2), in sector ministries (H3), and also at the permanent representations in Brussels, due to the intensity of participation in the EU committees (H7). H6 on the length of participation in EU committees was not empirically supported.

Few international organizations have created an executive branch with a strong functional and supranational autonomy. Most are structured primarily according to territory, with a fairly weak secretariat and a parliamentary assembly without an independent supranational mandate. Moreover, few international organizations have institutionalized a committee system that integrates external expertise and national civil servants to the same extent as the EU. Accordingly, the degree of interaction between community institutions and national administrations is stronger in the EU than in traditional intergovernmental organizations. This also implies that degrees of institutional fit and misfit across levels of governance have potentially greater implications in the EU than elsewhere. To sum up then, there are stronger functional and supranational dynamics, and there is stronger 'multi-levelness', within the EU than in intergovernmental organizations such as the UN, NATO and the WTO.

There is however evidence of institutional transformation within intergovernmental organizations. For example, studies of collective identities show that intergovernmental organizations such as NATO have contributed to changing images of national and democratic identities in Central and Eastern Europe in the 1990s, through a combination of mechanisms such as teaching and persuasion (Gheciu 2002). The European Council has also diffused norms that ultimately contributed to identity shifts in the former Soviet Union (Checkel 1999). Furthermore, Lerdell and Sahlin-Andersson (1997) reveal that the public management service of the Organization for Economic Cooperation and Development contributes to a partial convergence of the participants' world-views and conceptions of valid problems and solutions. Intergovernmental organizations are thus more than 'empty vessels that simply reduce transaction costs', but contribute to change in actors' preferences, cognitive maps and identity perceptions (Checkel 1998: 331). However, studies of the EU are currently more advanced than studies of other international organizations with regard to outlining, theorizing and empirically testing middle-range (operational) hypotheses on institutional 'mattering'.

Notes

1 The financial support of Agder University College and Sørlandets Kompetansefond (http://www.kompetansefond.com/) is gratefully acknowledged. Thanks to Elisabeth Griffiths and Annemarie Weitzel for improving my English.

2 The emergence of multiple roles and identities may reflect ill-coordinated processes. New roles and identities may be adopted without removing old ones, old identities and roles may be removed without adopting new ones, or the mix of and balance between existing identities and roles may simply be reorganized. From a sociological institutionalist perspective it may be easier to adopt new roles and identities than to remove old ones. According to the cognitive perspective, however, the mix of roles and identities is likely to be institutionally-contingent and efficient.

References

Alderson, K. (2001) 'Making Sense of State Socialization', *Review of International Studies*, 27(3): 415–33.

Barnett, M. (1993) 'Institutions, Roles, and Disorder: The Case of the Arab States System', *International Studies Quarterly*, 37(3): 271–96.

Barnett, M. and Finnemore, M. (1999) 'The Politics, Power, and Pathologies of International Organizations', *International Organization*, 53(4): 699–733.

Beyers, J. and Trondal, J. (2003) 'How Nation-States "Hit" Europe. Ambiguity and Representation in the European Union', Paper prepared for the Eighth Biennial International Conference, European Union Studies Association, March 27–29, Nashville, Tennessee.

Biersteker, T.J. (1999) 'Locating the Emerging European Polity: Beyond States or State?', in J.J. Anderson (ed.) *Regional Integration and Democracy*, Lanham: Rowman & Littlefield, 21–43.

Börzel, T.A. and Risse, T. (2000) 'When Europe Hits Home: Europeanization and Domestic Change', *European Integration online Papers (EIoP)*, 4; available: http://eiop.or.at/eiop/texte/2000–015a.htm.

Checkel, J.T. (1998) 'The Constructivist Turn in International Relations Theory', *World Politics*, 50(2): 324–48.

—— (1999) 'Social Construction and Integration', *Journal of European Public Policy*, 6(4): 545–60.

Christiansen, T. and Kirchner, E. (eds) (2000) *Europe in Change. Committee Governance in the European Union*, Manchester: Manchester University Press.

Cowles, M.G., Caporaso, J. and Risse, T. (2001) *Transforming Europe: Europeanization and Domestic Change*, Ithaca: Cornell University Press.

Egeberg, M. (1999) 'Transcending Intergovernmentalism? Identity and Role Perceptions of National Officials in EU Decision-Making', *Journal of European Public Policy*, 6(3): 456–74.

—— (2001) 'How Federal? The Organisational Dimension of Integration in the EU (and Elsewhere)', *Journal of European Public Policy*, 8(5): 728–46.

Egeberg, M. and Trondal, J. (1999) 'Differentiated Integration in Europe: The Case of the EEA Country Norway', *Journal of Common Market Studies*, 37(1): 133–42.

Eulau, H. (1959) 'The Role of the Representative: Some Empirical Observations on the Theory of Edmund Burke', *American Political Science Review*, 53(3): 742–56.

Fouilleux, E., Smith, A. and Maillard, J. (forthcoming) 'Council Working Groups: Their Role in the Production of European Problems and Policies', in G.F. Schaefer (ed.) *Governance by Committee. The Role of Committees in European Policy-Making and Policy Implementation*, Maastricht: European Institute of Public Administration.

Gheciu, A. (2002) 'NATO and the Construction of Liberal-Democratic Identities in Post-Cold War Central and East European Countries', in *Europe Transformed? The European Union and Collective Identity Change*, ARENA/IDNET International Policy Conference, Oslo, 11 October.

Hayes-Renshaw, F. and Wallace, H. (1997) *The Council of Ministers*, New York: St. Martin's Press.

Hooghe, L. (2001) *The European Commission and the Integration of Europe. Images of Governance*, Cambridge: Cambridge University Press.

Jacobsson, B. (1999) 'Europeisering ock statens omvandling', in K. Goldman (ed) *Politikens internationalisering*, Lund: Studentliteratur: 103–24.

Joerges, C. and Neyer, J. (1997) 'From Intergovernmental Bargaining to Deliberative Political Processes: The Constitutionalisation of Comitology', *European Law Journal*, 3(3): 273–99.

Kerr Jr., H.H. (1973) 'Changing Attitudes through International Participation: European Parliamentarians and Integration', *International Organization*, 27(1): 45–83.

Lerdell, D. and Sahlin-Andersson, K. (1997) *Att lära över gränser. En studie av OECD:s förvaltningspolitiska samarbete*, Stockholm: Svenska Offentliga Utredningar, 33.

Lewis, J. (1998) 'Is the "Hard Bargaining" Image of the Council Misleading? The Committee of Permanent Representatives and the Local Elections Directive', *Journal of Common Market Studies*, 36(4): 479–504.

March, J.G. (1994) *A Primer on Decision Making. How Decisions Happen*, New York: The Free Press.

—— (1999) *The Pursuit of Organizational Intelligence*, Massachusetts: Blackwell Business.

March, J.G. and Olsen, J.P. (1979) *Ambiguity and Choice in Organizations*, 2nd edn, Oslo: Universitetsforlaget.
—— (1994) 'Institutional Perspectives on Governance', in *Systemrationalität und Partialinteresse: Festschrift für Renate Mayntz / Hans-Ulrich Derlien*. Baden-Baden: Nomos, 249–70.
—— (1995) *Democratic Governance*, New York: The Free Press.
Pettigrew, T.F. (1998) 'Intergroup Contact Theory', *Annual Review of Psychology*, 49(1): 65–85.
Radaelli, C.M. (1999) *Technocracy in the European Union*, London: Longman.
Scheinman, L. and Feld, W. (1972) 'The European Economic Community and National Civil Servants of the Member States', *International Organization*, 26(2): 121–35.
Schneider, G. and Aspinwall, M. (eds) (2001) *The Rules of Integration. Institutionalist Approaches to the Study of Europe*, Manchester: Manchester University Press.
't Hart, P., Stern, E. and Sundelius, B. (1997) *Beyond Groupthink*, Ann Arbor: The University of Michigan Press.
Trondal, J. (2000) 'Multiple Institutional Embeddedness in Europe: The Case of Danish, Norwegian and Swedish Government Officials', *Scandinavian Political Studies*, 23(4): 311–42.
—— (2001) 'Is there any Social Constructivist – Institutionalist Divide? Unpacking Social Mechanisms affecting Representational Roles among EU Decision-Makers', *Journal of European Public Policy*, 8(1): 1–23.
—— (2002) 'Beyond the EU Membership – Non-Membership Dichotomy? Supranational Identities among National EU Decision-Makers', *Journal of European Public Policy*, 9(3): 468–87.
—— (2003) 'EU Committees as Sites of Europeanisation', Kristiansand: *Centre for European Studies Working Paper*, 2/03.
Trondal, J. and Veggeland, F. (2003) 'Access, Voice and Loyalty: The Representation of Domestic Civil Servants in EU Committees', *Journal of European Public Policy*, 10(1): 65–83.
Verdun, A. (2000) 'Governing by Committee: The Case of Monetary Policy', in T. Christiansen and E. Kirchner (eds) *Europe in Change. Committee Governance in the European Union*, Manchester: Manchester University Press, 132–44.
Wendt, A. (1994) 'Collective Identity Formation and the International State', *American Political Science Review*, 88(2): 384–96.
Wessels, W. (1998) 'Comitology: Fusion in Action. Politico-Administrative Trends in the EU System', *Journal of European Public Policy*, 5(2): 209–34.

Part VI

Policy windows

10 Sanctions in reaction to human rights violations

The impact of non-state actors on EU decision making

Hadewych Hazelzet

Introduction

In this chapter I analyse the conditions under which non-state actors (NSAs) have influenced European Union (EU) sanctions in reaction to human rights violations from 1989 to 2000. With the end of the Cold War, sanctions have become an often-used tool in a variety of cases that go beyond 'soft' politics. In fact, sanctions are one of the few foreign policy instruments at the disposal of the EU. The intricate mechanics of EU decision making on sanctions, however, are not well documented. Moreover, not much is known about the impact of NSAs on EU decision making in the area of foreign policy. Not-for-profit NSAs are well organized in the field of human rights and can therefore be expected to influence EU reactions to human rights violations, whereas profit-making NSAs can often be expected to have specific interests in preventing the imposition of economic or financial sanctions.

I will first outline how testable propositions can be derived from main approaches to international relations. Second, I will sketch the EU decision-making process on sanctions and the role of the various actors involved. Third, I will describe general NSA activity in the field of sanctions and human rights, and analyse its potential influence on EU decisions between 1989 and 2000 of whether or not, and if so, how, to react to human rights violations. Fourth, I will analyse the role of NSAs in one particular case, the Kimberley process, which resulted in an international certification system with regard to so-called 'conflict diamonds'. To begin with, however, a matter of definition is appropriate. I use the term *non-state actors* rather than *non-governmental organizations* (NGOs) in order to include both not-for-profit and profit-making actors.

Hypotheses

Theories of international relations differ in the potential impact they see for actors other than nation-states on the international system. They also differ in their assessment of the role of human rights in international relations. For (neo-)realism, the influence of NSAs on states can only be marginal. Realism dismisses human rights talk as mere rhetoric and provides an interest-based explanation. Traditionally brushed aside as belonging to the realm of 'low politics', human rights concerns will not prevail over security or economic interests. Liberal institutionalism has a more pluralist notion of international relations and explains the outcome of interactions between states as that of a struggle between a plurality of interest-driven actors with varying power resources (Moravcsik 1995; Kahler 1997). When trying to influence governmental decision making NSAs can be among the influential actors. Liberalism is more optimistic about possible cooperation between states, since international institutions and international law alter the costs and benefits of cooperation. In this light, variations in EU reactions to human rights violations could be explained by pointing to the varying degree of institutionalization. For instance, an increase in 'veto points' or potential breaches of agreement due to legal impediments to imposing sanctions could delay and complicate decision making. NSA access to, and therefore influence on, decision making would vary per institution and per issue.

Constructivism refuses to take interests as given and points to the emergence of a consensual norm through discourse and advocacy networks. Norms are not necessarily traded off against interests, because norms precede and constitute interests (Finnemore 1996; Klotz 1996; Risse *et al.* 1999). Hence, the increased use of the sanctions instrument could be explained by an increased acceptance of the norm of universal human rights. In this view the norm is part of the identity construction of modern democratic states. Indeed, by becoming a matter of principle human rights become 'high politics', affirming the liberal-democratic identity of states as opposed to the pariah status of those violating human rights. While not denying that states are pivotal actors in international relations, it points to the potential for non-state actors ('advocacy coalitions') to frame issues in such a way that states begin to perceive them as being in their interest (Keck and Sikkink 1998). The better NSAs manage to frame issues in line with states' interest perceptions, the more influential they can be.

The theories discussed above make causal claims about international relations rather than foreign policy. Therefore, any proposition derived from these claims is difficult to measure or verify. In order to unravel the potential impact of NSAs on EU decision making, it is necessary to formulate specific claims about the conditions under which NSAs are more or less likely to influence this decision making. In addition, their role in the decision-making *process* may be as important as their influence on the final *outcome* (Tieleman 2002). I hypothesize that the following factors could determine NSA influence on international decision making: the nature of the issue, access to the relevant actors, timing and power resources.

The power of EU institutions depends to a large extent on the issue at stake. Although the *European Parliament* would be most receptive to NSA input on human rights, it is formally the least powerful actor in this field. Agency theory focuses very much on the role of the *Commission* in the decision-making process, probably because most empirical studies have focused on regulatory, or first pillar, issues. The Commission (as an 'agent') has the right of initiative for second pillar, or foreign policy, issues, but acts very much under the control of the *Council* (representing the 'principals'). Verbeek (1998: 21) argues that the agent has more room for manoeuvre to influence policy outcomes: (1) the larger the number of principals (in this case the Council of the EU and its member states); (2) if unanimity is required (a coalition with one principal would therefore suffice to block decision making); and (3) the more asymmetrical the information distribution (the agent has more expert knowledge than the principal). At first sight, decision making on sanctions fulfils these conditions, albeit only during one stage of the process.

I will argue below that once the Council has decided whether it will react to human rights violations, the Commission has a more important role to play in the decision-making process. NSA influence thus depends on the type of decision they want to influence and, consequently, on which actor they gain access to, and at which stage of the decision-making process. I expect NSAs to be able to lobby the Commission with more ease than the Council, since the Commission speaks with one voice, whereas the Council consists of 15 member states. Potential NSA influence is further complicated by the fact that unanimity is required for the initial decision to impose sanctions. I thus expect that NSAs have more influence on the 'how' (Commission) than on the 'whether' (Council).

Potential NSA influence could also depend on the relative strength and power resources of NSAs *vis-à-vis* other NSAs, EU institutions and member states. According to Arts (1998: 266), NSA influence increases: (1) the better the quality of their interventions, (2) the more similar their demands to the aims of the principal, and (3) the higher the principal's dependency on NSA input. Hence, NSA influence will be greater the more coherent, well coordinated, and well documented their input, especially if decision makers depend on the information provided by NSAs. NSA influence will also be greater if they have means to pressure governments, for instance through large-scale campaigns and public shaming.

The EU decision-making process on sanctions

Three levels of decision making on sanctions can be discerned: the United Nations (UN) level, the EU level and the national level. The relative openness of EU institutions to outside influence depends to a large extent on formal voting procedures and competence in the area according to the Treaty. Since the Single European Act (1987), reinforced by the

Maastricht and Amsterdam Treaties, as well as several judgements of the European Court of Justice, sanctions have been coordinated at European level. As a matter of Community law, the European Community (EC) is responsible for the implementation of UN sanctions (Article 307 of the EC Treaty). Such legislation takes the form of Regulations by the Council and the Commission (decided upon by qualified majority vote, QMV), which are directly applicable within the EC as a whole.

Sanctions are an area in which foreign policy and commercial relations overlap (see for an overview and analysis of EU sanctions Hazelzet 2001). This means that *policy reasons* for action fall outside Community (i.e. Commission) competence. They are a matter of foreign and security policy (second pillar). Hence, prior consensus of the Council (unanimity) is required under the Common Foreign and Security Policy (CFSP) pillar. However, the *means of achieving that policy*, including an interruption, or reduction, of economic relations, fall within Community competence, requiring QMV by the Council (first pillar). Thus, the Commission's right of initiative for most types of sanctions and its expertise are its main powers – but only once the Council has decided whether it wants to react by means of sanctions. The Council also takes the ultimate decision on the type of sanctions.

Financial and economic sanctions, including on raw materials such as diamonds or oil, or flight bans, are covered by Articles 60, 133 and 301 of the Treaty on the European Union (TEU), following the adoption of a Common Position (unanimity). A visa ban also needs a Common Position. Sports relations are very much regulated by national associations and fall to a large extent outside the authority of the EU and its member states. The withdrawal of trade preferences (QMV) is regulated by Council Regulation 2586/2002 on the General System of Trade Preferences (GSP). The procedure for imposing arms embargoes is slightly more complicated and is in practice covered by TEU Articles 296 and 301 (unanimity). Decisions to (partially) suspend development aid depend on the agreement with the country in question and, on the part of the EU, are taken by QMV.

The formal role of the European Parliament (EP) is limited to its right of assent to the conclusion of trade and cooperation as well as association agreements. Before giving its assent, the EP has in the past very much insisted on the insertion of human rights clauses in such agreements. It can request that the Council allows the EP to give its opinion on proposals for a Council decision taken on the basis of Article 133, but this opinion is not binding on the Council. While controlling the budget for the European Initiative for Democracy and Human Rights (EIDHR), the EP does not hold the purse strings of the European Development Funds, since these funds are not part of the Community budget. The EP does play an important role in keeping the Commission and the Council alert to human rights issues. This is done through written and verbal parliamentary questions, debates in key committees or plenary sessions, and the adoption of resolutions.

This dispersed and complicated process of deciding on sanctions in practice means that it is extremely difficult for NSAs to influence the outcome of EU decision making.

NSA influence on EU decision making

What influence have NSAs had on EU sanctions decisions in the past decade? I will first discuss the role NSAs have played in the international discourse on sanctions, and then, in more depth, in the Kimberley process. The analysis of NSA influence on sanctions is based on over a hundred interviews conducted for a study on EU reactions to almost two hundreds cases of human rights violations from 1989 to 2000 (Hazelzet 2001).

From blunt to smart sanctions

In the past decade a change in the transnational discourse on sanctions has altered international decision making. What caused this change in discourse? First of all, research repeatedly pointed out that sanctions had not reached their goal in more than 30 per cent of cases (Hufbauer *et al.* 1990). The effectiveness of sanctions thus became disputed. Second, the humanitarian effects of the sanctions against Iraq created doubts about whether sanctions were the 'peaceful, silent remedy' which Woodrow Wilson had envisioned at the beginning of this century (for effects of sanctions on target state's populations see Hazelzet 1998). Former UN Secretary General Boutros Boutros-Ghali, in his 'Agenda for Peace' (1995), acknowledged that sanctions are 'a blunt instrument' that may impose hardships on a civilian population that are disproportionate to likely political gains (A/50/60-S/1995/1, 3 January 1995). On the other hand, the principle that respect for human rights is not just essential to liberal democracies but universal, and the position that violations cannot go unanswered, became virtually undisputed in the Western world. Politicians and business(wo)men alike felt the pressure from their constituents to pay more than lip service to human rights. Trade measures were indeed increasingly used in the 1990s to enforce broader foreign policy goals. Whereas before the UN had imposed sanctions twice (on Southern Rhodesia in 1966 and South Africa in 1977), in the 1990s it imposed them on at least 16 countries (Hazelzet 2001: 64).

Human rights advocates and business groups were left in a difficult position. Human rights advocates were resolved to act, yet reluctant to accept the side effects of the measures proposed. Business alliances, in a similar vein, were reluctant to accept the consequences of their engagement rhetoric and commit to substantial and independently monitored codes of conduct. However, while the business community's interests were served by the argument that increased, rather than reduced, commerce improved respect for human rights, human rights advocates saw themselves deprived of an important means through which to pressure authoritarian regimes. Two concepts aimed to resolve these diverging concerns and interests. The concept of 'constructive engagement' sought to combine elements of negative pressure with stimuli for positive change. Furthermore, the discourse and policy of sanctions changed from indiscriminate, or *blunt*, sanctions to targeted, or *smart*, sanctions.

Human rights advocates

Whilst strong in the field of human rights in general, NSAs appear to be weak when it comes to their proposals on *how to react* to human rights violations. The instrument of economic sanctions has caused major debates within NSAs. Many consider that, with globalization and increased interdependency, trade measures are an important tool for enforcing human rights policies (Keck and Sikkink 1998: 23; 201). Simultaneously, human rights advocates were also the first to lament the harsh impact on the populations of target states. They recognized that sanctions violated the social and economic rights of an already vulnerable population.

The aim of many advocates, such as Amnesty International (AI), is to expose human rights abuses rather than advocate specific policy responses, and they tend to build up a feeling that 'something should be done'. When push comes to shove, however, they lack a coherent and explicit stance on what that 'something' should be, albeit that the imposition of negative measures is often implied. Others, such as Human Rights Watch (HRW), after much internal debate, arrived at explicit stances on sanctions but judged them on a case-by-case basis using a list of criteria (see the testimony for US Congress, 8 September 1998, by HRW executive director Kenneth Roth). Instead of exerting pressure on governments, an increasing number of NGOs focus on multinational enterprises and demand withdrawal of their investments from countries violating human rights, combined with the introduction of ethical codes of conduct.

In a number of concrete sanction cases, such as Turkey,[1] the Ivory Coast, Togo and Niger, the Commission is said to have been approached by human rights advocates, albeit usually not in a coordinated manner and often *in situ* rather than in Brussels. This mainly took the form of providing evidence of human rights violations and pressuring for some sort of reaction from the EU, without specifying what type of reaction was required. In other cases human rights advocates were more explicit in their demands, such as with regard to Burma, Nigeria and China. However, none of the officials interviewed, either from the EU or the member states, had the impression that human rights advocates made a decisive impact on the ultimate decision of *how* to react to violations. One area in which human rights advocates have been very vocal and active is that of the arms trade. They lobbied heavily for a European code of conduct, but do not seem to have influenced the imposition of any particular arms embargo.

In the 1990s trade unions played a specific role in defending labour rights. Together with HRW and AI they were lobbying for the insertion of a human rights clause in EU trade and cooperation agreements. The International Confederation of Free Trade Unions (ICFTU) had an important part in filing complaints against Burma and Pakistan, which led to the withdrawal of trade preferences for Burma (Brandtner and Rosas 1998: 715; Hazelzet 2001: 86–7). The GSP regulation provides for a consultation mechanism with NSAs to this end. Despite this partial success, the enormous amount of paperwork required to file complaints discouraged the ICFTU from taking up other cases. According to one interviewee, the decision to lobby the EU to react to violations of labour rights depended on available funds, the likelihood of success, threats to affiliates in the target country, and the degree of human rights violations. The ICFTU found its efforts were most successful for targets with few allies within the EU.

Business coalitions

Within the business community opinions and interests with regard to sanctions diverge. The extra-territorial reach of US legislation rallied many more business lobbies against the unilateral use of sanctions by the EU than EU sanctions themselves have ever done, with a few exceptions. Businesses have tried to influence EU decision making on oil embargoes in a number of cases (Nigeria, Sudan, Libya), as well as on investment bans, flight bans and, more generally, EU reactions to the human rights situation in China. Feeling increased international pressure, the international banking community to an important extent influenced the development of financial sanctions.

In sharp contrast to their American counterparts, European companies do not seem to be that well organized or experienced in lobbying in this field. At the level of member states, companies concentrate on ministries of economic affairs, finance or defence rather than foreign affairs (the final decision maker on sanctions). Some approach members of their national parliaments, which in most countries have even less influence on final EU decision making. Companies mostly see it as the role of ambassadors to take their interests into account.

Many attempts at influencing occur at an informal level, which makes it difficult to unravel. One way of measuring the extent to which companies' interests are taken into account in EU decision making on sanctions is by assessing the extent to which the EU has been reluctant to impose sanctions on countries of greater economic importance. A statistical analysis of all EU cases for the years 1989–2000, controlling for economic interests, found that the severity of EU measures was dependent on the degree of human rights violations rather than on economic interests (Hazelzet 2001: 200–5). This is partly explained by the fact that the EU's most important trading partners are liberal democracies and therefore less likely to be potential targets of sanctions. Breaking down economic interests to the level of the member states shows that in the past certain member states have put profits before principles, at European level.[2]

Conflict diamonds: NSA impact on the Kimberley process

Diamonds from conflict areas have recently become subject to international import restrictions, because profits derived from diamond sales served to buy weapons and therefore prolonged conflicts in Africa. How have NSAs influenced the coming into being, content, and final outcome of the so-called Kimberley process that eventually led to a certification scheme for diamonds? And how did this influence differ from NSA influence on other EU decisions to impose sanctions?

Global Witness (GW), a London-based NGO focusing attention on how natural resources can fuel conflicts, has been particularly instrumental in the initiation of the Kimberley process (www.globalwitness.org/campaings/diamonds/). It started its research on the lack of corporate accountability in the international diamond trade in Angola in 1996. The publication of its report *A Rough Trade* in December 1998 marked the beginning of international attention on the link between trade in diamonds and continuing conflicts and human rights abuses. Its briefing to the UN Security Council in January 1998 led to the appointment of special ambassador R.R. Fowler. The Security Council imposed sanctions on Angola in June 1998 (UN Security Council Resolution 1176 of 24 June 1998). Fowler's first report on UNITA sanctions, published in July 1999 (S/1999/644), drew a lot of international attention.

In October 1999 GW, together with other organizations, launched Fatal Transactions, an alliance between various NGOs, to raise international public awareness and to call for a consumer boycott of conflict diamonds. Two days later De Beers, which controls the lion's share of world trade in diamonds, announced an embargo on the purchase of all diamonds from Angola and claimed to be reviewing its buying operations in the Democratic Republic of Congo and in Guinea. Other NGOs actively supported the process. Physicians for Human Rights launched The Campaign to Eliminate Conflict Diamonds, which is a coalition of human rights, religious, humanitarian, peace and development groups. The alliance against conflict diamonds soon included over 180 organizations worldwide.

The report *The Heart of the Matter: Sierra Leone, Diamonds and Human Security*, published by Partnership Africa Canada (PAC) in January 2000, marked the second crucial step towards an international ban on conflict diamonds. Until then the diamond industry, dominated by a very few players, had denied that conflict diamonds were an issue. The wide publicity of the PAC report, however, forced it to cooperate in the Kimberley process and to show the public its determination to guarantee clean diamonds (K. Shove, 'Trading diamonds for Guns', www.idrc.ca, 22 October 2001).

The final Fowler report was published shortly afterwards, in March 2000 (UN document S/2000/1125). Subsequently, US Congress held a hearing in May 2000 with representatives from major diamond traders as well as human rights advocates.[3] These hearings led directly to the first Kimberley process meeting in June. For that meeting, GW and AI produced studies challenging the diamond industry to present practical solutions to the illicit trade in diamonds. The Kimberley process negotiations, chaired by South Africa, brought together representatives from the EU and from producer and trading countries, as well as from the diamond industry and civil society. Exporters of 'clean' diamonds, such as Canada and South Africa, were very active in this process, keen as they were to distinguish their 'clean' diamonds from 'dirty' ones.

Following the PAC study and an open letter from a coalition of NGOs, the UN Security Council in July 2000 adopted Resolution 1306, prohibiting all states from directly or indirectly importing rough diamonds from Sierra Leone. The Council held a first-ever public hearing, chaired by ambassador A.K. Chowdhury, chair of the Security Council committee on Sierra Leone, and attended by representatives of member states, business and NGOs. That same month the World Diamond Council (WDC) was created, including representatives of producers, manufacturers, traders, diamond companies and civil society. Its mandate was to develop, implement and oversee a tracking system for the export and import of rough diamonds, to prevent the exploitation of diamonds for illicit purposes such as war and inhumane acts. Following the reports of the panel of experts on Sierra Leone in December 2000 (S/2000/1195), legislation was proposed to eliminate the trade in 'conflict diamonds' and to ban their import into the United States in January 2001. NGOs welcomed the initiative, but questioned whether it went far enough and started a consumer campaign on St Valentine's Day against buying conflict diamonds. The threat of a consumer boycott was a particularly powerful weapon in the hands of NGOs. AI USA run campaigns 'say "no" to conflict diamonds' and 'did someone die for that diamond?'. World Vision run a campaign 'Dying for a diamond? So are thousands of innocent children'. A network of 'clean' jewellery stores was subsequently created.

In April 2001, the report of the expert panel on the illegal exploitation of natural resources and other forms of wealth in the Democratic Republic of Congo called for sanctions on countries and individuals involved in illegal activities, including the diamond trade, singling out Burundi, Rwanda, Uganda and Zimbabwe (S/2001/357). In May the Security Council extended prohibitions on the import of diamonds to Liberia.

Meanwhile the Kimberley process continued its course, with meetings in Namibia, Angola, Canada, Britain and Russia. During this process the European Commission was very keen to negotiate on behalf of EU member states (on the basis of Article 133), something that was at times fiercely opposed by some of the main European countries involved in the diamond trade. Shortly before the expected adoption of the regulation, a link was alleged to exist between the financing of al-Qa'eda and the illicit trade in diamonds. The Kimberley process was already well under way and indeed in its final phase, and it seems unlikely that it would have stopped even without this alleged link between the diamond trade and financing terrorism.

While continuing their input and participation in the process, human rights advocates found themselves increasingly sidelined by the business community and state representatives, who were seeking to establish a monitoring mechanism that did not fulfil the strict standards urged upon them. The certification scheme, concluded on 5 November 2002 in Interlaken, Switzerland, sought to regulate the trade in diamonds by establishing guidelines and certificates for rough diamonds. From January 2003 diamond-producing countries were obliged to issue certificates proving that gems came from legitimate mines. Exporting countries failing to respect the certification scheme will be prevented from selling diamonds and risk international sanctions. Consequently, and after some thorny negotiations, the EU Council adopted a Regulation implementing the Kimberley process certification scheme for the international trade in rough diamonds (Doc. 15328/02, 16 December 2002).

According to NGOs, the final outcome of the Kimberley process was 'like a Christmas tree without lights' (*IRIN News*, Johannesburg, 6 November 2002). Ian Smillie, one of the authors of the PAC study, recalled that 'the one thing governments rejected was the one thing NGOs had insisted on from the start: regular, independent monitoring of all national diamond control mechanisms' (www.idrc.ca, 7 June 2002). According to Adotei Akwei, a senior negotiator for AI USA, 'the NGOs never had much power. We were allowed at the table but were seldom diners' (www.aiusa/amnestynow/diamonds). Despite this sobering assessment, their role in exposing the link between the trade in diamonds and continued human rights abuses and conflict was widely recognized, not least by the nomination of GW and PAC for the 2002 Nobel peace price.

Conclusion

The main questions were: under which conditions have NSAs influenced EU reactions to human rights violations over the past decade, and, to what extent was NSA influence determined by access to relevant actors at the right moment or by specific power resources? Interviews taught that NSAs seldom had a decisive role in EU decision making with regard to specific countries. Nevertheless, they contributed by fact finding and raising awareness and played an important role in shaping general EU sanctions and human rights policy. The main finding of my analysis, contrary to expectation, is that NSAs' greatest influence is in the initial stages of the decision-making process, when the EU contemplates *whether* to react, rather than later, when the EU decides on *how* to react.

This finding is explained both by NSA strengths and by the nature of EU decision making. On the one hand, NSA access to EU decision making is greater, and their input more specific and indispensable, early on in the process rather than in the final decision-making stage. Furthermore, the EU institution most accessible to NSAs, the European Parliament, is the least powerful in this field. On the other hand, few NSAs have a specific stance on exactly how the EU should react. NSAs seem to have more influence on the decision-making outcome when their campaign is focused on curtailing trade in particular products, rather than when they merely draw attention to human rights abuses without specifying what kind of measures they think should be taken.

The finding that NSA access to the EU decision-making process on sanctions is greater at the early rather than the final stage of decision making was in fact counterintuitive, since unanimity is required for the decision on *whether* to react, compared to QMV for *how*. It was hypothesized that lobbying 15 member states at the Council, each having the right of veto, would be more difficult than lobbying the comparatively unitary Commission. The thesis that the 'agent' (Commission) would have more power than the 'principals' (Council) thus proved to be confined to the decision on *how* rather than on *whether* to react. Even when only QMV is needed to adopt a decision, the Commission has tremendous influence through the wording of its initial proposal (unanimity is needed to change a proposal substantially). During this drafting process NSAs could, in theory, have an impact, but this would not necessarily be reflected in the final outcome.

How can one explain that the increase in players with a veto at Council level seems to facilitate rather than complicate potential NSA influence on decision making? This is all the more puzzling because the division of labour between national ministries as well as between European Directorates-General is such that NSAs could easily concentrate on actors that do not have a final say in the decision-making process. One would expect that under QMV NSAs need to lobby fewer players than under unanimity. The same was hypothesized for the Commission. Two factors explain this finding, both requiring further comparative study. First, the nature of the issue, human rights violations, has a highly emotional value, for both the public and the press. It might be easier to achieve consensus on human rights than on other, less high-profile, issues. An EU member state taking the position that it does not condemn human rights violations risks being portrayed as self-interested, insensitive and even acting against the principles enshrined in the Treaty and various Council decisions. Second, the grand gesture of deciding to impose sanctions has a higher news value than the nitty-gritty of how these sanctions are eventually designed. Also, the effective implementation of sanctions receives little attention, until the moment they fail to achieve their proclaimed goal. Contrary to agency theory, the Commission seems to have more autonomy under QMV because it is defending its own proposal. It is often easier to find a majority in favour than a blocking minority against. In this phase negotiations often get much tougher, especially since trade restrictions cost money and hurt specific constituents. Yet the Commission is unlikely to present a highly controversial proposal in the first place. In practice it rarely comes to a vote in the Council. While keeping the calculations in mind, the Presidency would try very hard to find consensus. Agency theory thus needs further study and redefinition in order to be applicable to foreign policy.

Returning to international relations theory, it can be concluded that liberal institutionalism with its pluralist focus helped to pinpoint why NSAs are more likely to influence EU decision making in the early stage. The neo-realist assumption that NSAs are inconsequential to decision-making outcomes was only confirmed for the end game. The final result, in this case the type of reaction, is less important than the very decision by member states on *whether* to react. The stage, where NSAs influence *how* states react, is also dominated by member states. The stakes of the game cannot be understood without first tracing the initial influence of NSAs in bringing human rights abuses to the attention of member states and the EU institutions. The constructivist assumption that NSAs influence interest *perceptions* thus seems correct. Having a general rather then a specific impact on EU policy is still hugely important.

A further explanation for the fact that NSA input is indispensable in the initial stage of decision making, yet inconsequential in the final stage, is that NSAs show their greatest strength during the initial stage, namely by presenting high-quality, credible and often unique accounts of human rights abuses. The phase in which NSAs have less influence (*how* to react) is also the phase in which human rights advocates, whilst traditionally forming a strong network in the field of human rights, have no unified position. Their role is therefore limited to awareness raising. The dependence on NSA reports and their high quality has increased NSA influence in the initial stages of the decision-making process. Moreover, because of the economic and financial costs of sanctions, human rights advocates have often faced powerful business coalitions lobbying against the use of sanctions, but this happens mainly in the second phase.

Notwithstanding the above, the campaign against conflict diamonds shows the strengths of NSAs when focusing on a single issue affecting consumers, industries and states alike. NSA impact was greater when they were explicitly included in the process. The same was true for the suspension of trade preferences under the GSP system. The threat of a consumer boycott proved particularly powerful. A similar NSA influence could be seen in the failure of negotiations on the Multilateral Agreement on Investments (Tieleman 2002) and in the ban on landmines (Anderson

2000). Also, by questioning the 'collateral damage' of embargoes on the population at large, NSAs have had an impact on the important policy shift from 'blunt' to 'smart' sanctions. In all these cases, however, the initial policy demands formulated by NSAs were not necessarily taken into account in the final result.

Finally, it can be concluded that the more open and transparent a political system, the more influence non-state actors are likely to have on the decision-making outcomes. Interviewees often quoted institutional impediments as the cause of the lack of specific NSA influence on EU decision making. These institutional impediments are in line with the claims formulated by liberal institutionalism. Whereas at member state level it is the foreign ministry that leads the decision-making process, NSAs often focus on the ministry of economic or development affairs, or the national parliament. Similarly, in Brussels they approach Directorate General (DG) Development or DG Trade rather than DG External Relations, and the EP rather than the Council. Apparently, human rights advocates and business alliances, with some exceptions, do not always know on which door to knock in Brussels. NSAs have themselves acknowledged the lack of institutional transparency as a reason for their limited influence. In recent years, however, some improvements have been observed in EU efforts to be more transparent, and to involve NSAs to a greater extent in the process of decision making through hearings and informal gatherings. Some Council working groups (e.g. the human rights working group) now provide NSAs with the opportunity to express their views on the margins of meetings. More power for the EP, and a more formal inclusion of NSAs in the decision-making process, would bring more influence to NSAs.

NGO influence on United Nations sanctions deserves further research. The publications, briefings and campaigns of Global Witness, together with a coalition of NSAs, triggered several UN reactions. Yet again, however, analysis of the Kimberley process showed that NGO influence seemed largely confined to the initial stages of decision making. But in this case NSAs' actions were a necessary condition to getting the process started. The commercial interests involved were another crucial characteristic of NSA success. Without the powerful reports and campaigns launched by human rights coalitions, it seems unlikely that the Kimberley process would have begun. The constructivist approach to international relations was instrumental in revealing NSA influence on states' interest perceptions. Human rights figures prominently on the national and international agendas of today's liberal democracies. Exactly how this initial NSA influence on interest perceptions is subsequently translated into states' action deserves further academic scrutiny. Empirical analysis of decision-making processes in the field of foreign policy is needed to further test and assess the validity of constructivism's claims. Such studies could usefully strengthen and specify the mechanisms that link international relations theory to foreign policy analysis.

Notes

1 The EP had the right to assent to the 1995 EU Customs Union with Turkey. Krauss (2000) illustrates that lobbying by member states probably was more important than Turkish or NGO endeavours to pressure the EP.
2 Hazelzet (2001: 205–10) measured specific interests of EU member states by comparing the extent to which former colonial powers tended to protect their colonies.
3 The US Congress never ratified the Clean Diamonds Act.

References

Anderson, K. (2000) 'The Ottawa Convention Banning Landmines: The Role of International Non-Governmental Organizations and the Idea of International Civil Society', *European Journal of International Law*, 11(1): 77–90.

Arts, B. (1998) *The Political Influence of Global NGOs. Case Studies on the Climate and Biodiversity Conventions*, Utrecht: International Books.

Brandtner, B. and Rosas, A. (1998) 'Human Rights and the External Relations of the E.C.: An Analysis of Doctrine and Practice', *European Journal of International* Law, 9(3): 468–90.

Finnemore, M. (1996) *National Interests in International Society*, Ithaca: Cornell University Press.

Hazelzet, H. (1998) 'Assessing the Suffering of "Successful" Sanctions: An Ethical Approach', in W.A. Van Genugten and J. De Groot (eds) *Effects and Effectiveness of UN Sanctions, Especially in the Field of Human Rights*, Groningen: Intersentia, 71–96.

—— (2001) *Carrots or Sticks? EU and US Reactions to Human Rights Violations (1989–2000)*. Dissertation European University Institute, San Domenico di Fiesole, Italy.

Hufbauer, G.C., Scott, J.J. and Elliott, K.A. (1990) *Economic Sanctions Reconsidered*, 2nd edition, Washington DC: Institute for International Economics.

Kahler, M. (1997) *Liberalization and Foreign Policy*, New York: Columbia University Press.

Keck, M. and Sikkink, K. (1998) *Activists Beyond Borders. Advocacy Networks in International Politics*, Ithaca: Cornell University Press.

Klotz, A. (1996) *Norms in International Relations. The Struggle Against Apartheid*, Ithaca: Cornell University Press.

Krauss, S. (2000) 'The European Parliament in E.U. External Relations: The Customs Union with Turkey', *European Foreign Affairs Review*, 5(2): 213–37.

Moravcsik, A. (1995) 'Explaining International Human Rights Regimes: Liberal Theory and Western Europe', *European Journal of International Relations*, 1(2):157–89.

Risse, T., Ropp, S. and Sikkink, K. (1999) *The Power of Human Rights International Norms and Domestic Change*, New York: Cambridge University Press.

Tieleman, K. (2002) *Negotiation as Transformation. Tracing the failure of the Multilateral Agreement on Investments (MAI) – Agency and Change in International Negotiations*, Dissertation European University Institute, San Domenico di Fiesole, Italy.

Verbeek, B. (1998) 'International Organizations: The Ugly Duckling of International Relations Theory?' in B. Reinalda and B. Verbeek (eds) (1998) *Autonomous Policy Making by International Organizations*, London: Routledge, 27–41.

11 Framing decisions in the United Nations

The exploitation of the political opportunity structure

Jutta Joachim

Introduction

How do non-governmental organizations (NGOs) influence decision making in international organizations (IOs)? Even though these non-state actors have gained tremendously in importance in international affairs, we still know relatively little about the ways in, and the extent to, which they shape outcomes in multilateral institutions. To help fill this gap in the literature, I examine the issue of reproductive rights and health, which women's NGOs successfully placed on the United Nations (UN) agenda in the 1990s, despite opposition from conservative forces and sections within the women's movement. At the International Conference on Population and Development (ICPD) in Cairo, Egypt, in September 1994, governmental delegates by consensus adopted a platform of action which identified greater control by women over their reproduction rather than demographic targets as a key to lowering population growth (UN 1994).

To explain the accomplishments of women's NGOs, I draw on various elements from both the agenda-setting and the social movement literature, which suggest that these organizations engendered governmental support for the issue of reproductive rights and health by (1) strategically framing problems and solutions, (2) seizing the political opportunity structure in which they were embedded, and (3) drawing on the mobilizing structures which they had at their disposal.

Following a discussion of the theoretical concepts and the agenda-setting process, I trace the role of women's NGOs in the case of reproductive rights and health within the UN by employing three different data sources: in-depth interviews with NGO representatives and UN officials; participatory observation of NGO and UN meetings and conferences; and UN and NGO documents, international newspaper accounts and secondary literature.

NGOs and UN agenda setting

NGOs play an important role in the agenda-setting process of international organizations such as the UN. This is not surprising. Because these civil society actors provide 'moral authority and knowledge about causal relationships, they are particularly crucial when it comes to paradigm shifts on the international agenda' (Risse 2002: 265). Of the various institutional agendas within the UN, those of the General Assembly (GA) are most relevant to this analysis. They address issues NGOs are primarily concerned with (e.g. human rights, the environment, development) and are adopted by the entire membership. More importantly, the agendas of the GA have a legitimization function, signalling to the international community which actions are considered appropriate and which are not (Risse and Sikkink 1999: 8). Hence, NGOs can use them to exert pressure on their own states to follow through on their international commitments (Keck and Sikkink 1998: 12–13).

To capture the agenda-setting process I employ the 'garbage-can model' developed by Michael Cohen and others (Cohen *et al.* 1972), which emphasizes the significance of chance and coincidence rather than comprehensive rationality in agenda formation (Gordenker *et al.* 1995: 41). The model suggests that different elements, ranging from problems and solutions to actors and opportunities, are thrown into the process just as 'trash' is dropped into a 'garbage can'. What an agenda will look like is therefore contingent on the contents of the 'can' and how these contents are linked or 'coupled' at various points in time (Kingdon 1984: 88). NGOs are participants in the agenda-setting process, struggling with others about the legitimacy of the problems and solutions they introduce at opportune moments. Drawing on various elements of the social movement literature, I detail the conditions under which they might be more or less successful in winning support for their ideas.

As they are short of material resources themselves, NGOs *frame* the problems they identify and the solutions they consider appropriate strategically, in order to mobilize governmental support for them. While intended to 'render ... events or occurrences meaningful', and 'to organize experience and guide action, whether individual or collective' (Snow *et al.* 1986: 464; also Rein and Schön 1991: 263), new frames tend to be contested, because they challenge or contradict already existing ones (Schön and Rein 1994: 29). Hence NGOs will have to 'align' or 'extend' their frames in such a way that they 'resonate' with the experiences and the empirical context of their targeted audience (Snow and Benford 1988). Two factors are critical in this process: the political opportunity structure in which NGOs are embedded and the mobilizing structures these non-state actors have at their disposal.

The *political opportunity structure* captures the national and international political context which imposes restrictions on and provides opportunities for framing processes (Tarrow 1994: 18; McAdam *et al.* 1996: 17). Structure is broadly defined here. It encompasses the material distribution of power and the formal institutional setting, i.e. the political space, in which NGOs aim to gain acceptance for their ideas, as well as the cultural and normative components which determine which actors and what frames are considered legitimate.

Three elements of the political opportunity structure are particularly pertinent. First, *access* to the agenda-setting process is essential. NGOs may obtain it through 'symbolic events' (Keck and Sikkink 1998: 22; Price 1998: 622), such as international conferences and meetings which provide opportunities for lobbying, or political crises which 'recast or challenge prevailing definitions of the situation, thus changing perceptions of costs and benefits of policies and programs and the perception of injustice of the status quo' (Zald 1996: 268). Second, the support of *influential allies* such as states (Weiss and Gordenker 1996), UN agencies and secretariats (Willetts 1996: 49), or the media (Klandermans and Goslinga 1996) is of vital importance because they possess resources or institutional prerogatives that NGOs lack. Third, *changes in political alignments and conflicts* can create opportunities for NGOs. Changes in political alignments may bring into power actors whose perspectives and beliefs are more in accordance with the frames advanced by NGOs (Tarrow 1994: 87), while conflicts can be fortuitous for NGOs because their frames might facilitate agreement among divided parties (Surel 2000: 501).

Together with influential allies and access, changes in political alignments and conflicts make up the political opportunity structure in which NGOs are embedded and which provides not only resources for influence, but also determines which frames are perceived as legitimate. However, political opportunities by themselves are not sufficient to mobilize broad-based support of initially contested ideas. NGOs need their own mobilizing structures, to actively seize and exploit these opportunities.

Mobilizing structures are 'those collective vehicles, informal as well as formal, through which people mobilize and engage in collective action' (McAdam *et al.* 1996: 3). They are the networks of NGOs. Mobilizing structures impart NGOs with agency. They enable them to engage in practices aimed at changing the international normative context and to manipulate information to their advantage, i.e. to be strategic. Mobilizing structures are the source of ideas and mobilizing energy (Smith *et al.* 1997: 60).

Three elements of the mobilizing structure are most relevant to NGOs in the UN context. *Organizational entrepreneurs* are an asset (Keck and Sikkink 1998: 14; Price 1998: 616). These are individuals or organizations who care enough about an issue to absorb the initial costs of mobilizing, bring with them a wealth of organizing experience, are well-connected, and frequently have vision and charisma (see, for example, Oliver and Marwell 1992: 252). Moreover, a *heterogeneous international constituency* (Smith *et al.* 1997: 62) is necessary. Comprised of people from diverse cultural and political backgrounds, it can enhance the legitimacy of a frame by (1) making it more difficult for opponents to discredit the frame as representing only the interests of certain groups, and (2) enabling NGOs to exert pressure at different levels with different strategies and tactics. Finally, *experts* are part of the mobilizing structure that NGOs have at their disposal. Among these are directly affected individuals who can provide testimonies based on their experiences (Keck and Sikkink 1998: 19), 'epistemic communities' consisting of scientists and academics who draw on technical knowledge (Haas 1992), and insiders who possess procedural knowledge in the sense that they are familiar with institutional rules and procedures.

In summary, the acceptance of frames developed by NGOs is contingent on both the mobilizing structures of these civil society actors and the political opportunity structure in which they are embedded. While the political opportunity structure mirrors political realities and institutional practices which provide resources and clues for action, the mobilizing structures are the seeds for framing efforts and enable NGOs to take advantage of institutional and international changes. Exactly how the dynamic interaction between the political opportunity structure and the mobilizing structure gives rise to consensual problem and solution frameworks in the agenda-setting process will be illustrated through the empirical case study of reproductive rights and health.

The case of reproductive rights and health

The inclusion of reproductive rights and health in the platform of action of the ICPD in Cairo was the culmination of a process which began two decades earlier. It started with (1) the definition of the problem in the mid-1980s, when Northern and Southern women conducted an international tribunal protesting against existing population control programmes which violated women's rights; continued with (2) the search for solutions in the late 1980s, when women's health activists engaged in a dialogue with members of the population establishment to develop more women-centred population policies; and concluded with (3) the 'coupling' of the problems with the solutions and the inclusion of women's reproductive rights and health on the international agenda at the ICPD in Cairo in 1994.

The problem: population control policies and the International Tribunal in Amsterdam, 1984

In 1984 a small group of Northern women entrepreneurs from the International Contraception, Abortion and Sterilization Campaign (ICASC) in London, as well as from the Dutch, Belgian and Luxembourg abortion campaigns, organized an International Tribunal and Meeting on Reproductive Rights, which took place in Amsterdam from 22–28 July. Bringing together nearly four hundred women from 65 countries, the meeting was an important symbolic event. It contributed to the expansion of the until then almost exclusively Northern constituency, to include women from Southern countries who had been marginalized due to their location, differences in culture and language, or lack of financial resources (Women's Global Network for Reproductive Rights 1986: 63).

The tribunal gave rise to an alliance between Northern and Southern women concerned about their reproductive rights and reproductive health. Women at the meeting were united in their opposition to international family planning and population control policies, which in their eyes violated their most basic rights and denied them their freedoms. Their alliance was grounded in newly established international networks such as the Women's Global Network for Reproductive Rights (WGNRR) in Amsterdam (Women's Global Network for Reproductive Rights 1986: 69), which facilitated the exchange of information and the conduct of international campaigns and future meetings.

The testimonies of Southern women were critical to the solidarity among tribunal participants. Moving and dramatic, the stories made Northern women aware of the problems women in developing countries were confronted with. They drew attention to the lack of access to basic health care and contraceptives as well as information. In addition, the testimonies made clear that the cause of the problem was not individual women but, rather, that it was structural in nature. On the one hand cultural and religious practices reinforced traditional notions of the family and women's subordinate status, while on the other international family planning agencies perceived women in developing countries in instrumental fashion, as a means of limiting population growth (Dixon-Mueller 1993: 57). Further, the testimonies had 'empirical credibility' (Snow *et al.* 1988: 208–10), corresponding to international developments.

Symbolic events rarely take place in isolation: it is their occurrence in conjunction with other events that enhances people's awareness and readiness to act (Keck and Sikkink 1998: 22). In the case of the tribunal, two events appear to have been particularly important in prompting women to organize internationally. The first was the dumping in the late 1970s by Northern family planning organizations and pharmaceutical companies of unsafe contraceptives, such as Dalkon Shield intrauterine devices (IUDs) and Depo-Provera injectable progestin, in developing countries. The distribution of these had been prohibited by the Food and Drug Administration in the United States, yet they were sold in developing countries under less than sanitary conditions, with the result that women suffered severe health problems and sometimes even died (Ehrenreich *et al.* 1979).

The United States (US) was also at the centre of the second symbolic event. At the UN Population Conference in Mexico City in 1984, its delegation announced that it would no longer fund international family planning organizations providing abortion services, and would reduce funding for international family planning more generally (Fox 1986). The announcement came as a surprise to many and sent shock waves through developing countries, because the US had been the main driving force behind population control efforts since the 1950s (Finkle and Crane 1985: 9). The US Mexico City policy reflected a change in government from relatively pragmatic administrations to one much more driven by an ideological agenda. In contrast to his predecessors Kennedy and Carter, who had perceived population growth as a threat to national security, Ronald Reagan depicted it as a 'neutral phenomenon', and the policies of the 1960s and 1970s as a 'demographic overreaction'. He preferred the free reign of market forces to continued support for family planning programmes (United States 1984: 4). In addition, the Mexico City policy was also indicative of the lobbying work of pro-life groups, to which the administration seemed particularly receptive due to the forthcoming elections (Cohen and Richards 1994). Together with the dumping of unsafe contraceptives and the testimonies of women at the Amsterdam tribunal, the Mexico City policy prompted women to act and to search for solutions.

The solution: women-centred population policies and dialogue meetings in the late 1980s

During the late 1980s several international women's organizations entered into a dialogue with individual members of the population establishment, with the intention of developing more women-centred population policies. The International Women's Health Coalition (IWHC) in New York emerged as an organizational entrepreneur, because it had close connections with the population establishment (McIntosh and Finkle 1995: 250), particularly with organizations which had a more liberal outlook and which played a major role in the formation and development of international family planning policies. These included the Special Programme of Research, Development and Research Training in Human Reproduction of the World Health Organization in Geneva, as well as the Population Council and the Rockefeller Foundation in New York. While the dialogue meetings helped women's health activists to garner the support of institutional allies, they were not without conflict.

The activists' experiences and views were initially incompatible with those of the physicians and scientists representing the population establishment, who saw the issue in a more technical light. For example, in contrast to women's health advocates who evaluated family planning programmes on their potential to improve the health and well-being of women, scientists and physicians measured their success on declining birth rates. Similar differences existed with respect to solutions for how to curb population growth. While members of the population establishment preferred *provider-controlled* methods (e.g. IUDs and injectables) because they were 'efficient' and 'safe', women's health advocates opted for *user-controlled* ones (e.g. diaphragms or condoms) owing to the freedom they give women to regulate their own fertility (World Health Organization 1991: 11). The conflicting priorities and standards reflected different sources of information. In contrast to women's health advocates, who drew on their personal experiences and encounters as counsellors with women in developing countries, the scientists and physicians relied on quantitative data from introductory trials, clinical assessments, laboratory tests and field studies (World Health Organization 1991: 12).

Despite these differences among the participants, the dialogue meetings resulted in a series of consensual solution frameworks. One of the most prominent of these was 'quality of care'. It linked women's experiences with technical knowledge, emphasizing, for example, the choice among a range of contraceptive methods or the availability of full information about all methods and side effects (International Women's Health Coalition and Population Council 1986). When women's health activists first introduced the framework in the mid-1980s, members of the population establishment questioned its feasibility. However, by the early 1990s major family planning organizations such as the UN Fund for Population Activities (UNFPA) and the private International Planned Parenthood Federation (IPPF) had integrated the framework into their programming activities.

Contributing to this shift in position were two factors. First, an article written by Judith Bruce of the Population Council, entitled 'Quality of Care: A Simple Framework' and published in the prestigious journal *Family Planning* in 1990, was crucial because it enhanced the legitimacy of the framework. The author grounded the quality of care concept theoretically and demonstrated its potential successfulness through references to field studies (Bruce 1990). Second, changes in the international climate following the Population Conference in Mexico City in 1984 were conducive to a shift. Political alignments within the population establishment began to move away from what Dixon-Mueller refers to as the 'supply-siders' of family planning – i.e. the Northern countries – and towards the 'demand-siders' of family planning – i.e. the Southern countries (Dixon-Mueller 1993: 69), whose views were more compatible with those of women's health activists. Contrary to Northern countries, which had been advocating the setting of population targets, Southern countries linked population growth directly to development (Joachim 2003). Also, the population conference in 1984 created a tactical incentive for women's health advocates and members of the population establishment to cooperate. They had a mutual interest in maintaining women's access to birth control, although for different reasons, and found a common enemy in the Reagan administration (Hartmann 1987: 31; Higer 1999). The integration of women into the population framework, though, was not unanimously supported in the women's health movement. Instead, it became a subject of conflict at the ICPD.

Coupling: reproductive rights and health as population and development issues, ICPD 1994

Following the first ICPD Preparatory Conference in Cairo, where women's rights had barely been mentioned in the draft platform of action, the IWHC organized the so-called London meeting in the spring of 1992, inviting a small group of friends from other international women's organizations. Agreeing that the forthcoming UN conference in Cairo presented an excellent opportunity to generate greater awareness of reproductive rights and health, participants formed what came to be known as the Women's Alliance and adopted *Women's Voices '94: The Women's Declaration on Population Policies*. This declaration specified seven ethical principles which population policies and programmes should honour in order to ensure the centrality of women's well-being (Antrobus *et al.* 1993). While *Women's Voices '94* had been intended by the Alliance as a lobbying instrument to mobilize support around the issue of reproductive rights and health, it proved to be highly divisive, triggering substantial criticism and counter-framing activities from the Vatican, as well as from sections within the women's health movement.

Reproductive rights and health challenged and was incompatible with the values and perspectives of the Vatican. It presented a 'fundamental threat to the family', violated the rights of the 'unborn life', and stood for a radical pro-choice position, namely the 'unrestricted right to abortion'. To prevent its inclusion in the conference agenda, the Vatican, together with Catholic countries, responded by entering into an alliance with fundamentalist Islamic countries, despite their ideological differences. The alliance blocked discussion on the issue of women's reproductive rights and health, making ample use of UN rules and procedures, such as making frequent oral interventions and the demand for brackets.

As regards the women's organizations expressing their discontent with the declaration, the most vocal were WGNRR, established at the tribunal in Amsterdam to facilitate cooperation and networking between Northern and Southern women, the Boston Women's Health Book Collective, the Feminist International Network of Resistance to Reproductive and Genetic Engineering (ICG-FINRAGE) from Hamburg, Germany, and the Committee on Women, Population, and the Environment (CWPE) based in Amherst, Massachusetts. These organizations criticized *Women's Voices '94* for the undemocratic fashion in which the document had been put together. In their eyes, the declaration had been 'drafted by an exclusive group of women whose perspectives were not representative of the entire women's movement, but rather that of its more pragmatic wing' (Telephone interview with Barbara Dutting, WGNRR, Amsterdam, 11 June 1996). Moreover, radical women's organizations objected to the document's content by publishing a 'Critical Appraisal of the Women's Declaration on Population Policies' in the January–March 1993 edition of the

WGNRR Newsletter. The authors disapproved of the declaration because of its 'lack of principled criticism of population policy', which did not address the major causes of population growth such as poverty and the uneven distribution of wealth. In contrast to members of the Women's Alliance, who saw the population policy framework as an adequate channel to gain acceptance for women's reproductive rights and health, the authors of the 'Critical Appraisal' considered it ill-suited because it reinforced the existing power structures, which they identified as fundamental causes of population growth. Moreover, working within the framework meant the threat of cooptation and of silencing women's voices (Telephone interview with Betsy Hartmann, CWPE, Amherst, Massachusetts, 11 August 1996). Together, the opposition of women's organizations and the religious alliance prompted the Women's Alliance to rethink its strategy.

Shortly before the ICPD took place the IWHC organized another symbolic event, in Rio de Janeiro in the spring of 1994: the International Women's Health Conference for Cairo entitled 'Reproductive Health and Justice' (International Women's Health Coalition (CEPIA 1994: 1). This conference signalled that the IWHC had learnt from its past mistakes. In contrast to the London meeting in 1992, the Rio conference was more inclusive. Despite budgetary constraints more than two hundred participants had been invited to the conference, with 'diversity' instead of 'friendship' being the criterion for selection (Interview with Rachel Kyte, IWHC, New York, 26 October 1995).

The Rio conference contributed to a more inclusive issue and action framework. First, it resulted in a change of strategy. In view of the Vatican's fierce opposition and the short amount of time left, participants at the Women's Health Conference decided to work together as a 'united front' and in 'solidarity'. This did not mean, however, that differences between the various groups had disappeared. Rather, women's organizations engaged in a division of labour, with pragmatic organizations lobbying inside the UN for women's reproductive rights and health, and radicals mobilizing political pressure on the outside (International Women's Health Coalition (CEPIA) 1994: 31–3). Second, participants drafted a 21-point statement which was considerably broader in scope than *Women's Voices '94*. On the one hand, the authors strongly voiced their opposition to population policies which control the fertility of women but fail to address their basic rights, such as a secure livelihood or freedom from poverty and oppression (International Women's Health Coalition (CEPIA) 1994: 4). On the other, they placed reproductive rights and health squarely within the development frame. Blaming inequitable development models as responsible for, among other things, the growing feminization of poverty and the marginalization of women, the authors of the 21-point statement called for 'alternative development strategies' and 'social development policies starting from the concerns and priorities of women' (International Women's Health Coalition (CEPIA) 1994: 5–6).

The solidarity among its members and the broadening of its frame helped the Women's Alliance to win influential allies in the ICPD process following the Rio conference. Among them was the US delegation, which supported women's reproductive rights and health, including the right to safe abortion. The position mirrored the liberal outlook of the Clinton administration, which was more receptive to the pressure exerted domestically by women's groups (McIntosh and Finkle 1995: 240). As well as the US delegation, the Secretary General of the ICPD, Nafis Sadik, was a vital ally. She engaged in a series of actions that worked to the advantage of women's organizations, highlighting the independence representatives of international organizations enjoy at certain points in the agenda-setting process *vis-à-vis* states. For example, using the prerogative of her office as Secretary General, she revised the platform of action more than a dozen times, until it had lost much of its demographic character and the rights of the individual had gained more prominence (McIntosh and Finkle 1995: 230), a frame that was more in alignment with that of reproductive rights and health. Moreover, Sadik initiated a series of preparatory meetings at regional, national and international level. Intended primarily to provide a forum for governments to air and resolve their disagreements before coming to Cairo (McIntosh and Finkle 1995: 229), these preparatory meetings gave women's NGOs ample opportunity to lobby. The leadership exhibited by the Secretary General and the US delegation on the issue of reproductive rights and health put the Vatican and its allies increasingly on the defensive.

With the growing support for the reproductive rights and health frame, ideological differences within the conservative alliance began to re-emerge, leading to its break-up midway through the conference. Not only many Islamic countries, such as Pakistan, Egypt and Iran, but also Catholic countries such as the Philippines, Mexico and Peru, held much more liberal views than the Vatican (McIntosh and Finkle 1995: 233). They were in favour of international family planning and needed the financial support of Northern countries for its implementation. In addition, governmental delegates grew tired of the delaying tactics and intransigence of the Vatican. In response to a request by the Vatican to continue the discussion on the reproductive rights and health chapter after negotiations had already been going on for three days and nights, some governmental delegates shouted 'no' and the rest booed, which, according to Cohen and Richards (1994: 275), constituted 'a virtually unknown breach of decorum at UN meetings'. In the light of the mounting opposition, and finding itself increasingly isolated, the Vatican reconsidered its position. For the first time in the history of UN population conferences it voted with the consensus, adopting the entire platform of action. However, its support was not unconditional. Even after having gained considerable concessions on many issues, the Vatican issued numerous reservations on the chapter on reproductive rights and reproductive health. This move left many governmental delegates sceptical as to whether its vote had been sincere or merely an attempt to redeem itself in the face of world opinion (McIntosh and Finkle 1995: 249).

To sum up, the radical positions of individual women's health organizations and the Vatican helped more moderate women's organizations win the support of influential allies and with it the inclusion of reproductive rights and health on the ICPD agenda. Apart from legitimizing women's demands at national level, the Cairo consensus has triggered institutional changes. Many development agencies and organizations have changed their family planning policies to ones on reproductive health. However, women's success at the ICPD has also given rise to new problems. In particular it has fuelled the opposition and determination of conservative forces. At the Fourth World Conference on Women in Beijing, China, in 1995, the Vatican sought to roll back the advances women had achieved in Cairo. In addition, the inclusion of reproductive rights and health has also reopened and deepened divisions within the women's health movement. In contrast to pragmatic organizations which perceive and celebrate the ICPD as a success, radical women's organizations feel that while the reproductive rights and health rhetoric has been adopted by the population establishment, nothing has changed in practice.

Conclusion

How, why and under what conditions can NGOs influence the agenda-setting process in international organizations? The case of reproductive rights and health highlights the explanatory power of both the 'garbage-can' model and the various elements of the social movement literature.

The 'garbage-can' model draws attention to the fact that agendas do not simply exist out there. They are the results of various streams: problems, policies and politics. It also highlights the role of policy entrepreneurs, who move in and out of the agenda-setting process with their ideas. They are pivotal in the coupling of the various streams. Finally, the model takes account of the timing as well. Agendas come about when the time is ripe, that is, when policy windows open.

The various elements of the social movement literature help us to determine more precisely how NGOs, as one particular kind of entrepreneur, can influence the agenda-setting process in international organizations. With only limited material resources, NGOs frame their issues in a strategic way, depending on the political opportunity structure in which they are embedded and the mobilizing structures they have at their disposal. In the problem definition phase, for example, women's organizations forged an alliance at the International Tribunal in Amsterdam between Northern and Southern women, whose experiences and testimonies provided evidence that international family planning programmes violated the fundamental rights of women. During the solution phase the IWCH, together with other organizations, seized on a shift in political alignments within the population establishment away from the supply-side and towards the demand-side of family planning to develop more women-centred population policies, drawing on the technical expertise of physicians as well as the experiences of women's health activists. In the politicization stage, the ICPD in Cairo in 1994 opened a policy window to place reproductive rights and health at the centre-front of the UN's agenda. Confronted with the opposition of conservative forces and of members within their own movement, the Women's Alliance mobilized the support of a heterogeneous constituency and influential allies. In this phase, women's organizations also benefited from the expertise they had gained during their campaign. In contrast to the early stages, when their framing activities still had an inchoate quality and seemed largely determined by changing political opportunities, these organizations worked more strategically by the time of the ICPD, using institutional rules and procedures as well as their own mobilizing structures to their advantage.

These findings give weight to recent calls by students of international relations to develop new approaches, borrowing from comparative politics, public administration, organizational theories and the social movement literature. In combination with conventional approaches, this promises to offer new and more nuanced insights into the nature of international organizations.

References

Antrobus, P., Correa, S., De la Fuente, M., Germain, A., Keysers, L., Madunagu, B. and Pitanguy, J. (1993) *International Conference on Population and Development (ICPD-Cairo '94). History and Process of Some Initiatives*, Buzios, Brazil: ICPD.

Bruce, J. (1990) 'Fundamental Elements of the Quality of Care: A Simple Framework', *Studies in Family Planning*, 21(2): 61–91.

Cohen, M., March, J. and Olsen, J.P. (1972) 'A Garbage Can Model of Organizational Choice', *Administrative Science Quarterly*, 17(1): 1–25.

Cohen, S.A. and Richards, C.I. (1994) 'The Cairo Consensus: Population, Development and Women', *Family Planning Perspectives*, 26(6): 272–7.

Dixon-Mueller, R. (1993) *Population Policy and Women's Rights: Transforming Reproductive Choice*, Westport: Praeger.

Ehrenreich, B., Dowie, M. and Minkin, S. (1979) 'The Charge: Gynocide; The Accused: The US Government', *Mother Jones*, 4(9): 26–37.

Finkle, J.L. and Crane, B.B. (1985) 'Ideology and Politics at Mexico City: The United States at the 1984 International Conference on Population', *Population and Development Review*, 11(1): 1–28.

Fox, G.H. (1986) 'American Population Policy Abroad: The Mexico City Abortion Funding Restrictions', *International Law and Politics*, 18(2): 609–62.

Gordenker, L., Coate, R.A., Jönsson, C. and Soderholm, P. (1995) *International Cooperation in Response to AIDS*, New York: Pinter.

Haas, P.M. (1992) 'Introduction: Epistemic Communities and International Policy Coordination', *International Organization*, 46(1): 1–36.

Hartmann, B. (1987): *Reproductive Rights and Wrongs. The Global Politics of Population Control*, Boston: South End Press.

Higer, A. (1999) 'International Women's Activism and the 1994 Cairo Population Conference', in M. Meyer and E. Prügl (eds) *Gender Politics in Global Governance*, Lanham: Rowman and Littlefield, 122–41.

International Women's Health Coalition (1994) *Women's Voices 1994. Women's Declaration on Population Policies (In Preparation for the 1994 International Conference on Population and Development)*, New York: IWHC.

International Women's Health Coalition and Citizenship, Studies, Information, Action (CEPIA) (1994) *Reproductive Health and Justice. Report of the International Women's Health Conference for Cairo '94, 24–28 January, Rio de Janeiro*, New York: CEPIA.

International Women's Health Coalition and Population Council (1986) *The Contraceptive Development Process and Quality of Care in Health Services. Rapporteur's Report of a Meeting Sponsored by the International Women's Health Coalition and the Population Council. New York, October 8–9, 1986*, New York: IWHC.

Joachim, J. (2003) 'Framing Issues and Seizing Opportunities: The UN, NGOs, and Women's Rights', *International Studies Quarterly*, 47(2): 247–74.

Keck, M.E. and Sikkink, K. (1998) *Activists Beyond Borders. Advocacy Networks in International Politics*, Ithaca: Cornell University Press.

Kingdon, J.W. (1984) *Agendas, Alternatives and Public Policies*, New York: Harper Collins.

Klandermans, B. and Goslinga, S. (1996) 'Media Discourse, Movement Publicity, and the Generation of Collective Action Frames: Theoretical and Empirical Exercises in Meaning Construction', in D. McAdam, J.D. McCarthy and M.N. Zald (eds) *Comparative Perspectives on Social Movements. Political Opportunities, Mobilizing Structures, and Cultural Framings*, New York: Cambridge University Press, 312–37.

McAdam, D., McCarthy, J.D. and Zald, M.N. (1996) 'Introduction: Opportunities, Mobilizing Structures, and Framing Processes – Toward a Synthetic, Comparative Perspective on Social Movements', in D. McAdam, J.D. McCarthy and M.N. Zald (eds) *Comparative Perspectives on Social Movements. Political Opportunities, Mobilizing Structures, and Cultural Framings*, New York: Cambridge University Press, 1–22.

McIntosh, A.C. and Finkle, J.L. (1995) 'The Cairo Conference on Population and Development: A New Paradigm?', *Population and Development Review*, 21(2): 223–60.

Oliver, P.E. and Marwell, G. (1992) 'Mobilizing Technologies for Collective Action', in A.D. Morris and C. McClurg Mueller (eds) *Frontiers in Social Movement Theory*, New Haven: Yale University Press, 251–72.

Price, R. (1998) 'Reversing the Gun Sights: Transnational Civil Society Targets Land Mines', *International Organization*, 52(3): 613–44.

Rein, M. and Schön, D. (1991) 'Frame-Reflective Policy Discourse', in P. Wagner, C. Hirschhorn Weiss, B. Wittrock and H. Wallmann (eds.) *Social Sciences and Modern States. National Experiences and Theoretical Crossroads*, Cambridge: Cambridge University Press, 262–89.

Risse, Th. (2002) 'Transnational Actors and World Politics' in W. Carlsnaes,

Th. Risse and B.A. Simmons (eds.) *Handbook of International Relations*, London: Sage, 255–74.

Risse, Th. and Sikkink, K. (1999) 'The Socialization of International Human Rights Norms into Domestic Practices, Introduction', in Th. Risse, S.C. Ropp and K. Sikkink (eds.) *The Power of Human Rights. International Norms and Domestic Change*, Cambridge: Cambridge University Press, 1–38.

Schön, A. and Rein, M. (1994) *Frame Reflection. Toward the Resolution of Intractable Policy Controversies*, New York: Basic Books.

Smith, J., Chatfield, Ch. and Pagnucco, R. (1997) 'Social Movements and World Politics: A Theoretical Framework', in J. Smith, Ch. Chatfield and R. Pagnucco (eds.) *Transnational Social Movements and Global Politics*, New York: Syracuse University Press, 59–77.

Snow, D.A. and Benford, R.D. (1988) 'Ideology, Frame Resonance, and Participant Mobilization', in B. Klandermans, H. Kriesi and S. Tarrow (eds) *From Structure to Action. Comparing Social Movement Research Across Cultures. International Social Movement Research*, Vol. 1, Greenwich: JAI Press: 197–217.

Snow, D.A., Burke Rochford Jr., E., Worden, S.K. and Benford, R.D. (1986) 'Frame Alignment Processes, Micromobilization, and Movement Participation', *American Sociological Review*, 51(4): 464–81.

Surel, Y. (2000) 'The Role of Cognitive and Normative Frames in Policy-Making', *Journal of European Public Policy*, 7(4): 495–512.

Tarrow, S. (1994) *Power in Movement. Social Movements, Collective Action and Politics*, New York: Cambridge University Press.

United Nations (1994) *Report of the International Conference on Population and Development, Cairo, 5–13 September 1994*, 18. A/CONF.171/13/Rev.1, Sales no. 95.XIII.

United States (1984) *Policy Statement of the United States of America at the United Nations International Conference on Population (Second Session, Mexico, D.F., August 6–13, 1984)*, reprinted in *Population and Development Review*, 10(4): 576 and 583.

Weiss, Th.G. and Gordenker, L. (eds) (1996) *NGOs, the UN, and Global Governance*, Boulder: Lynne Rienner Publishers.

Willetts, P. (1996) 'Consultative Status for NGOs at the United Nations', in P. Willetts (ed.) *'The Conscience of the World'. The Influence of Non-Governmental Organisations in the UN System*, Washington: The Brookings Institution, 31–62.

Women's Global Network for Reproductive Rights (1986) *Divided in Culture, United in Struggle. Report of the International Tribunal and Meeting on Reproductive Rights, Amsterdam 22–28 July, 1984*, Amsterdam: WGNRR.

World Health Organization (1991) *Creating Common Ground: Women's Perspectives on the Selection and Introduction of Fertility Regulation Technologies. Report of a Meeting Between Women's Health Advocates and Scientists, organized by the Special Programme of Research, Development and Research Training in Human Reproduction and the International Women's Health Coalition. Geneva, 20–22 February,* New York: WHO.

Zald, M.N. (1996) 'Culture, Ideology, and Strategic Framing', in D. McAdam, J.D. McCarthy and M.N. Zald (eds) *Comparative Perspectives on Social Movements. Political Opportunities, Mobilizing Structures, and Cultural Framings*, New York: Cambridge University Press, 261–74.

Part VII

Learning processes

12 Decision making in the International Maritime Organization

The case of the STCW 95 Convention

Jan Dirks

Introduction

In this chapter I discuss the decision-making processes which led to the *Standards of Training, Certification and Watchkeeping for Seafarers Convention, 1995* (STCW 95) of the International Maritime Organization (IMO). I ask why the IMO member states formulated and adopted this convention despite the wide range of interests and previously contradictory positions of the seafarers' unions and shipowners' associations, which were deeply involved in the formulation process. I utilize two basic theoretical research approaches on international relations – rational choice and social constructivism – which together explain the adoption and specific regulatory content of the STCW 95.

In the first section, a brief summary of the problem addressed by the STCW 95 Convention is given. The section also describes the kind of regulation represented by the STCW 95. The chapter then argues from a rational-choice perspective that a win-win situation emerged as a result of the bargaining processes between governmental and non-governmental actors that took place within the *arena* of the IMO. It continues from a social-constructivist perspective, by viewing the IMO as a *bureaucratic learning actor* which has induced its member states as well as the shipowners' associations and seafarers' organizations to redefine their interests in order to fulfil the IMO's primary task[1] (for social constructivism in international relations see Ruggie 1998a: 855–85; Ruggie 1998 b; also Finnemore 1996: 325–47). The IMO was able to do this because it underwent a process of organizational learning (for organizational learning in international organizations see Haas 1990 and Dirks 2001: 77–89). It questioned the theories that had previously guided its activity and facilitated the creation and further development of a consensual knowledge base. In the final section, both perspectives will be brought together and it will be shown that the IMO was able to take on new actor functions in the context of the STCW 95, because of its ability to learn and because its bureaucratic structures provided it with the legitimacy necessary to carry out influential actor functions.

The problem addressed by the STCW 95 Convention

In an era of dominant neo-liberal economic concepts, growing regional integration and expanding global economic activities, international organizations are faced with new challenges (for these challenges see, for example, Dirks *et al.* 2002: 12–14). The maritime sector in particular is affected by structural changes, because of the globalized nature of shipping (Dirks 2001: 97–135). Keywords include the growing number of ships registered under so-called flags of convenience (FOC) and on open registers, which allow non-national citizens to acquire nationally-registered ships without restrictions on the nationalities of the crew members (for statistical data on national fleet developments see Institute of Shipping Economics and Logistics 2001; for a historical discussion of the FOC-problem see Johnson 1996).[2]

It is often very easy to register a vessel under an FOC. Sometimes a fax message or even an e-mail, together with the remittance of a specified amount of money, is sufficient. Although the fees for registration and the taxes may greatly contribute to the flag state's balance of payments, they are usually very low compared to the fees and taxes of most industrialized states. Many shipowners previously committed to high-standard shipping registered their vessels under FOC or on open registers because of the strong competition in the shipping market during the 1980s and early 1990s.[3] This trend was accelerated by protectionist policies in many shipbuilding nations, low interest rates, and the opportunity to deduct the costs of running ships from taxable income in many industrialized countries. An extensive overcapacity of cargo tonnage was the result, which lowered freight rates and forced shipowners to cut labour costs.

Another challenge facing the IMO was the growing number of so-called manning agencies, which offer individual seafarers or whole crews to shipowners for specified periods of time. Often these crews are much cheaper than crews from the country of origin of the shipowner. The chance to hire cheap multinational crews, especially from developing countries, has been used extensively by many shipping companies from traditional maritime nations (for an account of the different wages for seafarers from different countries see ISF 1995, 1996, 1997, 1998 and 1999). In many cases such seafarers were badly trained and their qualifications were not verifiable, causing a downward spiral in the sailors' competence (Dirks 1998: 6), which endangered the safety of the ships and in some cases led to disastrous outcomes of shipping accidents (see Dirks 2001: 102–34).

However, an international IMO regulation on standards of training, certification and watchkeeping for seafarers did exist: the IMO Convention on Standards of Training, Certification and Watchkeeping for Seafarers, 1978 (STCW 78). Yet it did not bring the intended results. The STCW 95 is a complete review of the old STCW 78, which involved only principles to be observed 'to the satisfaction of the administration' in educating and certifying sailors. As a successor to the STCW 78, the new STCW 95 defines specific training and education modules, which all seafarer trainees have to pass regardless of whether the state in which the maritime training takes place has ratified the convention or not. It is a positive regulation, not only providing a framework which facilitates cooperation (negative regulation), but also defining specific measures to be taken by all national administrations of seafarer-providing states. It is a market-correcting convention, which has the aim of interrupting the downward spiral in maritime safety resulting from the growing number of ships registered on open registers and under FOC. It requires a lot of activity in every state, to adjust national maritime training, education and certification as well as develop control systems to monitor the new requirements. Theorists in international relations have often argued that such regulations are desirable but almost unattainable, because of the different economic interests of the states (for example, Scharpf 1996 and Zürn 1998).

The following section analyses the interests and positions of the IMO's member states and of the shipowners' and seafarers' groups. It investigates, from a rational-choice perspective, the reasons for the changing positions of the governmental and non-governmental actors during the bargaining process. In this perspective the IMO is understood to be an instrument for the realization of interests of governments and seafarers' and shipowners' organizations and an arena for negotiation in conflicts between these actors. The IMO is seen as a permanent diplomatic conference establishment, where all subjects of international concern may be dealt with (for the heuristic distinction between international organizations as instruments, arenas and actors see Rittberger 1994: 25–6), and as a provider of the contractual environment (see Zürn 1997: 56 on the necessity of a contractual environment for regime creation; also Zürn 1998). The analysis of actor groupings within the IMO arena and their interests facilitates the explanation of why member states finally adopted the STCW 95, despite previously different and sometimes contradictory positions on the part of all the actors involved.

Changing position pays

The review of the STCW 78 was carried out by an expert group of seven government representatives (Mexico, Spain, the UK, the Netherlands, Germany, Singapore and South Korea), one international shipowners' organization, one international seafarers' organization, one international ship masters' organization and four scientific institutes (for a summary of the processes of the revision of the STCW 78 see Morrison 1997: 1–20). What were the initial positions and interests in the field of international merchant shipping of the governments participating in the review (expert group), the other member states of the IMO, and the shipowners' associations and seafarers' unions, and why did they change their positions in most cases?

The behaviour of the *states represented in the expert group*, measured by the number of ratified IMO conventions, the safety performance according to the *Paris Memorandum of Understanding on Port State Control* (Paris MOU) during the period 1995–7, and the relatively high rate of inspections carried out by them, indicates a strong and enduring interest in improving ship safety. In most of these states shipowners are highly dependent on foreign seafarers to man their vessels, due to a lack of new recruits to the national maritime training and education systems. Measures to improve the quality of maritime training and education in labour-supplying countries are seen as a chance to reduce the risk of shipping accidents resulting from 'human error', especially in the territorial waters of the industrialized states. The industrialized states would not have been able to solve the problem by themselves, because they could not check the qualification of seafarers travelling in their waters before the STCW 95 standards came into force. The introduction of clearly defined standards for maritime education and training, as well as watchkeeping arrangements, in the STCW 95 enabled the industrialized states to effectively supervise the qualification of foreign crews themselves and to remove poorly qualified seafarers from ships. Therefore, international cooperation enlarged their scope for action.

The other IMO member states which participated in the Conference of Parties to the International Convention on Standards of Training, Certification and Watchkeeping, at which the STCW 95 was adopted, also show a high percentage of ratifications of IMO Conventions.[4] But their safety performance is slightly below average, according to Paris MOU statistics. This points to problems in putting IMO regulations into effect. Vessels from those developing countries which participated in the conference especially show a much higher rate of detention by state port authorities because of serious violations of international maritime conventions than ships from industrialized countries. Apparently, it was not lack of political will, but insufficient administrative capacity that hampered many governments of developing countries in implementing IMO standards.

The dependency of shipowners from industrialized countries on the labour force from developing countries led to the legitimate expectation by the latter to be able to participate in technical cooperation measures and transfers of technology (for example, simulators). Several projects to improve maritime education and training in labour-supplying countries have already been implemented by the IMO, the International Labour Organization (ILO), the shipowners' associations and the seafarers' organizations, as well as by the Norwegian government. It was a trade-off that brought most governments of developing and labour-supplying countries in line with the governments of industrialized states. The industrialized states gained more control over the maritime training and education systems of the labour-supplying countries for the price of investing in these systems and in the administrative structures of those countries.

Most states with flags of convenience agreed to the STCW 95, because they do not supply many seafarers themselves. They simply refuse to accept responsibility for ensuring compliance with international conventions on vessels registered under their flag and leave it to the shipowners to hire crews which are trained according to STCW 95 standards.

Although the IMO is an intergovernmental organization in which trade unions and shipowners' organizations only have observer status, these organizations had a strong influence on the regulatory content and the structure of the convention. The shipowners' associations and seafarers' organizations were the main providers in the expert group of information on the situation regarding political, economic and structural developments in merchant shipping, the qualification of seafarers and practices of non-compliance with STCW 78 standards. They also supported the implementation of the STCW 95 standards by carrying out missions in labour force-supplying countries, for example in the Philippines,[5] and by sponsoring capacity building in maritime education and training institutes.

Until the mid-1990s the seafarers' organization, the International Transportworkers Federation (ITF) was in a deep conflict with the shipowners about the system of open registers and FOC which had been in existence for decades. Their approval of the STCW 95 was due to their perception of structural changes in international merchant shipping that had taken place during the 1980s and 1990s. While their political activities were formerly concentrated on the abolition of the system of open registers and FOC, they now accepted the new realities of the growing number of FOC vessels. Today the ITF concentrates to a far greater extent on improving the working and living conditions of seafarers on all merchant ships, because the number of sailors employed on FOC vessels has constantly grown. Their representatives were aware that the implementation of the STCW 95 might cost some of their colleagues their jobs because they lacked the education necessary to comply with STCW 95 standards. Nevertheless, the goal of improving safety for as many seafarers as possible appeared to be very important to them. Therefore, in order to maintain their position as an organization representing all sailors, they had to concentrate on the protection of seafarers employed on board FOC vessels.

The shipowners' organization, the International Shipping Federation (ISF), supported the STCW 95 because the shipowners had an interest in improving the safety of ships by halting the downward spiral in the quality of crews. The deputy general secretary of the ISF argued that competition from substandard shipowners had increased so much during the previous decade that even those owners committed to employing highly qualified crews were no longer able to withstand the financial pressures resulting from the employment of cheap crews by substandard owners (Interview David Dearsley, August 1998). According to the ISF *Wages Surveys*, a shipping company might save several hundred thousand US dollars per vessel in wages each year by hiring a crew from Bangladesh, for example, rather than seafarers from Germany or other northern European states (see ISF 1995; 1996; 1997; 1998; 1999). Although the ISF was aware of the problem of substandard crews, it was in favour of maintaining the system of open registers and FOC. The reason for this position is that most of its members are European shipowners, who themselves register ships on open registers and under FOC. Therefore in the STCW 95 context, the shipowners' organization had an interest in improving ships' safety within the framework of existing structures, but not in changing these structures.

The seafarers' and shipowners' organizations also had to resolve their conflict, because they wanted to be accepted by the IMO as reliable and supportive partners whose contributions to the IMO's activities justified their observer status. For organizations with observer status, participation in standard-setting processes in an intergovernmental organization such as the IMO always requires a compromise between the goals of their members and the requirements of the member states. By participating in the policy-formulation processes, the international seafarers' organizations and shipowners' associations (as well as the scientific institutes) are able to gain potential advantages, that is, they are in a position to influence decisions made in the IMO to the benefit of their members. However, in order to retain the right of being accepted as an observer in the IMO, the transnational actors also have to adapt their behaviour to the norms of the international organization.

To summarize, from a rational-choice perspective the decision to formulate and adopt the positive regulations of the STCW 95 was taken because a win-win situation emerged during the bargaining process. The bargaining process in the IMO arena on the increasing problems of seafarers' qualifications led to the discovery of the following new possibilities.

- On the part of the industrialized states, the improvement of ship safety by being able to regularly inspect the crews' qualifications, regardless of their nationality, according to a uniform list of minimum standards.
- On the part of the developing countries, the improvement of the quality of their maritime education and training systems through technical and financial assistance from industrialized states and seafarers' and shipowners' organizations.
- On the part of both the seafarers' and shipowners' organizations, instead of confrontation over the system of open registers and FOC, the improvement of safety and living and working conditions within the framework of existing structures.

Organizational learning: A key factor in fulfilling the primary goal

Although the rational-choice perspective convincingly explains *why* the seafarers and shipowners supported the formulation and implementation of the new convention, and *why* the IMO member states adopted it, it fails to explain the specific outcome of the discussion processes. The rational-choice perspective treats ideational factors as given and does not investigate their origins (see Ruggie 1998b). It states that actors pursue their interests in international bargaining processes, without explaining how the constituent actors (in the IMO's case the member states) acquired their current identities and the interests that are assumed to go with them (Ruggie 1998a: 863). This is where the social-constructivist analysis comes in. There is growing empirical evidence that in addition to states' identities, normative factors stemming from the participation in international contexts shape their interests and behaviour in international relations.[6]

The following section focuses on the IMO's actor function, thereby viewing the IMO as a bureaucratic learning organization that influenced the interest formulation of its member states and seafarers' and shipowners' organizations. It is argued that the IMO questioned its own activity-guiding theories-in-use and its own understanding of its role. In the STCW 95 context, the IMO acted as an idea-generation centre, which allowed the member states and seafarers' and shipowners' organizations to identify new activity options for solving the qualification problem of the seafarers (for international organizations as idea-generating centres see Katzenstein *et al.* 1998: 675). In order to influence the interest formulation of the member states and to act as an idea-generating centre, the IMO as an organization has to undergo a permanent process of organizational learning.

One specific characteristic of any intergovernmental organization – including the IMO – is that it is at the same time a decision-making body within a particular policy field, a service agency and a mechanism for self-evaluation, which is exhibited in the particular relationship of each international organization to its respective environment, described by Haas (1990: 27) as 'hyperdependency'. Unlike international companies, intergovernmental organizations with universal membership are dependent on the support of their environment in the shape of the member states, which are at the same time the targets of the regulations. It is necessary for the IMO to consciously examine and deal with the processes of change in its environment. This examination and organizational adjustment is unavoidable, because of the hyperdependency of international organizations on their members. The way in which this task is carried out, however, is determined by the organizational culture and the commitment of the organizational leadership – be it the Secretary General, staff members and constituents, or networks with new actors (for the role of leadership in international organizations see Reinalda 1998: 42–61).

In the literature about organizational learning two different, but not always separate, lines of theoretical paradigms can be distinguished (for this distinction see Mahler 1997). One theoretical approach investigates organizational activities with its focus on the rational processing of information and disturbances in these processes which are inherent in the systems (see, for instance, March and Olsen 1976; Duncan and Weiss 1979). Others centre attention on the interpretative outputs and judgements of the organizations' members when organizational knowledge is generated (see Argyris and Schön 1978; Dülfer 1991; Schein 1991). The development of new consensual knowledge about a problem or policy field is at the forefront in the present approach. The aim is to analyse whether, how and why new central ideas and conceptions of issues, which are relevant to the political process of the formulation and adoption of the STCW 95, arise. These new ideas and notions are translated into political decisions in the IMO's fields of activity, i.e. the interactive fields of norm-setting and technical cooperation.

There are several indicators that may help explain the processes of IMO organizational learning in the context of the STCW 95 and the impact of that learning on the adoption of the convention:

- development of the IMO's knowledge base and basic assumptions pertaining to the problem area;
- development of the priorities of the IMO in the STCW 95 context;
- development of the criteria for successful implementation in the STCW 95 context;
- changes in the IMO's understanding of its own role.

From the early 1990s onwards the IMO has begun to change its basic assumptions about the nature of the problems, moving from technical issues towards human element questions. These changes are strongly related to the participation of a growing number of non-governmental organizations and scientific institutes which deal with humans in labour processes. To improve its knowledge base on issues in the maritime sector, the IMO set up a constantly growing network of communications with United Nations and intergovernmental organizations, non-governmental organizations and scientific institutes. The continual enlargement and development of this knowledge base – coordinated by the IMO staff – facilitated discussion processes on appropriate measures for solving the problem of seafarers' qualifications. It enabled the identification of the solutions to this problem as documented in the STCW 95. While the Convention contains new methods for training, certification, watchkeeping and supervision of its implementation, it also reflects the previously formulated interests of the member states and seafarers' and shipowners' organizations. The efforts of the IMO to foster the knowledge base made a major contribution to the generation of *consensual knowledge*, a precondition for international regulation which not only eliminates the identified problems but also their causes (see Haas 1990: 24).

Due to the changing basic assumptions about the causes of shipping accidents, the priorities in the IMO's activities have also changed. Until the early 1990s the IMO always reacted to shipping accidents by creating new technical standards. 'There is another lesson to be learned from these studies and it is that mistakes are usually made not because of faulty, deficient or inadequate regulations, but because the regulations and standards that do exist have been ignored' (O'Neil 1994: 1). The new priorities in the technical cooperation programmes of the IMO therefore focus on the strengthening of national administrations and the promotion of national implementation of existing norms through education and technology transfers. The IMO has recognized that the problems are primarily due to the inadequate implementation of the conventions and less so to a lack of standards (IMO 1996: 5).

The new focus on implementation influenced the criteria for measuring successful implementation of the norms. While the organization formerly interpreted high ratification percentages and lower numbers of shipping accidents as signs of success, it concentrates today more on structural changes in the member states. A high ratification figure is only one of several criteria for success. More important in the STCW 95 context is the number of states appearing on the white list of nations that have adapted their maritime education and training systems to STCW 95 standards.

This enables the IMO to identify arising problems at an earlier stage. The new criteria are in line with the organization's new understanding of its own role. In the course of its history, the IMO has changed from an organization completely dominated by the interests of a few maritime states which wanted an organization that created favourable conditions for their national economic interests, to a 'pro-active' (O'Neil 1994) organization with almost universal membership, dedicated to improving shipping safety and the protection of the maritime environment. The new understanding is reflected in the goals of the organization for the new millennium, formulated in Assembly Resolution A.900:

1 to focus more on humans;
2 to support more strongly the effective implementation of already existing IMO standards and regulations;
3 to develop a safety culture;
4 to avoid over-regulation;
5 to strengthen its technical cooperation programmes (IMO 1999: 6; translated from the German).

Despite the constraints imposed on the IMO by its statutes, the organization was able to take on actor functions, a development which certainly had not been foreseen at its foundation in 1948. In the context of STCW 95 the General Secretary (William O'Neil) had a strong influence over the review process of the STCW 78. First, he proposed the establishment of an expert group for the review, instead of having the work carried out by the Maritime Safety Committee (MSC) itself, which would have taken a lot of time. Second, he accelerated the adoption process by combining the conference to accept the STCW 95 with that for the STCW Fishing Convention. Finally, he suggested speeding up the implementation process by reducing the tacit acceptance time limit from 24 to 18 months.[7] As a result, the STCW 95 was adopted two years earlier than would have been the case if the usual procedures had been followed.

To summarize, the IMO actively sought to include information from a variety of sources in its knowledge base. On the one hand this facilitated the development of consensual knowledge. On the other hand, the processing of new information and its inclusion in the already existing knowledge base enabled the staff, and the General Secretary in particular, to put into practice their ideas for the review of the STCW 78. Both the way in which the information from the different sources was processed and the use of this information by the IMO to redefine its own role, as well as the active steering of the discussion process by the General Secretary of the IMO, led to the extension of the actor function of the IMO by the member states.

Conclusion

The combination of the two approaches – rational choice and social constructivism – has proved to be very useful in explaining the IMO decision to adopt the STCW 95. A perspective that views the IMO as a learning actor facilitates the discovery of the various possibilities for solving identified problems, from which rational actors can choose. The solutions put forward by international organizations may be related to the processes of norm-setting, the regulatory content and the implementation of standards. In the present case the process of norm-setting was strongly influenced by the IMO Secretariat, while the regulatory content was mainly determined by the social partners. The question of implementation had, of course, already been dealt with by the member states during the norm-setting process. In the event, the member states for the first time granted the IMO an actor function, which may lead to a situation in which the organization passes judgement on national policies and could refuse to issue certificates of competency if it is not satisfied with the national maritime education system.

Research on international organizations points out the influence on national law of regulations set by international organizations. As early as 1973 Cox and Jacobson argued that the stronger the impact of these regulations on national law, the lower the degree of independence of international organizations from national decisions, particularly where these decisions are mainly determined by the most powerful states (Cox and Jacobson 1973: 371–436). Krasner argues in a similar way in his analysis of the roles of industrialized and less developed countries in maritime standard-setting processes (Krasner 1985: 196–226). In the present case, these contentions do not fit. First, the member states made the STCW 95 a very influential, international, positive regulation with a strong impact on national law. Second, they decided to charge the IMO with the supervision of the STCW 95. From a rational-choice perspective it can be argued that it appeared to be the only way of avoiding a prisoners' dilemma situation, such as had arisen over the implementation of the STCW 78. At that time the maritime states were unable to verify the qualifications of foreign seafarers travelling within their territorial waters and, therefore, could not determine whether other states had implemented the STCW 78 standards.

From a social-constructivist perspective it can be argued that the IMO gained the authority to monitor the implementation of the STCW 95 standards because of the legitimacy of its bureaucratic procedures and rules on the one hand, and its technical expertise and access to information on the other. Barnett and Finnemore have shown that bureaucracies can acquire the authority to act independently in the name of generally accepted rules through their inherent rationality, in the sense of rule-setting based on socially recognized knowledge (Barnett and Finnemore 1999: 707–9). Therefore the suggestion to assign the task of monitoring the implementation of the STCW 95 to the IMO was not rejected by the member states, because of the generally accepted bureaucratic (long-term) performance of the IMO. This performance influenced the member states and other actors in their perception of the nature of the problem, because they regarded the knowledge provided by the IMO as reliable. As a result a stronger actor function for the IMO was legitimate from the perspective of the member states. In order to retain this legitimacy the IMO has to continually undergo organizational learning processes, which enables it to keep up with the challenges of globalization.

In conclusion, the STCW 95 Convention was made possible by a combination of a positive actor group, which allowed the development of overlapping interests in the bargaining process, and an international bureaucratic organization that was able to act as an idea-generating centre, because it constantly underwent organizational learning processes. It therefore legitimately adopted actor functions to prevent possible problems arising from an inadequate implementation of the STCW 95 standards. Whether the Convention will be effective depends also on the development of a convergence of interests, to which the IMO must continue to contribute by providing information and technical cooperation.

Notes

1 The term primary task has been developed in the tradition of the Tavistock Institute in London. Compare Rice 1958: 32. Rice 1963: 13 redefines the term as 'what an institution or system has to carry out in order to survive'.

2 There is no standard definition of the term flag of convenience. In most cases the Rochdale criteria are applied to determine the characteristics of FOC. For the Rochdale criteria see Lindemann 1983: 5. Usually FOCs are differentiated from the so-called open registers, which also allow the registration of ships owned by non-nationals. The difference between the two is a qualitative one. While FOCs are generally characterized by little political will or administrative capacity to implement even the basic international standards for seafarers, open registries implement at least some minimum standards and, therefore, show a better safety performance.

3 For a summary of these developments in the 1980s see ILO 1987; for recent developments see ILO 2001: 1–26; for an account of possible competitive advantages of registering ships as FOC or on open registers see OECD 1996.

4 The participating states have ratified 48.84 per cent of all IMO instruments (2000), while the average rate of ratification is 36.44 per cent.

5 Roughly 25 per cent of all seafarers in international merchant shipping come from the Philippines (for an analysis of the global seafarer supply and demand situation see BIMCO/ISF 2000).

6 See Ruggie 1998a: 864; this has been shown, for example, by Finnemore (1996); for the influence of national interests on states' identities and international interest formulation see Moravcsik 1997: 519; also Gourevitch 1996: 350; for a summary see Zangl 1999: 55–60.

7 The tacit acceptance procedure means that states do not have to explicitly accept a protocol or amendment to a convention. Under tacit acceptance a regulation comes into force when a specified number of states with a specified nationally-registered tonnage (adding up to 50 per cent of world tonnage), which have signed the principal convention, do not reject the protocol or amendment.

References

Argyris, C. and Schön, D. (1978) *Organizational Learning. A Theory of Action Perspective*, Reading, Mass.: Addison-Wesley.

Baltic and International Maritime Council and International Shipping Federation (2000) *Manpower Update*, London: Baltic and International Maritime Council and International Shipping Federation.

Barnett, M.N. and Finnemore, M. (1999) 'The Politics, Power, and Pathologies of Internal Organizations', *International Organization*, 53(4): 699–732.

Cox, R. and Jacobson, H. (eds) (1973) *The Anatomy of Influence*, New Haven: Yale University Press.

Dirks, J. (1998) *Universales Positives Regieren jenseits des Nationalstaats. Zwei Fälle im Maritimen Sektor*, Bremen: Forschungszentrum Arbeit–Umwelt–Technik.

—— (2001) *Positives Regulieren in der Handelsschifffahrt im Kontext der Globalisierung*, Münster: Lit-Verlag.

Dirks, J., Liese, A. and Senghaas-Knobloch, E. (2002) *Internationale Arbeitsregulierung in Zeiten der Globalisierung. Politikveränderungen der Internationalen Arbeitsorganisation in der Perspektive Organisatorischen Lernens*, Bremen: Forschungszentrum Arbeit–Umwelt–Technik.

Dülfer, E. (ed.) (1991) *Organisationskultur, Phänomene, Philosophie, Technologie*, Stuttgart: Poeschel.

Duncan, R. and Weiss, A. (1979) 'Organizational Learning. Implications for Organizational Design', *Research in Organizational Learning*, 1(1): 75–123.

Finnemore, M. (1996) 'Norms, Culture, and World Politics: Insights from Sociology's Institutionalism', *International Organization*, 50(2): 325–47.

Gourevitch, P. (1996) 'Squaring the Circle: The Domestic Sources of International Cooperation', *International Organization*, 50(2): 349–73.

Haas, E.B. (1990) *When Knowledge is Power. Three Models of Change in International Organizations*, Berkeley: University of California Press.

International Labour Office (1987) *Report of the Director General, International Labour Conference, 74th Session*, Geneva: ILO.

—— (2001) *The Impact on Seafarers' Living and Working Conditions of Changes in the Structure of the Shipping Industry, Joint Maritime Commission, 29th Session*, Geneva: ILO.

International Maritime Organization (1996) *IMO's 50th Anniversary: A Record of Success*, London: IMO.

—— (1999) *Assembly Resolution A.900*, in: *IMO News*, 4/99, London: International Maritime Organization.

International Shipping Federation (1995–1999) *ISF Wages Survey*, London: ISF.

Institute of Shipping Economics and Logistics (2001) *Shipping Statistics Yearbook 2001*, Bremen: ISEL.

Johnsson, L. (1996) *Funny Flags. ITF's Campaign – Past, Present, Future*, Falköping: Utbildningsförlaget Brevskolan.

Katzenstein, P., Keohane, R. and Krasner, S. (1998) 'International Organization and the Study of World Politics', *International Organization*, 52(4): 645–85.

Krasner, S. (1985) *Structural Conflict. The Third World Against Global Liberalism*, Berkeley: University of California Press.

Lindemann, D. (1983) *Das Übereinkommen Nr. 147 der Internationalen Arbeitsorganisation vom 29. Oktober 1976 über Mindestnormen auf Handelsschiffen*, Baden-Baden: Nomos.

Mahler, J. (1997) 'Influences of Organizational Culture on Learning in Public Agencies', *Journal of Public Administration Research and Theory*, 7(4), 519–40.

March, J.G. and Olsen, J.P. (1976) *Ambiguity and Choice in Organizations*, Bergen: Univeritetsverlag.

Moravcsik, A. (1997) 'Taking Preferences Seriously: A Liberal Theory of International Politics', *International Organization*, 51(4): 513–53.

Morrison, W.S.G. (1997) *Competent Crews = Safer Ships. An Aid to Understand STCW 95*, Malmö: World Maritime University Publications.

O'Neil, W. (1994) *Better Standards, Training and Certification – IMO's Response to Human Error*, World Maritime Day 1994, London: International Maritime Organization.

Organization for Economic Cooperation and Development (1996) *Competitive Advantages Obtained by Some Shipowners as a Result of Non-Observance of Applicable International Rules and Standards*, Paris: OECD.

Reinalda, B. (1998) 'Organization Theory and the Autonomy of the International Labour Organization: Two Classic Studies Still Going Strong', in B. Reinalda and B. Verbeek (eds) *Autonomous Policy Making by International Organizations*, London and New York: Routledge, 42–61.

Rice, A.K. (1958) *Productivity and Social Organization*, London: Tavistock.
—— (1963) *The Enterprise and its Environment*, London: Tavistock Publications.
Rittberger, V. (1994) 'Internationale Organisationen – Politik und Geschichte', in U. Alemann, L. Kißler and G. Simonis (eds) *Grundwissen Politik*, Opladen: Verlag Leske + Budrich: 14–33.
Ruggie, J.G. (1998a) 'What Makes the World Hang Together? Neo-Utilitarianism and the Social Constructivist Challenge', *International Organization* 52(4): 855–85.
—— (1998b) *Constructing the World Polity. Essays on International Institutionalization*, London and New York: Routledge.
Scharpf, F. (1996) 'Politische Optionen im vollendeten Binnenmarkt', in M. Jachtenfuchs and B. Kohler-Koch (eds) *Europäische Integration*, Opladen: Leske + Budrich: 109–40
Schein, E.H. (1991) 'Organisationskultur. Eine neues unternehmenstheoretisches Konzept', in E. Dülfer (ed.) *Organisationskultur, Phänomene, Philosophie, Technologie*, Stuttgart: Poeschel, 23–37.
Zangl, B. (1999) *Interessen auf zwei Ebenen: Internationale Regime in der Agrarhandels-, Währungs- und Walfangpolitik*, Baden-Baden: Nomos.
Zürn, M. (1997) '"Positives Regieren" jenseits des Nationalstaats', *Zeitschrift für Internationale Beziehungen*, 4(1): 41–68.
—— (1998) *Regieren jenseits des Nationalstaats*, Frankfurt: Suhrkamp.

13 Social learning with the precautionary principle at the European Commission and the Codex Alimentarius

Jim Dratwa

Introduction

The phrase 'precautionary principle' has been incorporated into international texts since the 1980s. Although it arguably originated in the *Vorsorgeprinzip* of German federal environmental legislation in the 1970s, it is often traced back to the Rio Declaration, which states in its Principle 15:

> In order to protect the environment, the precautionary approach shall be widely applied by States according to their capabilities. Where there are threats of serious or irreversible damage, lack of full scientific certainty shall not be used as a reason for postponing cost-effective measures to prevent environmental degradation.
>
> (Rio Declaration on Environment and Development, 1992)

Various parties relate to the 'precautionary principle' with diverse interpretations, demands and hopes, even if they agree that lack of full scientific certainty ought not be used as a reason for postponing political decision making, which could be an expedient way to delineate it. One of the ways to comprehend the multiplicity of meanings is to examine the formation of this problematic normative claim – this 'essentially contested' norm (Connolly 1993), the precautionary principle – in the social and institutional settings where it occurs. In this chapter, I discuss its formation in the European Union (EU) institutional domain with the European Commission's *Communication on the precautionary principle* (Commission 2000a), paying particular attention to the work within its Directorate-General (DG) for consumer policy and its DG for the environment from 1998 to 2000, and its extension to the Codex Alimentarius Commission, the international organization serving as the expert wing of the World Trade Organization (WTO) in matters relating to food.

Building on March and Olsen's (1998) study of institutional dynamics, the chapter's principal claim is that norms emerge and evolve in international organizations through particular patterns of learning, in a process that ties together social learning, creation of meaning, and decision making. Moreover, in an interplay of centrifugal and centripetal forces, various actors within the institutions attempt to direct the norms' substance towards features they favour, while at the same time striving towards a common understanding.

The substance of the norm: in the making

The elaboration of the precautionary principle concerns a number of issues of transnational or multi-level governance, expertise, legitimacy and sovereignty. It involves a series of tangled 'internal' concerns (to the European Union, to the EU institutions, etc.) and 'external' concerns (as exemplified by the beef stories: BSE disease and US hormones). It is also underpinned by further frames: risk analysis, science versus policy, a given policy domain – environment – in relation to others. In this chapter I will scrutinize these interests, which hold and pull the precautionary principle in several directions (for a historical background, see Boutonnet and Guégan 1999; Dratwa 2000a). This is well summarized – and illustrated – by two Commission officials at the October 1999 interservice working session on the precautionary principle in Brussels:

> We are under pressure in terms of food legislation, for instance, and in terms of member states invoking the precautionary principle. One should also consider the international level – for instance the Codex Alimentarius. And also in other parts of DG Enterprise, to do with chemical and also pharmaceutical industries. We would like to see this move as quickly as possible.
>
> 'Qui trop embrasse mal étreint.' Note that we too have been impressed by the contribution of the Legal Service. Now there are *so* many different aims here. We should (1) consolidate the precautionary principle on human health and internal affairs, (2) extend it to the environment, (3) extend it to the international/external level.
>
> (Interview, Commission officials, Brussels, 20 October 1999)

In these fields, while the precautionary principle comprises numerous ins and outs, it does pertain explicitly to situations of scientific – and political – uncertainty, to the integration of expert knowledge into decision making. Furthermore, this chapter on the precautionary principle relates to the integration of normative and ideational factors into decision making.

In addition to the crucial importance of states as well as non-state actors, and indeed of institutions, in the study of international relations and decision making, a growing body of literature has highlighted the role of ideas (see Majone 2000 for an indicative listing). Such ideas are generally conceived of as 'shared' (McNamara 1998: 4) from the outset, leading to neglect of the important constitutive dynamics that this chapter examines. Even in recent studies on norm dynamics (as reviewed in Finnemore and Sikkink 1998), which examine with remarkable finesse the emergence and 'life cycle' of normative and ideational factors, 'norm entrepreneurs' do engage in the framing, renaming and dramatization of issues, but it is *only the fate – not the substance – of the norm* they promote that is discussed. The assumption here is one of equivalence between the phrase, the substantive norm and perhaps even its operationalization. While this may seem adequate in the case of 'women's suffrage', it certainly is not for the 'precautionary principle'. If the discussion of the formulation and content of norms only pertains to their success or failure in being adopted, there is however an acknowledgement of this lack of attention to the 'process of "norm building"' (Finnemore and Sikkink 1998: 896) and the influence thereof. In the present chapter I address the very issue of *how this common understanding is arrived at, or striven for*. I argue that in order to study the impact of this norm, or how the precautionary principle structures international decision making, one must pay attention to the precautionary principle *in the making*.

Social learning

I propose to view international organizations as collective cognitive setups ('dispositifs cognitifs collectifs', following Favereau 1994) with norms as their pivotal inner structure. Favereau's procedural theory of implicit and explicit norms[1] places their emergence and impact in a twofold dynamics. On the one hand, a dynamics of formalization, thematization, or narration ('mise-en-discours') and of reconfiguration, application or situating ('mise-en-situation') of knowledge and norms. On the other hand a dynamics of collective – or social – learning, the point of crystallization thereof being the norm (as selective summary or formalization of previous learning, but also as the interactive substratum for further situations). I assert that, through social learning, norms emerge in the course of regular international organizations' decision making and that such norms take on a set of meanings and have certain roles and impacts.

This (theoretical) claim about norms and decision making is refined theoretically by bringing *social learning* – understood as actors learning from one another in situations of interaction, but see below – to bear on the development of the precautionary principle. It is tested and further substantiated empirically, in the subsequent section, by studying the arguments over the Commission's *Communication on the precautionary principle* at the European Commission and then at the Codex Alimentarius.

'Social learning' has a long history in political science (Deutsch 1963; Haas 1964; Heclo 1974) and has given rise to studies confronting issues of knowledge production and its role in international politics. Its bearing on the production of meaning and decisions is also important to my argument. As a first approximation, it might clarify matters to advance a typology defining three kinds of social learning, which are interdependent and come together in international organizations: (1) social learning by individuals *in* international organizations ('socialization', 'individual learning'); (2) social learning *by* international organizations ('institutional memory', 'organizational learning'); and (3) social learning by states, polities or societies assembled in international organizations ('states socialization', 'societal learning'). The limitations of this typology, with tensions and overlaps between types, are set out below, together with its heuristic potential. I will then establish how the precautionary principle has emerged and evolved as a result of these three types of learning.

From knowledge to interpretative frameworks

Social learning, as it emerges in international relations theory and the study of international organizations in the work of Ernst Haas, is precisely associated with the integration of scientific and technical expertise into decision making. Haas is concerned primarily with 'social learning' as the process through which consensual knowledge influences policy (E. Haas 1990: 23). The emphasis on consensus is problematic, however, when it takes the form of a *presumption* of expert consensus (be it only on single issues). This leads to *ignoring* decisions made in situations of scientific uncertainty, those numerous decisions where one would expect the precautionary principle to come into play. Moreover, Haas persistently separates science and policy, knowledge and power, and thus expert advice and the domain of politics. Nonetheless, the most important agents of institutional innovation and social learning, according to Ernst Haas, are 'epistemic communities'. As developed by Peter Haas, one of the benefits of this notion is the recognition of social learning as a deeply political process, rather than the result of the application of knowledge (P. Haas 1992: 17). Drawing social learning further towards the second type of my unpolished typology, Hugh Heclo uses the concept to draw attention to the importance of the historical and institutional context of decision making. Policy change is shaped and limited by the legacy of past decisions, or 'policy inheritance', and this is a process he calls 'social learning' (Heclo 1974: 308–15). It is these notions of social learning and policy legacy that are developed in Peter Hall's work on ideational 'policy paradigms' (Hall 1993).

As regards the question 'what is it that is learnt?', some of the ways it is addressed take us past the content/process dichotomy. They stress that some of the most important learning pertains not only to the incorporation of new knowledge, but also to superordinate factors such as norms, values, and indeed the interpretative frameworks that have been studied as the 'problematization' of actor-network theory in science and technology studies (Callon 1986), or 'policy frames' (Jachtenfuchs and Huber 1993), or 'policy paradigms': 'a framework of ideas and standards that specifies not only the goals of policy and the kind of instruments that can be used to attain them, but also the very nature of the problems they are meant to be addressing' (Hall 1993: 279). This is of particular interest in the study of bureaucratic politics or of expertise in international organizations. These thus become, in March and Olsen's work on the logic of appropriateness and the creation of identities, 'not only *decision-making* institutions but also institutions for *socializing* individuals and *creating meaning*' (March and Olsen 1998: 964). It is precisely these three practices – decision making, socialization, creation of meaning – that are involved in the shaping of the precautionary principle. This is a central claim in my argumentation, one which I will further scrutinize and elaborate upon in the empirical section.

From states to societal learning

International relations studies on social learning by states, even in refined constructivist accounts, bring with them the classic troubles of referring to states as if they were unitary, individual actors. There is always a temptation to combine the whole and the part, however far removed that part might be. In these studies, moreover, individual learning sometimes serves as a paradigm for state learning, down to the psychological microfoundations (Finnemore and Sikkink 1998: 904). State learning, therefore, is sometimes equated to 'elite learning' (Checkel 1998) in settings where state elites regularly meet and their socialization is facilitated.[2]

A number of observations are in order here. First, international organizations are first-rate settings for the development of such social learning. Second, since the matter at hand is an intersubjective process of social learning amongst individuals, non-state actors will partake in it as well as state representatives, provided they have access. Third, studies of bureaucratic behaviour and of experts in international organizations emphasize the creation of international and organization-specific or epistemic community-specific identities. If socialization of states occurs through individuals (with their rich identities), states are not the only ones around the table. This is even more obvious at the European Commission, as the officials are not even meant to represent their nation(s) and as it is the interests of the Union that are looked after rather than merely those of the member states. From that perspective, though maintaining the focus on states, another valuable presentation of state learning (rather than mere socialization) is offered by Stephen Toope: 'Common endeavour, even common debate, can give rise to shared meanings which crystallize into norms. States participating in such regimes "learn"' (Toope 2000: 105). The emphasis here is more on mutual learning, such as through legal transferences and exchanges of best practice, between and within polities. This is what I have termed *societal learning*.

Making decisions with the precautionary principle

Having claimed that norms emerge and evolve in international organizations through a process that ties together social learning, creation of meaning and decision making, I will now scrutinize that threefold connection in the field. What is more, as regards social learning itself I expect all three types to play specific roles in the shaping of the precautionary principle.

At the European Commission

The work of the Commission which led to the *Communication on the precautionary principle* developed in an EU institutional context already stimulated by this notion and which became – during the drafting of the *Communication*, from 1998 to 2000 – increasingly pressing.[3]

In scrutinizing the drafting process of the *Communication*, a fundamental feature to illuminate is the variety of approaches to the precautionary principle expressed during the deliberations by the various actors, and the fields of study from which they emanate: judicial theory, risk analysis and political science. In turn, each can variously relate to issues of environment, public health, consumer policy, science studies, participatory democracy, etc. Each refers to a particular notion of the precautionary principle, i.e. to particular cases, texts, institutions and historical frameworks.[4] Specific circumstances also apply to individual member states. Britain, for instance, has had a special situation with regard to BSE. France has been affected by the 'scandale du sang contaminé', the HIV-infected blood transfusions and their judiciary aftermath. The debate in France – as in every other country – is linked to national legislation (notably the 'Loi Barnier' on the reinforcement of environmental protection) as well as European and international law.

With the development of the *Communication*, there occurs precisely such a meeting of particular notions of the precautionary principle, of cases, texts, institutions and specific historical frameworks. One can trace, for instance, the exchanges, contributions and spill-overs between the environment Directorate and the other sectors, and notably, although only briefly, the relationship between (concerns of) DG XXIV (or SANCO: consumer policy and protection of the consumer's health) and DG XI (or ENV: environment, nuclear safety and civil protection). The environment is the privileged field in which the precautionary principle is anchored (experimentally, historically, internationally, etc.): 'The Community has already relied on the precautionary principle. Abundant experience has been gained over many years in the environmental field, where many measures have been inspired by the precautionary principle, such as measures to protect the ozone layer or concerning climate change' (*Communication*: 9); 'Although the precautionary principle is not explicitly mentioned in the [Amsterdam] Treaty except in the environmental field [in Art.174, ex-130R of the Maastricht Treaty], its scope is far wider' (*Communication*: 10, also 3). The narrative here, and indeed the undertaking, is one of policy learning across policy domains – and of a coalition of forces. It is the expression 'the environment and [/or] human, animal or plant health', widely used in the document, which bridges any gaps between the issue areas. Section 4 of the *Communication* traces the history of the precautionary principle through certain international texts, with its birth in the environmental field and its progressive consolidation and extension, leading to the WTO and to the *Agreement on the application of sanitary and phytosanitary measures* (SPS) of 1994. It is at that juncture in the text and at that moment in the discussions associated with the writing process that the usage based on historical heritage (environmental germination, growth extending into the other fields) was found to be no longer sustainable. This is how an official of DG XI expressed it: 'Of course the precautionary principle is crucial for health, but it is for the environment that the Treaty mentions it. And it is in the environment that it was born in the Seventies in Germany. It is not desirable that the Communication – of general scope – be unbalanced in this respect' (Interview, Commission official, Brussels, 20 October 1999). In earlier deliberations – on an earlier draft – the same official had voiced dissent over the mention of the need to 'respect the international commitments when these are binding', suggesting instead to 'respect the international commitments in their respective domains' (same interview). This is reflected in the final text as well, where this usage across policy domains (one common precautionary principle across all policy sectors) is held to be incoherent:

> The principles enshrined in Article 5.7 of the SPS [which translate the precautionary principle without mentioning it, JD] must be respected in the field of sanitary and phytosanitary measures; however, because of the specific nature of other areas, such as the environment, it may be that somewhat different principles will have to be applied.
>
> (*Communication*: 12; also 20)

It is only the possibility of a carefully circumscribed difference that is granted, however. Furthermore, while the most intense interaction was between environmental policy and various aspects of consumer policy, other sectors and DGs like those of international trade (with the consequent place of the WTO) or of the internal market also made their importance felt.[5]

In the construction of the precautionary principle at the European Commission, the overarching issue was to stabilize or consolidate a problematic normative claim, to reach a common understanding and to extend its reach. The first step – as exemplified above – was thus to find agreement between the three officials drafting the text so as to build a consensus among the various DGs within the Commission, thereby paving the way for a common position among the EU institutions as well as a common understanding among the member states. In turn, by renewed use of this incremental leverage, the guidelines and harmonized approach were extended to the international scene, notably to the WTO (through numerous localized negotiations, arrangements and inclusive involvements – such as within the Codex Alimentarius, as will be seen). It thus appears that this forming of the precautionary principle took place through the different types of social learning. What is more, apart from that *process* aspect, the *substantive* aim of the operationalization of the precautionary principle was explicitly social learning of the third, i.e. societal, type. It is in the perspective of societal learning that the precautionary principle can be used to produce better decisions, by drawing lessons from previous – and current – decisions. And it is thus aimed – by structuring international decision making with entangling and innovative procedures such as the continual re-evaluation of policies and scientific evidence – at making the most of the collective experimentations on acting while doubting, in taking risks while taking precautions.

Throughout the production of new decision-making procedures and norms – i.e. the production of the meaning of 'precautionary principle' – the interests and identities of the actors are constantly renegotiated. So are those of the organization as a whole. Hence, in the course of the elaboration of the *Communication on the precautionary principle*, the interests and the identity of a variety of Commission officials, units, DGs, and indeed those of 'the environment' and of 'Europe', were at stake. This follows from the social, institutional, individual and expert learning that occurs in the course of the European decision-making process and is an indication of bureaucratic politics within an international organization, as suggested in the previous section. Not only were there dynamic interrelations between different policy sectors, scrutinized above, but the official from DG Enterprise involved early on in the drafting of the *Communication* did not only 'change her mind' but ended up changing jobs, moving to DG Environment. Furthermore, some cases, texts, institutions and historical frameworks are part of an *EU-specific* experience with the precautionary principle. One such case is the traumatic European failure over hormones in beef, in the wake of which one could view the precautionary principle as part and parcel of an elaborate strategy to 'beat the SPS': by calling for the right amount of risk assessment, the adoption of provisional measures and their re-evaluation, it both follows and subverts the language of the SPS agreement so as to avoid the pitfalls that had caught the European Community in the hormones dispute. That proposition is yet another push for convergence and/or divergence of the precautionary principle (in this case a push for EU-level convergence and divergence beyond the EU). The tensions between divergence and convergence are played out between different policy sectors, as shown above, as well as between different polities, as discussed in the following section on the Codex Alimentarius. This interplay of centrifugal and centripetal forces is one of the ways to describe the development of the precautionary principle at the European Commission and beyond. Divergence occurs because each actor has his own ambitions with regard to the precautionary principle, while convergence is necessary because the actors have to produce a collective document, which means restraining – themselves and others – from free-riding or pulling too hard on the common thread. I will further illustrate, in the following section, the emergence of a 'European precautionary principle identity' on the international scene, denoting the sustained attempt at presenting a united front: an acceptable stabilization common to all levels. One should note that, in a context of recurrent (food) safety crises, this 'European precautionary principle identity' is also geared to the consumers or the European public in order to foster the legitimacy and credibility of European public authorities, although member states – albeit through their 'independent scientific agencies' – are quick to leave that fold.

At the Codex Alimentarius

Besides the *Codex Alimentarius Commission* (CAC), which meets in session every other year and adopts standards by consensus, the Codex Alimentarius also has committees that prepare draft standards for submission to the CAC. One such is the CCGP, the *Codex Committee on General Principles*, meeting annually in France.

For the April 2000 session of the CCGP, the Codex Secretariat had circulated a *Conference Room Document* (CAC 2000) from the United States, which was meant to provide comments and a list of questions on the European Commission's *Communication*. DG SANCO later offered a response to it, in a document made public in September 2000. On page 2, the American document plays the 'either science or policy' trick on the Commission, along the fault-line of the modernist fallacy indicated above: 'In its *Communication*, the Commission states that the decision to act or not, i.e. to exercise precaution or not, is a "political decision." Does this characterization mean that the decision need not also be science based ?' Throughout, the Commission endeavoured to accommodate the policy-making innovations enmeshed with the precautionary principle as well as (the use of) their counterparts' language and divides. This was their answer:

> The term 'political decision' used in the *Communication* means 'risk management decision' taken by the responsible regulatory authorities. This decision must be science-based, but . . . is essentially a political or a societal value judgement to be taken by the responsible regulatory

> authorities . . . The Commission's *Communication* and the guidelines proposed therein are intended precisely to avoid unwarranted and arbitrary risk management decisions.
>
> (Commission 2000b)

In line with the Commission's design to establish a *common understanding* of the precautionary principle, a conciliatory exercise of justification and explanation is always attempted. It is thus a case of handling *divisive language*. The divides are always addressed by the Commission, both in these responses and in the *Communication*: the conciliation can take the form of subverting or bridging the divides (such as the 'science-based versus precaution' argument above), or can consist of endorsing the divides. A striking example of this is in the *Communication* in section 6.3.5 on 'Examination of scientific developments', which indicates: 'Research could also be conducted for the improvement of the methodologies and instruments for assessing risk, including greater integration of all pertinent factors (e.g. socio-economic information, technological perspectives)' (*Communication*: 21).

Now this innovative prospect should be compared to the Commission's orthodox answer to the antepenultimate question of the American document: 'How does the Commission intend to use "all pertinent factors (e.g. socio-economic)" to improve a risk assessment, which is science based ?' (CAC 2000: 5). The United States' questioners had identified a passage were the *Communication* fosters the innovative aspects of the precautionary principle, its capacity to transform existing institutional and procedural set-ups. Indeed, it highlights the challenge it brings to classic risk assessment by calling for 'taking into account', i.e. by calling for a broadening of the base of expertise and inputs. American critics therefore employed the divide card: science and policy are sharply divided, risk assessment and risk management are similarly sharply divided, and nothing but science, sound science, can be used in risk assessment. Pushed, the Commission relented:

> There is no such reference in the *Communication*. The *Communication* does not claim that socio-economic factors are or can be used in order to improve the risk assessment. The Commission Services believe that such factors can be taken into account, where relevant and appropriate, in the risk management phase.
>
> (Commission 2000b)

Learning can be a lengthy and uncertain process. While the proponents of the precautionary principle can draw strength from previous stabilization work, any further 'diffusion' of the principle entails detailed negotiations in which its very substance really is at stake, as in this new situation, where new actors with different perspectives on the norm attempt to reshape it.

In the absence of a 'tipping point' (as students of norm diffusion, such as Finnemore and Sikkink 1998: 901, call the norm's breakthrough) the snowballing effect has to happen in various key settings, if a shared understanding is to be more widely achieved.

Conclusion

I have shown that the precautionary principle is an area of both fencing off and integration of issues, actors and domains. This is an important way in which it structures international decision making, while at the same time being itself constructed and coming 'into good currency'. In these twin processes – decision using it and decision on it – one observes that it is not a 'final decision' that is made, but rather *a series of deciding acts* which are – to diverse extents – reversible and flexible. Furthermore, these deciding acts are not only made in series but also in parallel (in different policy sectors as well as in different polities).

It is important to recall that, as evidenced in the empirical cases, the forming of the precautionary principle occurs at the convergence (or divergence) of a number of interests, fronts or aspirations, which hold it and pull it in several directions. These interests include the (governance of) international trade disputes and negotiations, as an *external* dimension so to speak; the *internal* intra-European policy coordination or harmonization; the singularity, demarcation and integration of the environment and other policy domains; the taking into account of public participation, of 'other legitimate factors' in scientific risk assessment and decision making, etc. Conversely, the precautionary principle can be understood as a complex set-up intended to address or resolve these predicaments. It is worth noting that not only the precautionary principle, but also the emergence of the European Food Safety Authority can also be understood in those terms. The legitimacy and the autonomy of the European Commission, and indeed its 'rapports de force' with the EU member states, are thus being displaced to the arena of scientific expertise.

My conclusions, like the precautionary principle that I probed, bring together decision making, creation of meaning, and social learning. In their attempts to establish 'a common understanding' (*Communication*: 3, 8) regarding the precautionary principle, its formulators in the European Union institutional sphere and beyond have great difficulties in maintaining a balance between the solidity of a general definition and the long-prevailing flexibility of being attuned to specific policies or sectors (as was shown in respect of the environmental domain). At the European Commission, individual, institutional and societal learning worked together in such a way that ambiguity (or multiplicity of meanings) was still possible – even in the finalized *Communication*. But efforts to promote a new norm take place within the standards of the 'logic of appropriateness' set by prior norms, as indicated by Finnemore and Sikkink (1998: 897). Indeed, as I showed at the Codex Alimentarius, underscoring the difficulties of learning among individuals within but also across international organizations, the precautionary principle is constrained by the legacy of past decisions and has to *come to terms* with the policy paradigm, for instance, of risk analysis. Currently, because policy making consists of making judgements about trade-offs between various risks and benefits (judgements that the precautionary principle calls upon decision makers to acknowledge), it should come as no surprise that different – or divergent – policies will be made in different situations and in different polities. Despite its drawbacks (for the internal market and international trade), the coexistence of different regulatory circumstances, of different experimental conditions, can, however, have 'learning benefits' from the perspective of societal learning – provided that equity is not forfeited and that the set-up is appropriate for learning from one another's mistakes and successes.

Notes

1 Or rules, I do not differentiate here.
2 Furthermore, be it as a presumption rather than as a process to investigate, the socialization of states into wider international systems is common to mainstream international relations theories (notably Waltz 1979: 127).
3 A detailed account of the institutional and legislative situation can be found in Dratwa 2000a and Dratwa 2001. Dratwa 2000b and Dratwa 2002 provide a critical scrutiny of risk analysis and the other frames in/with which the precautionary principle is drawn.
4 Thus, in a genuine reversal of environmentalisms' history, Michel Setbon (1999: 22) states that the precautionary principle – as in the French 'Loi Barnier' – 'only extends to the environment practices that are customary in the field of sanitary risks'.
5 'The search for a high level of health and safety and environmental and consumer protection belongs in the framework of the single market, which is a cornerstone of the Community' (*Communication*: 9). Note that this sentence was introduced at the end of the interservice consultation concluding the drafting process in late 1999, at *cabinets* level.

References

Boutonnet, M. and Guégan, A. (1999) 'Historique du principe de précaution', in Ph. Kourilsky and G. Viney (Rapport au Premier Ministre présenté par), *Le principe de précaution*, Paris: Services du Premier Ministre: Annex 1, 1–17.

Callon, M. (1986) 'The Sociology of an Actor-Network: The Case of the Electric Vehicle', in M. Callon, J. Law and A. Rip (eds) *Mapping the Dynamics of Science and Technology*, London: Macmillan, 19–34.

Checkel, J. (1998) *Norms, Institutions and National Identity in Contemporary Europe*, ARENA Working Paper, 98/16, Oslo: ARENA.

Codex Alimentarius Commission (2000) *Codex Document CX/GP 00/3-Add.6, for the 15th Session of the Codex Committee on General Principles, Paris, 10–14 April*, Paris: CAC.

Commission of the European Communities (2000a), *Communication from the Commission on the Precautionary Principle*, COM(2000)1, 2 February, Brussels: EC.
—— (2000b), *Comments from the European Commission Services to the Codex Secretariat*, September, Brussels: EC, available at http://europa.eu.int/comm/food/fs/ifsi/eupositions/ccgp/ccgp01_en.html.
Connolly, W. (1993) *The Terms of Political Discourse*, 3rd edn, Princeton: Princeton University Press.
Deutsch, K. (1963) *The Nerves of Government. Models of Political Communication and Control*, London: Free Press.
Dratwa, J. (2000a) *The Precautionary Principle. Options for Policy Making*, Brussels and Luxembourg: European Parliament STOA.
—— (2000b) 'Prendre des risques avec le principe de précaution ou Comment l'incertain se communique', in E. Zaccaï and J.-N. Missa (eds) *Le principe de précaution: Significations et conséquences*, Brussels: Editions de l'Université de Bruxelles, 50–71.
—— (2001) *The Precautionary Principle and the European Union*, Brussels and Luxembourg: European Parliament STOA.
—— (2002) 'Taking Risks with the Precautionary Principle: Food (and the Environment) for Thought at the European Commission', *Journal of Environmental Policy and Planning*, 4(3): 197–213.
Favereau, O. (1994) 'Règle, organisation et apprentissage collectif', in A. Orléan (ed.) *Analyse économique des conventions*, Paris: PUF, 113–37.
Finnemore, M. and Sikkink, K. (1998) 'International Norm Dynamics and Political Change', *International Organization*, 52(4): 887–917.
Haas, E. (1964) *Beyond the Nation-State. Functionalism and International Organization*, Stanford: Stanford University Press.
—— (1990) *When Knowledge is Power. Three Models of Change in International Organizations*, Berkeley: University of California Press.
Haas, P. (1992) 'Introduction: Epistemic Communities and International Policy Coordination', *International Organization*, 46(1): 1–35.
Hall, P.A. (1993) 'Policy Paradigms, Social Learning, and the State. The Case of Economic Policy Making in Britain', *Comparative Politics*, 25(3): 275–96.
Heclo, H. (1974) *Modern Social Politics in Britain and Sweden*, New Haven: Yale University Press.
Jachtenfuchs, M. and Huber, M. (1993) 'Institutional Learning in the European Community: The Response to the Greenhouse Effect', in J.D. Liefferink, P.D. Lowe and A.P.J. Mol (eds) *European Integration and Environmental Policy*, London: Belhaven Press, 36–58.
McNamara, K. (1998) *The Currency of Ideas. Monetary Politics in the European Union*, Ithaca, NY: Cornell University Press.
Majone, G. (2000) 'Public Policy and Administration: Ideas, Interests and Institutions', in R. Goodin and H.-D. Klingemann (eds) *A New Handbook of Political Science*, Oxford: Oxford University Press, 610–27.
March, J. and Olsen, J. (1998) 'The Institutional Dynamics of International Political Orders', *International Organization*, 52(4): 943–69.
Setbon, M. (1999) 'L'action publique face aux risques sanitaires: Responsabilité et incertitude', *Revue française des affaires sociales*, 53(1): 21–30.
Toope, S.J. (2000) 'Emerging Patterns of Governance and International Law', in

M. Byers (ed.) *The Role of Law in International Politics*, Oxford: Oxford University Press, 91–108.

Waltz, K. (1979) *Theory of International Politics*, Reading: Addison-Wesley Publishing.

Part VIII
Conclusion

14 Patterns of decision making within international organizations

Bob Reinalda and Bertjan Verbeek

Introduction

The individual chapters in this volume all testify to its central claim that a renewed interest in decision making within international organizations can help in accounting for the extent to which international civil servants make use of the policy freedom they enjoy and for the contents of the organization's policies. In this chapter we will first explore the usefulness of the suggestion we put forward in chapter 1, namely that a focus on decision making requires the recognition of a so-called principal–agent baseline, a pragmatic attitude towards the rationalist–constructivist divide and a fresh interest in middle-range theories. Next, we will discuss the results of the individual contributions in terms of the six elements of decision making this volume has focused on, as well as some themes not covered. Finally, we will address the research questions formulated at the outset of this journey.

The principal–agent baseline

The international organizations discussed in this volume enjoy considerable policy discretion. Unsurprisingly, this is the case for supranational international organizations such as the European Union (EU), but interestingly also for organizations of a more intergovernmental character, such as the Council of Europe. At the same time, in every instance it is clear that within international organizations permanent tension exists between the member states and the institutions they have created. Member states want these institutions to accomplish various tasks and accept that they thus have to be granted some freedom of manoeuvre. The contributions to this volume suggest that an international organization's policy discretion is rooted in at least four aspects of the principal–agent relationship.

One is the formal delegation of authority. Kerremans underlines that the European Commission has the power to withdraw proposals or simply not to conclude an agreement. Another is the peculiar circumstance that the agent (the international organization) faces many different principals (its member states). This allows the playing off of principals against each other. Joachim holds that the Secretariat of the United Nations International Conference on Population and Development thus outmanoeuvred a coalition of conservative states led by the Vatican, which was forced to be part of the consensus. Policy freedom can also be produced by the member states' unwillingness to deal properly with problematic issues. Freitas's analysis of the problem of internally displaced persons suggests that member states were actually very keen for the UNHCR to assume formal responsibility for an issue they found too hot to handle. Finally, policy discretion can be rooted in an organization's technical expertise. This is exemplified by the monetary and macroeconomic experts at the World Bank and the International Monetary Fund (IMF), who derive their policy discretion largely from their expert knowledge. Yet, as Woods demonstrates, an agent's expertise is partly the product of a principal's willingness to provide relevant data. The desk officers at the two institutions have to engage in a subtle process of negotiation with a member state about the release of confidential data, often resulting in a compromise.

Because member states know that an international organization may slowly expand its freedom of manoeuvre, or implement decisions ineffectively, they are prepared to invest in devices to monitor international bureaucracies. But they only do this to a limited extent. Kerremans shows how the EU Council of Ministers created Committee 133 to monitor the way the European Commission handles its freedom of manoeuvre in negotiating international trade agreements. And Marcussen demonstrates how within the Organization for Economic Cooperation and Development (OECD) the Economic and Development Review Committee, composed of member state representatives, closely follows the production of OECD country reports. In both examples, however, the agents have devised strategies to limit the effects of the member states' monitoring mechanisms. The European Commission actually uses Committee 133 to shape opinion in the member states and the OECD plays the 'idea game' in order to persuade state representatives of its macroeconomic arguments.

International organizations are aware of their policy freedom, but they also are keen not to antagonize their masters too much. In chapter 1 we argued that international civil servants are unlikely to step beyond the so-called baseline, which may not always be clearly defined. Kerremans's analysis of the role of the European Commission in EU trade negotiations stresses the inherent vagueness with which member states formulate negotiating mandates for the European Commission. This vagueness gives the Commission some leeway and allows member states to display some flexibility in their own position. Both the Commission and the member states are permanently aware that their actions may risk a violation of the baseline and thus endanger European consensus, while the precise contours of the baseline remain officially unspecified. Lovecy's account of the Council of Europe's policy to promote democracy and human rights suggests that in practice the baseline can be even more restricted than expected. Although the Committee of Ministers could in principle vote on the basis of a qualified majority, it has informally decided to do so on the basis of unanimity, thus limiting even further the freedom of manoeuvre for organs such as the Assembly and the Secretariat. As can be expected, the agents enjoying least freedom of manoeuvre are keenest on anticipating the boundaries envisaged by their principals. Bayne argues that the sherpas in the G7/G8 institutional framework will not prepare policies that they expect to be vetoed by the heads of government. At the same time, however, the sherpas assume a different type of freedom, namely preventing their political masters from adopting proposals that have not been prepared in advance.

For various reasons, the baseline can shift. First, because international organizations are embedded in different international regimes, changes in this external environment may affect an agent's policy discretion. Kerremans shows how changes at the level of the World Trade Organization (WTO) changed the relationship between the European Commission and the EU member states, increasing the Commission's policy discretion considerably. Second, international civil servants can be part of a winning coalition of member states which changes the norms and rules of the international organization. Joachim's analysis of coalition building in the UN International Conference on Population and Control demonstrates a change of norms and rules after the Cairo conference in 1994. This created a different understanding of which types of policy would be considered unacceptable. Given the fact that after the heated 'politicization' debates of the 1980s no state has actually left an international organization out of frustration with its performance, it seems that most states have been prepared since then to accept shifts in the baseline created by external or internal developments.

The rationalist–constructivist divide

In chapter 1 we argued that the study of decision making within international organizations would benefit from a 'pragmatic' attitude towards the discussions between rationalists and constructivists. The contributions to this volume support the constructivist notion that international organizations can affect member states' preferences through the constitutive effect of norms and ideas. This may even lead to a shift in the baseline. Moreover, ideas and norms often account for the preferences put forward by international bureaucracies themselves. They thus help solve the frequent puzzle of explaining in which way international organizations make use of the policy freedom granted them within a principal–agent relationship. However, the role of norms and ideas cannot be investigated in disassociation from more rationalist insights into the role of power in international politics.

In some cases decision making within international organizations takes place in the context of norms or rules that have not been explicated at all. Schemeil shows how informal notions guide deliberations within the World Meteorological Organization (WMO) and the WTO: their decisions should be compatible with the principles of equality and fairness. Moreover, participants in both organizations have been socialized into an even less precise, yet weighty, norm: WTO and WMO should at all costs avoid becoming as politicized as many UN organizations were in the past. In other cases international civil servants have been motivated by, and have been putting forward, specific norms and values in order to affect their member states' preferences. Lovecy shows that the Parliamentary Assembly of the Council of Europe, cooperating with its Secretariat, pushed for a specific reading of the term democracy. Once adopted, this principle had the constitutive effect of setting the boundaries of what was a breach of the Council of Europe's human rights regime. In that sense, the Assembly and the Secretariat set the agenda, or framed the regime. Similar processes of framing can be found in Hazelzet's analysis of the EU sanctions policy towards human rights violations and Joachim's case study of UN decision making on reproductive rights. Dratwa, in his account of the evolution of the precautionary principle in the EU and the Codex Alimentarius, makes clear that norms themselves, once adopted, remain subject to changes in their meaning. Framing thus is part of a potentially permanent battle over the meaning of a norm. Once consensus over a new meaning has been reached, however, this new meaning defines the rules within the game that is being played.

The constructivist emphasis on norms and ideas helps to understand specific positions taken by international civil servants. As a matter of fact, rationalist accounts often have difficulties in explaining an international bureaucracy's policy preference. Unless an international organization's very survival is under threat, it is often difficult to attach a clear-cut material interest and an ensuing policy preference to an international organization. However, common positions can be recognized. In her analysis of the UNHCR Freitas shows that subagencies may develop very specific perspectives. The powerful Division of International Protection within UNHCR, for instance, developed a very legalistic approach to the issue of internally displaced persons, which cannot be linked easily to any material interest UNHCR itself might have. Similarly, policy preferences of bureaucrats within the OECD, the World Bank and the IMF seem linked to the shared professional training in economics and accountancy of their civil servants.

At the same time, research into the impact of norms and ideas can often benefit from traditional insights in international politics offered by rationalist accounts. Lovecy emphasizes that institutional factors, especially decision rules, affect the possibilities for framing of policies in the Council of Europe. Hazelzet reaches the same conclusion regarding the EU. Dirks, in his account of decision making at the International Maritime Organization (IMO), demonstrates that the specific norm on maritime safety preferred by the IMO could only be successfully adopted because of a carefully organized strategy of monitoring changes in maritime transport and reporting these persistently to the IMO's member states. Likewise, Joachim notes that policy framing by international civil servants in the reproductive rights case could only take place because of their alliance building with like-minded states and non-governmental organizations.

Middle-range theories

Our third claim is that the study of decision making within international organizations would benefit from renewed attention to so-called middle-range theories. This would be in line with those constructivists who have a preference for what they call 'small-t research', investigating a limited group of phenomena. Several such middle-range theories surface in the contributions to this volume. Some of them seek an explicit application of such theoretical frameworks (e.g. in the chapters by Freitas, Kerremans, Trondal and Woods), whereas others prefer to be more generally informed by these theories. Various authors apply (neo-)institutionalist theories. In this volume they come in four varieties: two-level games, the importance of path dependency, the impact of formal and informal rules, and garbage can theory.

Kerremans makes use of two-level game theory in order to investigate the relationship between the European Commission and the member states in negotiating and carrying out a mandate regarding WTO trade negotiations. This theory predicts that a negotiator possesses ample leeway with regard to both his domestic constituents and his international opponent. Kerremans demonstrates that the European Commission enjoys this policy discretion, but does not exploit it fully *vis-à-vis* the member states because it would render more difficult future battles over its negotiation mandate. Kerremans thus defines iteration as a qualification to the application of two-level theory to EU trade policies. Before him Meunier had already formulated another qualification: which negotiating party is closest to the status quo (Meunier 2000).

Path dependency is the second neo-institutionalist theory. It refers to the idea that the formation of an institution or a policy is likely to have a lasting effect on that policy well into the future (Peters 1999). Bayne argues that even the decisions of a highly intergovernmental and infrequently meeting body such as the G7/G8 are partly the product of decisions reached at previous summits.

The third neo-institutionalist theory focuses on the impact of formal and informal rules. Institutions, defined as formal and informal rules, structure the decision-making process by distributing advantages and disadvantages to various actors. In an extreme form this may result in actors occupying veto points, such as the domestic constituents in two-level games. Hazelzet and Joachim demonstrate how formal rules within international organizations affect the opportunities for NGOs to make an impact on decision making within the EU and during UN conferences. Interestingly, however, contrary to institutional theory Hazelzet finds that NGOs were successful in affecting EU decision making on human rights policies during the first, and not the second, stage of the policy process. She suggests that the stages in EU policy making may differ in their vulnerability to the effects of media exposure. Trondal argues that within the EU specific institutional arrangements evoke particular role definitions and identities with national civil servants participating in EU committees. The more committees are gatherings of sector specialists, the more supranational are the roles and identities national civil servants adopt. The same is true for committees that advise the European Commission rather than the Council and for civil servants who come from federal political systems and have thus grown accustomed to conflicts of loyalty already.

Joachim applies the garbage can model, an institutional theory that aims at explaining change rather than continuity. She chose not to focus exclusively on the role of policy entrepreneurs in bringing together 'policy streams' at accidental 'windows of opportunity'. Rather, she shows how NGOs made use of the political opportunity structure offered to them by the UN International Conference on Population and Control and of the mobilization of specific resources, in order to forge a consensus on women's reproductive rights. At the same time, these attempts at influencing the outcome cannot be understood without the role of the most important policy entrepreneur of the conference, Secretary-General Nafis Sadik.

Some authors refer to the concept of epistemic communities in order to explain decision making within international organizations. These actors are driven by certain policy ideas rather than by national or organizational interests. Decision making within international organizations is thus the product of a majority of like-minded actors prepared to ignore other loyalties they might have. Bayne adamantly states that the sherpas of the G7/G8 system cannot be considered an epistemic community. Despite their frequent meetings throughout the year, the sherpas do not share substantive policy views. International bureaucrats at the WMO and the WTO, however, do share a sense of identity based on substantive policy considerations, even though they are perfectly aware of the political limits to their view, as Schemeil demonstrates. The same is true for international civil servants at the OECD, the World Bank and the IMF. Marcussen and Woods show how these international bureaucrats share similar perspectives on macroeconomics and how they form alliances with like-minded officials within their member states.

Notwithstanding this like-mindedness, an expert group's policy consensus can be detrimental to policy making within international organizations.

The shared policy views, in combination with their relative isolation within the IMF and the World Bank and the advent of a crisis situation, contributed to the development of tunnel vision in the country desk officers during the 1994 Mexican currency crisis. Woods's application of groupthink theory offers a rare insight into IMF and World Bank decision making. Her contribution shows that groupthink theory can and should be applied to policy domains in international relations other than security studies alone.

Finally, Freitas's analysis of UNHCR decision making shows that bureaucratic politics theory may be a relevant tool for understanding decision-making processes within international organizations, which often consist of many subdivisions. Bureaucratic politics theory has been an obvious tool for analysis. Nevertheless, very few such studies of international organizations exist, not even of the EU. Interestingly, Dratwa points to bureaucratic politics within the EU when observing that the development of the precautionary principle requires consensus among three Directorates-General of the European Commission. Freitas's study suggests that intra-organizational rivalry may hinder the organization's exploitation of the room for manoeuvre. The internal battle between DIP and other subunits prevented UNHCR from assuming a formal mandate over the issue of internally displaced persons. Moreover, substantive policy differences between an international organization's subunits may help explain the specific contents of policies adopted. In the case of UNHCR an internal compromise was reached, brokered by the High Commissioner, leading to the actual development of policies for internally displaced persons on a case-by-case basis without incorporating the outcome into UNHCR's formal mandate.

Decision-making themes

The individual chapters in this volume each contribute to a better understanding of six characterizing elements of the policy process of international organizations.

Leadership

International organizations and their subunits are often able to exploit their relative policy freedom and make their member states accept policies the latter would not have judged acceptable at the outset. Their leadership may result in making member states adopt entirely new policies. This is clear in the case of the Assembly and the Secretariat of the Council of Europe, which succeeded in founding a specific human rights regime in the 1940s and in updating that regime at least six times up to the 1990s. An international organization's leadership may also take the form of setting the agenda. This is the case in the WTO, where the core group consisting of the secretary-general and the directors have important agenda-setting powers. An organization's leadership may also show in resolving intra-organizational stalemates, such as in UNHCR over the issue of internally displaced persons, or may involve tipping the balance in favour of particular coalitions of state and non-state actors, such as in the case of the secretary-general's leadership in brokering a women's rights regime during the UN International Conference on Population and Control. A caveat is in order, however, because an international organization's leadership may have no positive effects at all, as was shown in the 1994 Mexican peso fiasco.

The power of the international bureaucrats is seldom formal. Only the IMF and the World Bank can be said to possess official instruments of leverage because of their financial resources. The European Commission also has formal competencies. The OECD, however, as Marcussen observes, only has arguments to fight with. Most of the time therefore an international organization's leadership is rooted in forms of 'soft' power, such as expertise (IMO, UNHCR, WMO, WTO), coalition building (European Commission, OECD, UN International Conference on Population and Control) or shaming (OECD). And even then international organizations are careful not to antagonize their masters too much. Kerremans emphasizes that the European Commission uses Committee 133 to mobilize the member states behind its policies, but is very aware of the danger of pushing the member states too hard. The core group within the WTO may have agenda-setting powers, but it operates in tandem with the representatives from important member states. All in all, the contributions to this volume stress the institutional conditions of an international organization's leadership, whereas other recent studies tend to focus on individual characteristics of secretaries-general (Kille and Scully 2003; Smith 2003).

Consensus building

Consensus building appears to be the core business of decision making within international organizations. Deadlines of conferences or annual meetings impose a sense of urgency on participants to reach consensus, no matter how shallow. The individual chapters in this volume bear out that it is very difficult to actually see a consensus. This is caused by the vagueness of many decisions taken within international organizations. Schemeil points out that often there are no formal decisions, but only vague understandings or *de facto* postponements of official decisions. Marcussen stresses the point that the OECD has no formal regulatory powers. In that sense the organization does not take decisions. But in its consensus-building process with a member state under scrutiny, the OECD contributes to consensus on the required macroeconomic policies of the country and thus to final decisions. The methodological lesson here should be that future studies of decision making within international organizations need to distinguish between various types of consensus building and decision making and should formulate theories accordingly.

The chapters by Schemeil and Marcussen show that international organizations whose decision making is done in committees perform better, in terms of consensus building, than those that are organized in assemblies. This is especially the case where regulatory rather than distributive policies are concerned. Committees prefer to avoid formal voting, something which is more difficult to accomplish in assemblies. At the WTO and the WMO informal meetings in green rooms, which are nevertheless officially announced as taking place, prepare the ground for consensus. Training programmes help establish a common policy perspective among national and international civil servants. At the OECD the idea game is being played in 42 committees and 98 working parties and groups. Nevertheless, as Bayne argues in his account of G7/G8 sherpas, preparation is the key to success. Consensus cannot be reached without proper preparation. Sherpas keep their eyes open and try to keep unprepared issues off the politicians' agenda, although not always successfully. Woods's analysis of the World Bank and IMF's crisis decision making teaches us that under specific conditions informality and consensus seeking may be disastrous. Similarly, consensus may be blocked by bureaucratic stalemate, such as in the case of UNHCR. It requires leadership by the organization to resolve such a situation of misinterpretation or deadlock.

Organizational dynamics

Several chapters in this book stress the importance of paying attention to what happens within international bureaucracies. The machinery of international organizations seems to expand. Bayne and Lovecy argue that this is even true for such relatively intergovernmental organizations as the G7/G8 and the Council of Europe. At the same time, apart from on the EU, studies of intra-organizational dynamics remain an underdeveloped theme. Curiously, many studies of international organizations tend to treat them, in parallel with nation-states, almost like unitary actors. Nevertheless, the chapters by Freitas, Woods and Joachim show that several middle-range theories offer the opportunity to relax the unitary actor assumption. Bureaucratic politics theory portrays international organizations as an environment in which different agencies compete among each other and thus affect decision making. Groupthink theory points to socio-psychological and politico-psychological factors affecting the performance of small units within organizations. Garbage can theory provides a framework for explaining what at face value seem erratic policy changes, by making a distinction between different actors within the organization and their motives. Relaxing the unitary actor assumption would make it easier to develop further Cox and Jacobson's notion of the participant subsystem, which conceives of an international organization as consisting of many different and influential actors.

Conflicts of loyalty

International organizations are environments in which national and international civil servants experience claims of loyalty from various sides. Much of what goes on within international organizations can be described as socialization processes, sometimes deliberately designed in order to open up individual civil servants to what constructivists would call particular policy frames. Schemeil describes the training programmes at WMO and WTO, aimed at integrating newcomers into both the policy outlook of the organizations and their preferred procedures of informal meetings. The OECD regularly invites national civil servants to Paris and thus attempts to socialize them. The development of specific training programmes is a device also employed by other international organizations, such as the International Atomic Energy Agency and the European Court of Justice (Joensson and Bolin 1988; Alter 2001). The success of the WTO programmes can be measured by the distrust that Schemeil reports many trade diplomats display towards their national peers from other departments. At the same time nation-states try to maintain strong bonds of loyalty with their diplomats. Marcussen points out that OECD member states call home their civil servants from the OECD after four or five years in Paris.

Trondal demonstrated that, on the whole, the more supranational an international organization is, the more likely it is that civil servants develop loyalties to that organization. Participants in working groups of the European Commission display a more supranational outlook than those participating in Council committees. Indeed, the most intergovernmental organization in this volume, the G7/G8, does not command loyalty from the sherpas. They remain *national* civil servants. In addition, Trondal argued that loyalty also depends on the political system in the civil servant's own country (federal or unitary), as well as on the degree of sector specialization characterizing EU advisory committees. This mixture of pressures produces multiple roles for national civil servants and a variety of possible role conflicts. Analyses of bureaucratic politics at international organizations, such as by Freitas, may offer promising links to loyalty conflicts, because traditional bureaucratic politics theory assumes that civil servants experience no conflicts of loyalty and look on the bureaucratic organization as their primary focus of loyalty.

Policy windows

The occurrence of policy windows is the topic of various contributions to this volume. Several factors are at play. Institutional conditions seem to determine the occurrence of many policy windows. Hazelzet points to the legislative process within the EU, which provided several opportunities to put human rights issues on the agenda. Contrary to her expectations, however, the first phase, involving the difficult-to-lobby Council of Ministers, proved a better policy window than the second phase, involving the easier-to-approach Commission. She points to the role of the media in this. The decision on whether or not to take action is much more sensitive to media exposure than the decision on how to take action. Joachim also acknowledges the role of the media when NGOs began to table women's rights issues through the strategy of symbolic politics. Yet institutional conditions are of considerable importance, as the NGOs' success ultimately depended on a coalition with the international bureaucracy, in particular the secretary-general, who used her agenda-setting and brokering power to put forward a resolution that remained close to the NGOs' position.

Learning processes

International organizations are political systems and thus contain feedback mechanisms, such as learning. In this volume two types of learning are discussed: learning by (groups of) individual civil servants and learning by the international organization as a whole. Schemeil shows how at the WMO and the WTO technical experts learn that negotiations also involve political games. Simultaneously politicians learn to appreciate the technical side of the issues they deal with. Their learning thus contributes to the successful WMO and WTO practice of informal consensus building. Woods, however, warns against too large a degree of informality. If informality is embedded in strongly hierarchical relations, learning may be difficult to accomplish. At the World Bank and the IMF hierarchical relations produced so-called directive leadership, which in turn prevented individual civil servants from learning the proper lessons from previous monetary crises and contributed to their failure to heed the warning signals of the Mexican currency crisis.

International organizations may also be capable of learning. Dirks argues that the IMO learned from its earlier failure to promote a specific maritime safety convention. It decided to reorganize its operations and started to closely monitor developments in its immediate surroundings. Its resultant authority on the causes of shipping accidents contributed to its development as a well-respected, idea-generating centre producing new consensual knowledge on ship safety. This explains its success in promoting the adoption of a new and stricter maritime safety convention in 1995. Marcussen predicts that the OECD will have to learn soon to adapt to a changing environment with stronger competition from the EU and IMF, which have also started to play the idea game and which have more carrots and sticks than the OECD.

Themes not covered

A book on decision making within international organization cannot address all relevant matters. Which themes have been omitted that nevertheless might have contributed to answering our research questions? One is the interrelationship between international organizations. In adopting and implementing specific policies international organizations may be mutually interdependent. They may display cooperative as well as competitive interaction patterns. However, member states of the interacting organizations may well be influencing the various organizations in political terms due to the interests they themselves are pursuing, whereas the organizations may stress the interests of the entire membership and bring forward administrative and bureaucratic considerations, such as budget concerns. This will be the case within the UN family of organizations and in regions where states and various organizations need to cooperate (see Feld *et al.* 1994: 203). Given the restricted budgets of international organizations, it can be expected that organizations try to avoid superfluous activities and to prioritize their common preferences among themselves. Although at face value they may seem natural allies, evidence surfaces pointing to increased competition between international organizations. Marcussen observes that the OECD is facing competition from the EU and the IMF. In Europe the International Labour Organization is sometimes considered less relevant now, because the EU has become a more important standard setter in specific social policy areas. Given the proliferation of international organizations, the subject of their interrelationship and its effect on their decision making merits future attention.

Our focus within this volume has been on political public leadership. Private influence such as exercised by NGOs and business has been touched on, but the relevance of transnational corporations in the context of multilateral decision making needs more analysis. Bayne refers to an increased involvement of business in the preparation and follow-up of the G8 summits, relevant because of a greater legitimacy of these international gatherings. Legitimacy, as Dirks argues, also played a role in binding the employers to the debates within the IMO, where they provided expert information during the process of standard setting and offered contacts to domestic institutions and their constituencies during the implementation phase of the new IMO convention. Whereas NGOs mainly act as transnational advocacy networks that use their consultative status within international organization for public purposes, corporations may use the lobbying tool more intensively to represent their sectoral interests. This is reflected in the chapter by Hazelzet, where it is assumed that profit-making non-state actors have specific interests in preventing the imposition of economic or financial sanctions. It should be noted, however, that business-oriented NGOs also acquire consultative status within international organizations and thus, within those arenas, may collide with more critical NGOs. During the 1990s business in fact became more active within certain international organizations as a reaction to critical public actions by transnational NGOs. The change in the attitude of international corporations with regard to multilateral decision making can be described as a shift from defensive and reactive to more supportive and proactive (see Reinalda 2001: 34–5). Yet, simultaneously, transnational corporations continue to prefer voluntary action and if necessary the creation of private authority arrangements, rather than submit themselves to internationally agreed public conventions or codes of conduct (Ronit 2000). It is this multifaceted approach by corporations (lobby, participation and evasion) that should be analysed more deeply, including the aspect of public opinion as mobilized by critical NGOs.

In the context of neo-functional integration public opinion for a long time remained a largely irrelevant aspect, notwithstanding the general idea that more intense international cooperation would promote common feelings among citizens, which in turn would support international cooperation. This irrelevance disappeared not only with the further development of integration in Western Europe, but also along the continuum of internationalized governance (Niedermayer and Sinnott 1995). The international relevance of public opinion was enhanced by Amnesty International, which in the 1960s began to combine the monitoring of public international standard setting with transnational activism in order to attract public attention to violations of internationally agreed norms. It thus added the use of transnational pressure from citizens to affirm norms of government in various issue areas and to involve the mass media more strongly in the genesis and results of international decision making to the functioning of international organizations (Clark 2001). Greenpeace built on this new attitude by making international environmental violations 'visible' through daring actions which the media wanted to cover. This combination of apparently bureaucratic and dull multilateral decision making and worldwide effective calls for international attention remains a puzzle to be solved.

Finally, the issue of domestic politics surfaces only seldom in the contributions to this volume. Kerremans's use of the two-level game to analyse the relationship between the European Commission and the EU member states implies that domestic politics may be part of the ratification process guiding the (re-)formulation of the Commission's trade negotiating mandate. On the whole, however, domestic politics remains an absentee in this book. Nevertheless, recent studies suggest that international organizations are affected by member states' domestic politics and *vice versa*. As a matter of fact, the new wave of transnational studies suggests that international organizations have become part of transnational advocacy networks, trying to have an impact on international negotiations by putting pressure on nation states through their domestic democratic processes (the boomerang effect) (Risse-Kappen 1995; Keck and Sikkink 1998). These sources of influence deserve close attention in future studies of international organizations' decision making.

Similarly, international organizations may attempt to make an impact on member states' national policies, and thus become entangled in domestic politics. This may be particularly the case if they have been given the authority to monitor the national implementation of internationally agreed policies, such as is the case with the European Commission. In this volume Marcussen's study of the OECD comes closest to discussing these implementation processes. He argues that the OECD frequently succeeds in making member states respect internationally agreed macroeconomic targets and standards by playing the idea game. Interestingly, this is a case in which the influence of an international organization is gained through keeping the network as closed as possible, by limiting it to international and national civil servants with similar macroeconomic perspectives. In many other instances international organizations get a foot in the door of member states by increasing the number of participants to such an extent that decision making becomes hard to control for the states.

Conclusions

The principal conclusion of this book, not surprisingly, is that a focus on decision making within international organizations contributes to a better understanding of whether and how international organizations exploit the freedom of manoeuvre they possess. Following Cox and Jacobson, the analytical starting point must be that an international organization is two things simultaneously: a representative subsystem and a participant subsystem. In a representative subsystem the international bureaucracy is the instrument of its member states. In a participant subsystem the international organization is a more pluralistic arena with many actors, state and non-state, in which the actual outcome cannot simply be predicted by pointing at the interests of the most powerful member states.

The contributions to this volume have shown that the principal–agent approach helps in delineating the borders of the representative and participant subsystems. Because international bureaucracies provide services that would cost more if states produced them individually, member states delegate tasks to international bureaucracies. They accept that this gives the bureaucracies a certain degree of policy discretion. This volume demonstrates that the principal–agent approach is helpful because it highlights the constant tension between member states and the organization. In addition, it points to several sources of influence international organizations have. At the same time, however, it was shown that the so-called baseline is seldom clearly defined and that this can also be changed throughout the initiative of international bureaucracies.

Principal–agent theory can account for the policy freedom an international organization is enjoying. It cannot, however, easily account for the organization's failure to exploit that policy freedom or for the specific policies it pursues. Because an international organization's preference is seldom defined in terms of material interests, unless its survival is at stake, constructivist accounts can supplement rationalist insights into international organizations. Constructivism points to the impact of norms and ideas. It thus helps account for the policy preferences of international organizations. Thanks to its notion of constitutive effect, it can also contribute to explaining changes in the preferences of member states, and thus of the so-called baseline.

The contributions to this volume have shown that middle-range theories, or small-t approaches, may be the best way forward to generate knowledge of decision making within international organizations. First, many middle-range theories formulate claims that are related to decision-making processes at national level. Applying them to international organizations opens up a huge tool kit. Second, middle-range theories allow stepping beyond general claims about the impact of international organizations. Their further development will permit the formulation and testing of more precise claims regarding specific types of organizations, specific types of policies, and specific elements of decision-making processes. The individual contributions to this volume testify to these possibilities. Ultimately, however, this requires the development of specific research designs that go beyond the single-case study which is the predominant methodology in this volume, with the exception of the contributions by Schemeil, Dratwa and Hazelzet. A major future challenge therefore is a comparative case study design theoretically informed by such middle-range theories as applied in this volume.

References

Alter, K.J. (2001) *Establishing the Supremacy of European Law. The Making of an International Rule of Law in Europe*, Oxford: Oxford University Press.

Clark, A.M. (2001) *Diplomacy of Conscience. Amnesty International and Changing Human Rights Norms*, Princeton: Princeton University Press.

Feld, W.J., Jordan, R.S. and Hurwitz, L. (1994) *International Organizations. A Comparative Approach, Third Edition*, Westport: Praeger.

Joensson, C. and Bolin, S. (1988) 'IAEA's Role in the International Politics of Atomic Energy', in L.S. Finkelstein (ed.) *Politics in the United Nations System*, Durham: Duke University Press, 303–23.

Keck, M.E. and Sikkink, K. (1998) *Activists Beyond Borders. Advocacy Networks in International Politics*, Ithaca: Cornell University Press.

Kille, K.J. and Scully, R.M. (2003) 'Executive Heads and the Role of Intergovernmental Organizations: Expansionist Leadership in the United Nations and the European Union', *Political Psychology*, 24(1): 175–98.

Meunier, S. (2000) 'What Single Voice? European Institutions and EU–U.S. Trade Negotiations', *International Organization*, 54(1): 103–35.

Niedermayer, O. and Sinnott, R. (eds) (1995) *Public Opinion and Internationalized Governance*, Oxford: Oxford University Press.

Peters, B.G. (1999) *Institutional Theory in Political Science. 'The New Institutionalism'*, London: Pinter.

Reinalda, B. (2001) 'Private in Form, Public in Purpose: NGOs in International Relations Theory', in B. Arts, M. Noortmann and B. Reinalda (eds) *Non-State Actors in International Relations*, Aldershot: Ashgate, 11–40.

Risse-Kappen, T. (ed.) (1995) *Bringing Transnational Relations Back In. Non-State Actors, Domestic Structures and International Institutions*, Cambridge: Cambridge University Press.

Ronit, K. (2000) 'The Good, the Bad, the Ugly? Practices of Global Self-Regulation Among Dyestuffs Producers', in K. Ronit and V. Schneider (eds) *Private Organizations in Global Politics*, London: Routledge, 83–101.

Smith, C. (2003) 'More Secretary or General? Effective Leadership at the United Nations', *International Politics*, 40(1): 137–47.

Index

Made in the USA
Las Vegas, NV
31 October 2024

10663445R00151